ALSO BY JOSHUA MOHR

FICTION

Some Things That Meant the World to Me

Termite Parade

Damascus

Fight Song

All This Life

NONFICTION

Sirens

MODEL CITIZEN

MCD
FARRAR, STRAUS AND GIROUX
NEW YORK

MODEL CITIZEN

A MEMOIR

JOSHUA MOHR

MCD
Farrar, Straus and Giroux
120 Broadway, New York 10271

Library of Congress Cataloging-in-Publication Data
Names: Mohr, Joshua, author.
Title: Model citizen : a memoir / Joshua Mohr.
Description: First edition. | New York : MCD / Farrar, Straus and Giroux,
    2021. | Summary: "The intimate, gorgeous, garish confessions of Joshua
    Mohr—writer, father, alcoholic, addict" —Provided by publisher.
Identifiers: LCCN 2020046546 | ISBN 9780374211721 (hardcover)
Subjects: LCSH: Mohr, Joshua. | Novelists, American—21st century—
    Biography. | Recovering addicts—Biography. | Substance abuse—Biography. |
    Fatherhood—Biography.
Classification: LCC PS3613.O379 Z46 2021 | DDC 813/.6 [B]—dc23
LC record available at https://lccn.loc.gov/2020046546

Designed by Gretchen Achilles

Our books may be purchased in bulk for promotional, educational, or business
use. Please contact your local bookseller or the Macmillan Corporate and
Premium Sales Department at 1-800-221-7945, extension 5442, or by email at
MacmillanSpecialMarkets@macmillan.com.

www.mcdbooks.com • www.fsgbooks.com
Follow us on Twitter, Facebook, and Instagram at @mcdbooks

1   3   5   7   9   10   8   6   4   2

To those of us who want to do better

AUTHOR'S NOTE

This is a true story, though some names and details have been changed.

PART I

COLUMBUS & COLUMBUS

PROLOGUE

When I was in kindergarten I stabbed myself with a pencil, on purpose—one minute sitting in class holding the thing in my hand wondering what it would feel like to be stabbed, the next, hitting my open palm with the pencil's tip, screaming and sobbing and bleeding, the teacher taking me to a water fountain to clean the wound, asking, "Why why why, Josh, why on earth would you do that?"

I still have the graphite lodged in my palm. I'm looking at it right now. And for the next ninety thousand words, you'll be staring at it, too.

1

It's six in the morning on New Year's Day and Ava cries from the crib, which means my wife says something to me like, "Your turn," and I say something whiny like, "Bottle, fine," and stumble into the kitchen and spill milk on the counter and don't wipe it up, leave it for later, after coffee, after caffeine makes my mind fire right. I tuck the bottle in the waistband of my drawers so I can hoist Ava up with both arms, and she says, "Let's play," a new phrase for her, and I carry her back into our bed and lay her in the middle and get back in myself, Lelo and I flanking her, the three of us lying like a happy family, and for twenty seconds that's what we are.

Then the numbness starts.

I notice it first in my right arm, then realize it's creeping into my leg, too. *That's weird*, I think, *two limbs falling asleep at the same time.*

Soon there's no feeling on that entire side of my body, from shoulder to toes.

I shift positions, rolling onto my back, so blood can flow freely.

Five seconds. Ten. Twenty.

Still numb.

Fear spills out of me like the milk rolling down my daughter's chin. I shake my dead hand back and forth, back and forth, and say to Lelo, "Something's wrong," and she says, "What?" and I say, "911."

She's to the phone fast and I roll over onto my stomach, a gesture that Ava interprets as an invitation to play and she's straddling my back and yelling, "Hop on Pop! Hop on Pop!"

My frantic wife doing her best to conjure the paramedics and me knowing beyond any doubt that the numbness will zip over me like a body bag and Ava keeps chanting, "Hop on Pop! Hop on Pop!" and I am crying uncontrollably, grieving a girl I'll never get to see turn into a woman, and if this is the end of my life, I wish it had ended sooner. Wish I had died before meeting Lelo, before ever seeing Ava on the ultrasound, the size of an orange seed, our nickname for her until she was born.

I wish I'd never gotten sober, never tried to be a better person. Why endure so much harrowing improvement to die like this at thirty-eight years old?

◘

In 2004, while I was in grad school at the University of San Francisco, I volunteered at a halfway house in the Mission District, teaching creative writing.

Kae was one of my students at the halfway house. He had spent fifteen years in San Quentin and was out two weeks when I met him. One of the conditions of his parole was that he had to stay clean or he'd be busted back to prison. After the first session we had together, he came up to me and said, "Gonna be the first American Indian to win the National Book Award for nonfiction."

It made me like him immediately. Here he was fresh from the penitentiary and he had no fear of odds, no concept of how remote the chances were of that happening. Or he did know and didn't care. Maybe winning the National Book Award seemed easy after pulling all those years in prison.

The first essay he handed in made me think he might actually do it. The scene was short, maybe four or five paragraphs that dramatized Kae sitting on the sidewalk, against the front of a twenty-four-hour donut shop in San Francisco's Tenderloin District, the part of town where junkies roamed in an animal refuge, no police, no poachers, so long as they kept their chaos in a contained radius. This is changing as the city gentrifies, but back then, the TL was an addict asylum.

In the scene, Kae was out of heroin and he wore only an undershirt and he'd never been so cold in his life, so hungry, so depleted. A taxi parked out front of the donut shop, the driver talking on his cell, arguing with someone. Kae watched words explode from the driver's mouth and then he saw the exhaust puffing from the tailpipe, looking like a steam room, giving him an idea. Freezing, Kae crawled, pulled himself across the sidewalk to the cab's back, first warming his hands in the exhaust, finally submerging his head in that toxic cloud, lathering himself in the car's warmth and affection.

The story ended there, the reader sucking carbon monoxide right along with Kae, smelling the acrid poison, but also feeling its billowy tenderness.

I finished it and started right back at the beginning, reread it a few more times. This guy was good and needed help, needed someone to treat him like he wasn't just another convict.

"You might do it," I said to Kae, handing his essay back with my notes, ways I thought he could make it even better.

"Do what?"

"Win the National Book Award."

He eyeballed me. Kae was in his fifties, dark complexion set off with pale patches of eczema that he constantly scratched. His head was kept in a crew cut. Old and faded tribal tattoos on his forearms.

"Course I'll do it," he said.

They were always calling out, screwing around, and I dug their chaos during our classes. They didn't have to front tough; no one was a gangster while we wrote. Nobody had felonies hanging from their necks like nooses. We were people talking about storytelling, and that was all we were.

I had one student who was illiterate. She came up to me and said, "Do you have to know reading for this class?"

She was in her forties. I stayed after our sessions and read our assignments to her. Usually, she didn't like the stories I chose, saying something like, "These people is snobs." She was right. My first batch of stories was too much head, not enough heart. All the characters brandished vocabularies like weapons, but all it really did for them was provide more words to describe their disappointments in life.

Everyone was in some sort of halfway house.

One time, I was scheduled to teach the morning after Valentine's Day. My ex-wife—well, not my ex yet when this all happened, Blue was still my disappointed wife, my why-did-I-pick-this-guy wife—decided that we should go out for a fancy Valentine's Day dinner. It was only one meal, after all, and what could go wrong?

I went from martinis to a few beers and we drank a couple bottles of champagne during the meal and don't forget after-dinner drinks. We had to cocktail hard, otherwise there was this whole conversation thing. Couples have to talk, they say. We hadn't been talking much at all because earlier that week we'd had a huge fight.

I'd done another dumb thing so I bunked at Shany's house, making up maudlin and self-sympathetic remixes of what had happened. Shany was my best friend, and even she thought I was in the wrong.

"Have you even apologized to her?" she said.

"We both need to say we're sorry."

"So no."

"Not yet."

"If you want to fix this, go home."

So I slunk back. I don't even think Blue took her eyes off the TV when I rolled in. Blue needed to believe in something and I wasn't giving her much. We spent pretty much every night in one Mission District bar or another. Hell, we had fallen in love in dive bars, but recently she'd grown weary of going at it so hard every night, which didn't make sense to me.

Weary?

Of what?

Of whiskey and jukeboxes and free peanuts? Of friends and adventures and bummed smokes? Of giving a kiss to an angel you'll never see again? Of all singing along when "Sister Christian" played from cheap speakers?

I'm not one of those sober cats who looks back and demonizes everything from when they were dirty. I'm glad I embarrassed myself all those nights because I learned what shame was.

What shame is.

It's impossible to describe real shame to somebody who hasn't thrived on self-destruction.

Kae wasn't having it. We met at a café close to the halfway house, around 15th and Mission. Talking about his donut shop essay. I had made a bunch of suggestions for how to make it better, but he didn't think it needed any improvements.

"Already wrote it," he said. "It's done."

"You can make changes. Writers revise."

"That's the whole story already on the page."

He was distracted, looking out the window, scratching his eczema. I was mad that he wasn't taking this meeting more seriously. I didn't get paid to teach there, so I sure as hell didn't get any money for sitting in a café listening to someone say he wouldn't edit.

"Are you waiting for somebody?" I said, knocking on the window.

He didn't even look at me. "Ain't got nobody to wait for."

"Your story is pretty good," I said, trying to make him focus, "but it can be great."

"Used to grind right down there," Kae said, pointing up 16th Street. There was a BART station and everyone knew if you needed opiates or crack or crank in the Mission that was where you scored. I knew it intimately, buying bindles there myself, though I never told Kae. "Selling shit and getting high," he said. "How am I supposed to stay clean living a block away?"

"You do it so you don't go back to prison," I said.

"Easy as that, huh?" He still wasn't looking at me, staring out the window like he sat on an airplane and there was something panoramic down below, the Grand Canyon, the Rocky Mountains, heroin. "Most of my life was standing on those corners."

"Do you want to talk about your essay?"

"No," he said, "I don't."

Here was what had caused my fight with Blue earlier that Valentine's week: I was super coked up and had at least ten Fernets swimming in me when I met her and a couple of girlfriends (I'd been bartending around the corner and got off at midnight and hoofed to Laszlo) so we could all cocktail. I knew the guys slinging drinks there pretty well, Rick and Brian, who had a whole *Brokeback Mountain* thing going on, except instead of illicit fishing trips they blew dunes of coke and slow danced while the sun came up, much to the chagrin of Brian's wife.

Me walking over and kissing Blue and saying hey to her friends and immediately heading to the bar to buy the table a round, having a quick pop with the Brokeback brigade and striking up a conversation with the woman next to me, some debutante all dressed up, slumming it in the Mission. I dealt with these posh ladies all the time on the weekends behind my own bar, as they turned our neighborhood into the Dirty Marina—the rich seeing how the paupers lived, or that's how it was back then; now the Mission *is* the Marina—and I hated these crosstown tourists but also dug making them want to screw me, and cocaine made me a charming chauvinist who some women found irresistible and apparently this lady was one of those because she flirted right off, and I looked her up and down and she wore these crazy jeweled shoes that looked like chandeliers and some belligerent carnival barker in my head demanded I drink whiskey from one of them stat.

Which I said to her, making her giggle and bite her bottom lip, and I said, "What's funny?" and she said, "You're crazy," and I said, "You've got that right, pretty lady" and leaned down slipping off one of her shoes and my wife was at a corner table having no idea that I was being such a scumbag, simply chatting with her friends, waiting for me to come back with a round of drinks, enjoying a normal night cocktailing until the moment she couldn't stand me anymore, though that was still minutes away, me trying to convince one of the Brokeback blokes to pour whiskey straight in this girl's shoe and either Rick or Brian asking her, "You okay with this?" and she pointed at me and laughed and said, "He's crazy," and Rick/Brian already knew that, of course, and poured whiskey in her shoe, my chalice, and the music thumped some Chicago break beats, and most people at the bar started cheering when I brought the shoe to my lips and slurped out all the booze and the woman whose shoe it was clapped and made some sorority-style squeals and I asked the debutante if she wanted to dance and she said, "Sure," and I said, "Not here," and she said, "Where?"

I still had her shoe in my hand and I knocked on the bar with it and said, "Up there," and she squealed again and I jumped on the bar and pulled her up there too and we let the music take over, dancing terribly, me flying the shoe all about, doing my whole king-of-the-bar shtick, dancing with spirits and blow and a squealing debutante.

I wonder if Blue saw me herself or if one of her friends had to point toward the bar and ask, "Is that your husband up there?"

I wonder what went through her mind turning to look, having witnessed countless of my idiotic shenanigans, each of them tangling together, creating a huge ball of humiliations, too much for one wife to take, and it was over, I was over, we were over, I'd gone too far not with the outlandishness of this one incident per se, but the speeding boulder of all the times I embarrassed Blue, and I bet she didn't even answer her friend, bet she simply stood and stormed and all the ire coursed through her and out her fingertips.

I never saw her coming, one second dancing and zooming the shoe in zigzags and the next feeling pressure on the backs of my legs.

Feet leaving the bar.

Weight flipping in a slow-motion tumble.

I must have dropped the shoe, must have brought my hands up to protect my face, must have thought it was the debutante's beau or a jilted one-night stand, it never occurred to me that Blue might mastermind this violent fate, still falling, still feeling my legs whipping up until I was upside down. I crashed face-first to Laszlo's floor. Landed and lay there. And then it was like the whole room vanished. All the other people gone. Except the two of us. Blue and me. Music nixed. The shining shoe sitting on the floor. Blue standing above me. The look in her eyes was all anger. At this drunk she'd tethered herself to. At this person too dense to treat other people with dignity.

I lay there bleeding and my head all sideways, shocked but also proud of our life's chaos. Loved all the shoves I never saw coming.

The shoe-chandelier should have been my headstone, a lighthouse, tossing watts to mark the grave of a lousy husband. A whimpering eulogy flitting on the wind, saying *a parasite, a wrecking ball, a waste.*

Kae and I met before or after class for the next couple weeks. I'd worn him down about revision, about the idea that a story needs more work after its initial conception. I did this by sharing a couple of my short stories with him: I showed him the rough drafts, and then the final, published products.

"Which is better?"

"These is shit," he said, meaning the rough drafts. "These is solid," he said, pointing at the finals.

"So will you revise the donut shop piece?" I said. "I can help you publish it."

"Why do you help me?"

"I want you to win the National Book Award."

"I was playing about that," said Kae. "Can't win."

"You can," I said. "You're super talented."

Kae smiled. "You think?"

Back to Valentine's Day, where Blue and I were stuck with wonderful French food in front of us and having a terrible time. She could barely look at me. From her perspective, dancing on the bar with that woman was the latest example of me disrespecting her. I had bad boundaries with the opposite sex. I knew it and she knew it and everyone we ran around with knew it, and that was what made her so pissed: how public it all was.

A couple free Fernets with the bartender on our way out the door. He and I had watched the sun rise a few times, telling our war stories at mach speeds, the cocaine making us sprint through our life's woes. I can't remember his name, but I can tell you his mom used to beat him with a hair dryer.

Blue and I were specifically calling it an early night so I could be semi-coherent at the halfway house in the morning. I had to be there at 9:00 a.m., and I didn't want to show up stinking of booze. The people there worked so hard to clean up their lives, and I liked pretending that I was trying, too.

But the cops had other ideas of how this Valentine's Day was going to end. Sirens and a failed field sobriety test. Blue taking a cab home and me heading to the drunk tank. Another night wedged in a cell with a bunch of hammerheads. The highlight was always a peanut butter and jelly sandwich early in the morning. Did I really like them, or is that only how I'm remembering it now? I remember those sandwiches tasting like they were made by god, the almighty creator sticking a knife into each jar, getting the proportions just right.

I brought a couple books that I thought would help Kae dig into his rewrite. The first was Denis Johnson's *Angels*. The other was Amy Hempel's *Reasons to Live*. Those writers did emotional filth like few others. They'd be good role models on the page for Kae.

Somebody buzzed me in the halfway house and one of the supervisors called me into the office. She collated a huge mound of pages into a bunch of smaller stacks. She was fast at it. In another life, she would have been the most sought after dealer in Vegas.

"Kae got busted back," she told me.

"What?"

"He failed a piss test."

"So he's in jail?"

"In county now, then back to the pen."

"For how long?"

"For the rest of his suspended sentence," she said, not looking up at me, just slamming new pages down in her stacks. "That was a provision of his parole."

"How long is his suspended sentence?"

"I got no idea," she said.

"But it could be years?"

She actually laughed at this. "Oh, it's definitely years," she said. "Do you know what he did to get locked up in the first place?"

"Why?" I asked her. I knew she wouldn't be able to tell me

anything, certainly not what I needed to hear. The information I was after could only come from Kae.

She stopped collating that massive stack of papers. "Why what, Josh?"

"Why did he relapse?"

The woman shrugged.

"There has to be a reason," I said.

"No," she said, "there doesn't. Happens every day."

She kept slapping pages down on her swelling stacks.

I left the office and went into the room the students and I met in and wrote *Class Canceled* on the dry-erase board. I stormed out of the halfway house and threw the books I brought for Kae in the trash. On the days I didn't have MFA classes, I tended bar at a place over on Valencia. I was scheduled to work that day but my shift didn't start for like seven hours. Time suddenly delegated to a wake, a funeral, a proper send-off for Kae.

I hit the closest dive bar and ordered a shot of tequila, a beer in a can; I made a cheesy eulogy-cheers for Kae and downed my shot.

"What's going on?" the bartender said once I chugged the whole beer. He wanted to chum it up since we were the only people there. Without asking, he got me another tequila and Tecate.

"He's gone," I said and threw the tequila back. Kae had quit. He had one last shot to get his shit together, and he couldn't, and all those years in prison that could have been avoided regenerated around his body, steel bars, cement, sealing him away from any future. If the stakes were that high for him and he couldn't stay clean, what chance did I have?

Sure, I ruptured a marriage, but that was nothing compared to Kae or the others at the halfway house. Maybe I'd get divorced, fired. Neither of those offenses would lead me to San Quentin.

Without any serious penalties, I was going to keep punishing my-self. It was the *punishment* that got me high.

In my early twenties, living in a punk house in the Sunset District, I suggested a game of beer-bottle baseball. I handed somebody a bat in our living room and stood like fifteen feet in front of him and I lobbed a beer bottle and he hit it and smashed it and shards of glass flew everywhere, cutting the shit out of my face, and I was laughing like the animals laughed once they realized Noah's ark was going to float, and I kept pitching bottles and people kept club-bing the glass to bits and each and every cut on my face was where it was supposed to be, each cut was perfect.

"Another?" the bartender asked, probably wondering what was taking me so long with the new tequila shot.

"I'm going to drink until I black out."

"I've heard worse ideas," he said.

The morning after my failed field sobriety test, the heavenly PB&J, they let me out of jail about 8:00 a.m. I had time to get to the half-way house to teach. I really wanted to go that morning. It felt important, doing something for other people.

I stopped by a store and bought a pack of gum and a bottle of Gatorade. There was no time to take a shower or brush my teeth. I knocked on the halfway house's door and somebody buzzed me in. The class started in two minutes.

The number of students fluctuated based on who had job inter-views, who had to work, who had house responsibilities. The week before we had fifteen students, which was a record, and I thought the class was our best yet and we'd build on it and things would get stronger.

Which made it even worse the day I came straight from jail. That morning, I walked into the classroom and no one was there. Not one student. It was 9:00 a.m. and I figured I'd give them a grace period. We all need a grace period.

It was impossible that nobody would show. We'd had small classes before, maybe four or five. Never zero, though. That couldn't happen.

I sat there by myself until 9:30, and the only reason I got up was that I started crying. There I was, drunk in the bathroom of a halfway house, the biggest wreck on the premises, and I didn't even live there. I had to get out. The longer I stayed, the better the odds that I was going to be discovered. Exposed for who I really was.

I heard Shany's voice saying, "If you want to fix this, go home."

"I don't know how," I said to the empty bathroom.

◻

Me, you, any stranger standing around and watching, we would have messed up that morning at the donut shop. We'd have seen sadness as Kae crawled across the sidewalk to warm himself in a fart of carbon monoxide.

See, to Kae there was no tailpipe. No taxi. No driver. Kae didn't take in any of that.

He saw a house. Saw a mother making singsong syllables to a baby in a bathtub. Saw kindness coming out of the exhaust pipe. Saw nourishment, grace, saw exactly what he needed to survive another day, and isn't that all any of us are after? Won't we do anything to survive?

There's no such thing as the long view when you're freezing, when you're broken. There's only the shortest path to the tailpipe. Life isn't about the comforts we covet. It's about the kinds we can crawl inside.

2

What's that one thing in your life that you wish to control, yet the compulsion spins constantly, relentlessly? We all have that seductive adversary, the voice in our head calling us to calamity. What's yours?

Like Odysseus and the Sirens. Everyone knew it was a death sentence, sailors passing by and getting liquored up on the Sirens' melodies, losing any semblance of themselves, abandoning their jobs, standing mesmerized and smiling—

It was romantic; it was religious, seemed like the Sirens knew the secret to end suffering.

And Odysseus wanted to hear them.

He instructed his crew to tie him to one of the masts, fasten him so tightly that he couldn't break free. Then he told all of them to lodge beeswax in their ears, so they couldn't hear a sung note. He instructed them to sail close to the Sirens.

When their perfect, terrifying music began, Odysseus fought to free himself, ropes cutting into his skin, hurting him, but he didn't care—it was the music, a call to reach deeply into the heart of his world and jerk the organ out, stomp it to pulp. His crew navigated the ship safely, and Odysseus heard the Sirens' debauched propositions and lived to tell.

It's that piece of cake you shouldn't eat, that stranger you shouldn't kiss. That bet you shouldn't place. That cocktail that's the same as swallowing smallpox. That bug you chase. That computer you can't close. That nicotine parching your lungs, turning them to jerky. That blade you wanna run across your skin. That finger down a throat. That line of drugs. That blaring self-hate racing around your skull, screaming its dreary predictions. That pill that's supposed to help, so why isn't it—why can't anything fucking help us?

I'm thirty-nine, writing this as a father, someone sober six years, writing this wondering if a look backward can make sense of who I am, what I am. Maybe writing this can make sense of my parents, too.

Because if I don't tell this story I might wake up in a week or a month or a year alone in bed, beckoning for my second wife and daughter, only to see them by the front door with their bags packed. I might have that mildew reek of a dive bar draining from my pores, might have shame snaking around my beaten-up face like smoke.

If I don't tell this, there's the chance I'll forget to fear my Sirens. Ava and Lelo will leave with their pulverized hearts and suitcases, slamming the door behind, but they might as well be closing me in a coffin.

Everyone said that our baby would be the best reason to stay sober. Intellectually, I grasped the concept and agreed with the sentiment. But the baby also seemed the best reason to relapse.

I felt trapped. Overtired, on call 24-7, thanklessly worked, no seeable end to the madness. All these things brought out the worst in my nature. They made me petulant, made me want to get whiskey and bask in beautiful failure.

I wanted a lurid, loud affair, not with a woman, but with a bottle, a baggie, a syringe. I wanted to check into the most squalid motel I could find and drink so much that I threw up. And then drink some more. Then do every drug. Then drink some more. And then let the next wave of alcohol poisoning spray out of me like a reverse baptism.

I lived in San Francisco, one of the most enchanting spots on the globe. I was married to my second wife, Lelo, the kindest person I'd ever known. We had a daughter, whom I adored when she wasn't confusing the hell out of me. I'd gotten sober, sure, but I'd taken myself with me, that fraction of my mind that worshipped ruin.

Even now, typing that line, I can feel it kick like a demented baby.

Saying *hey stupid, let's be stupid.*

I still think about booze and drugs every day, triggered by all sorts of ubiquities. For instance, Ava and I play acoustic guitar together. I strum and she sits on my lap, gnawing on the top of the guitar. Her teeth marks in the wood are some of my favorite things.

Every now and again she rips the pick out of my hand and tosses it inside the guitar. Now, there's no graceful way to get a pick out of the instrument, so I hold the guitar over my head, hole down, shaking it back and forth, the pick rattling around in there. And as it ricochets from side to side, I always think about pills. Maybe the pick has turned into oxy. Or Norco, codeine, Demerol. Maybe it's a pill and when it falls out I can gobble it up.

I never think it's anything else while I shake the guitar over my head, listening to the rattle. I never think there's a penny in there. A glass eye. A nail. Never think it's a bullet. And I'm momentarily disappointed when the pick falls out, and I'm momentarily disgusted about that disappointment. And then it's over. There's simply a guitar pick on the floor. So what?

There are the times I make her a bottle, heaping formula into water. Invariably, some powder falls onto the counter and it's cocaine, and I want to line it up with a credit card, roll up a dollar.

There are these triggers, and there are more, all the normal things that become drugs because that's how I see the world.

That's the guitar pick rattling around inside me.

Ava was born in the morning, and by the time eight o'clock rolled around that night, Lelo was out cold, exhausted from the difficulties of childbirth. Ava was awake. I was awake. I sat in a rickety chair, next to Lelo's hospital bed, and read my daughter *Franny and Zooey*. I only expected to read her the first few pages, but she was content. I finished thirty while she cooed and kicked on my lap. I read the next fifty after doing my first solo diaper change, a humbling experience. I woke Lelo for a quick breastfeed, and after a burp, Ava and I returned to our lumpy chair—the place where I was supposed to "sleep"—and picked the book up where we left off. Ava dozed on my chest, and I kept reading aloud and finished the thing, sharing one of my favorite novels on her first day here.

A couple weeks after her birth, my mom and I decided to give Lelo a break—take a shower, take a nap, take a breath—so we bundled Ava up and put her in the stroller.

I was freaking out, wondering why I'd voluntarily ruined my life. What would happen if I dropped Ava off at the fire station's Safe Surrender site? How angry would Lelo be?

That's the thing about being an older dad: you've engineered a day-to-day life that you dig, deriving pleasure from the narcissism of your routine. Since 2009, I had published four novels, writing every day and earning a living teaching other misguided romantics to churn out pages. I worked out; I traveled around doing readings; I spent time with Lelo, my best friend and favorite author.

I pushed the stroller, Mom walking next to me.

"I keep crying," I said to her.

"That happens."

"I've made up these little lullabies for her and I can't get through one without crying."

"It makes sense."

"How do you figure?"

"You're in a new style of love," she said. "One you've never known before."

We were up at Holly Park on Bernal Heights. It's a small, circular park that has a concrete walkway running around the outside of it and we pushed the stroller in this circle, doing laps.

"It's harder than I thought it would be," I said.

"Being a parent?" she said.

"I might not be able to do it."

"You're already doing it."

"That's not what I mean."

"It will get easier," my mom said, "and it will get harder."

"Super."

"Josh, she'll never know you the way you knew me," she said, stopping.

I stopped too, the stroller fixed in front of me.

"She'll only know you sober," she said. "Do you know how fortunate that makes you?"

"Who knows if I'll stay sober?" I said.

"Don't you dare."

"You know what I mean."

"Only sober: I wish that was how you knew me. Can you imagine?"

I didn't want to construct some fiction about our past, didn't want to worry about what had already happened. I wanted to stop circling the carcasses of all those years, which was one of the reasons I loved drugs in the first place: they yanked me into a paradise nude of memory. And it worked. Drugs helped me for years. That's what nobody tells you. Drugs help until they don't. But by then, you can't stop.

Nothing is my mom's fault. Sure, there's some genetic junk floating in me, unseen but dangerously there, like plastic in the ocean. But I ate that acid, smoked that heroin, shot that Special K, bought those bindles.

My mom and I were still stopped in the park. A jogger whizzed by.

She had waited ten seconds for me to answer, and when she realized I wasn't going to say anything, she added, "Look at the baby," putting her hand on the stroller, right next to mine. "Just look at her."

Ava slept, my three-week-old miracle, my three-week-old mindfuck.

"She'll only know you sober," my mom said. "Just don't be stupid."

"Okay."

"As long as you're not stupid," she said, "everything will be fine."

◇

It starts like this: Ava and I are in the hallway, and I am locking the front door to our apartment. We live on the top floor, the third floor. It's an old building with brown carpet that looks like burned bacon. No padding underneath it. The white walls are barely painted, scuffed and gouged. But the apartments themselves are nice. The best thing about our building is the smell: there's a laundromat on the ground floor, and our apartment is always perfumed by fabric softener.

Granted, that fabric softener's lovely stink is noxious and probably carcinogenic, but this is where we live.

Ava is jimmied between me and the front door as I fumble with the keys, as I'm loaded down with the diaper bag, our lunches, our jackets. She's fighting to free herself, and I say, "Hold on, sweetie, almost done," and she says, "No!" and I drop the keys, lean down to retrieve them, and say to her, "Wait," and she says, "No!" and the diaper bag falls from my shoulder and Ava keeps fighting to free herself, and I say, "Please," trying to keep her wedged in front of me, and she says, "No!" and I work to keep her contained, to make this as easy as it can be, though nothing about this is simple, the ordeal of getting a kid out the door who doesn't want to cooperate, even when the destination is someplace fun, someplace she wants to end up, and the last twenty minutes have been a constant fight, "Let's put on your socks and shoes" and "No!" and "Let's get some snacks together" and "No!" and, to be honest, I'm wondering why I'm even working so hard to get out the door, lumbering us to the Peek-a-Boo Factory, which I know sounds like a German fetish bar with glory holes and adult-size changing tables, but in actuality is an indoor play structure, a three-story hamster cage that kids can run around in and lose their minds, and she likes it, so we go, that's the gig, that's one of the tenets of being a parent, putting their happiness before your own, so what if the Peek-a-Boo Factory is my worst nightmare, piping horrific music, all campfire songs sung by a gaggle of medicated children, and it's not easy being in a hamster cage/insane asylum that's flush with hyped-up kids and bored parents pecking iPhones on the periphery, using the Factory as a padded nanny, granting them an hour-long break from the day's barked demands for food and toys and the incessant messes accumulating around the house, sprouting up, seemingly spontaneously, *didn't I just put that goddamn thing away!?* and maybe you did, maybe you didn't, maybe it doesn't matter because it's there again.

So:

My daughter doesn't dig running around the hamster cage by herself, no, she's a bit too young to want to venture into the upper stories without me, so I am forced to scramble around the cage as well, sweating and puffing and evading other children. I'm often the only adult hamster pushing past the padded walls, navigating up and down the narrow passageways, cramming my six-feet-two frame down on slides between hanging plastic stalactites, but a deal is a deal: Ava adores this, and I love watching her, each trip there revealing a new move for her, a new accomplishment, venturing into a small plastic room, sitting in there and clapping and laughing and looking at me and saying, "Echo!" and I lean my head in and say, "Echo!" and the first time she does the big red slide by herself, the first time she spins around on what can only be classified as a Sadistic Revolving Vomit Machine. I watch her do all these new things with each subsequent visit to the Factory and it's fun, if not a dash humiliating, but I'll embarrass myself day after day if it means being around her pure joy.

As adults, we think we know happiness, but all we really possess is a tangled, lodged remembrance of it, like hair in a drain. Being around a child, that's what joy looks like.

Today, however, we are far from the Factory. Today, we're struggling. Ava has been waking up at 4:30 a.m. for some reason, and about an hour ago I limped in the bathroom to pull a piece of sleep from my eye that was the size of a crouton, was so exhausted that then I rubbed lube on my face instead of lotion.

Coffee. Send coffee.

So I'm down on the old brown carpet, on a knee in front of our apartment's door, trying to gather the keys and trying to hoist the diaper bag back up on a shoulder and Ava escapes my grasp and she's running toward the stairs and I say, "Stop!" and she doesn't answer, though I expect her to at least pause at the top of the stairs, expect her to feel an unconscious tug toward self preservation, a fleck of survival instinct, but there is no pause, there is no acknowledgment of me saying "Stop!"; there is nothing but an eighteen-month-old launching herself off the top step and tumbling down the stairs.

Time does this odd division—on one hand, there's a slow-mo look to everything as Ava goes over the lip of the stairs: I see her head, her shoulders, her arms flap as gravity begins to take her down, and it's anguishing, this swath of time, taking forever, and yet on the other hand, there is an assaulting velocity to this moment as well, Ava's body moving away from me at the speed of light, and I can't move fast enough to save her, despite the desperate commands screaming in my mind, *your daughter is falling, the person you're tasked to protect, the girl you love more than anything, why are you the worst, most worthless parent in the world with your kid falling down the stairs?!* and I drop everything, the keys and jackets and lunches and the diaper bag, all of it plummeting to the burned-bacon carpet, and I take two steps and follow her, diving down the stairs headfirst, hoping I'm tall enough, hoping with my long arms I'll be able to snatch her halfway down, and I smash my knuckles on the banister and I feel a sharp pain in my balls, and I am as stretched out as I can, like Superman flying, though that's the shittiest simile I've ever conceived; there is nothing heroic about a hapless dad trying to right a situation that never should have happened in the first place. I shouldn't have been trying to do so many things at once. I should've put all my cargo down, locked the door while holding her tight. I should've made two trips.

Poor Ava with the dumb dad sliding down the stairs with his bashed hand and hurt nuts and she's only three or four steps ahead of me, the carpet so trampled the floor feels like cement, Ava rolling down them, which is better than a headfirst somersault-style plunge, her whole body hitting one step before flipping down onto the next; she has gone down about eight of them, she is making these noises—these terrible panting noises—and I can hear them—I still can hear them—each time I walk these stairs, I hear phantom pants.

Reaching my hand out.

Grabbing ahold of her thigh.

Stopping her.

She's safe, and I've saved her.

But too bad the human body doesn't have air brakes. Too bad that a sturdy grip on her thigh doesn't trump the apathetic rules of momentum, inertia. Too bad that despite my best intentions we fall down the remaining three or four stairs together, roll to a stop on the landing.

Her wide eyes. The terror.

I can't smell the fabric softener.

I sit up and pull her onto my lap and check her little body, squeezing her limbs, combing over her head, looking for any blood, any damage, but I'm the only one bleeding, from my hand.

Then she starts crying.

Something is really wrong with her. I know it. Internal bleeding. A broken bone. A dislocation. A traumatic brain injury. I remember reading about a child who hit her head in a bouncy house—a bouncy house!—and died, and if something like that can happen, there's no doubt that Ava is badly injured and it is all because of my incompetence and negligence and she keeps crying those desperate animal noises, and I grab my cell from my back pocket, and it isn't cracked or damaged, and I dial 911 and I have to explain it, have to admit it, have to tell a total stranger that I let Ava fall down the steps, and I begin by saying, "We need an ambulance," and the operator asks exactly what happened, and I say, "A child needs medical attention," and she says, "What specifically happened, sir?" and I say, "She fell."

Now a 911 operator isn't a priest, but I confess my involvement, trying to make her understand that I'm not one of those intentionally negligent parents, I am one of those doing-my-best-but-things-still-happen parents.

Ava continues to cry and kick on my lap, and I continue to hope for an over-the-phone absolution, but all the operator says is, "Ambulance, on the way."

"We were going to the Peek-a-Boo Factory," I tell her.

"Would you like me to stay on the line until they arrive?"

"It's her favorite place."

"I can hold the line with you until emergency services get there."

"She loves it."

"Okay, sir."

"We go there all the time together."

Back about fifteen years, me and V: We had a platonic, polluted relationship, one running on booze. We both liked to black out, dug talking shit and smoking cigarettes. We'd been in North Beach all night and were walking to wherever we were going. I have no idea, probably one of the bars on Columbus Street.

Let's talk about Columbus for a second. It had grown famous in our alcoholic circle because of Kerrie's ex-husband, Alan. Legend has it that one night Alan was wasted and called Kerrie begging for a ride home, and she agreed to pick him up, asking, "Where are you?" and he said, "I'm at the corner of Columbus and Columbus," and she said, "Those aren't cross streets. Where are you?" and again he said, "Columbus and Columbus," and that became a way to communicate when you were too fucked up to find yourself.

You were at the corner of Columbus and Columbus.

So that was where V found herself on the night I'm trying to tell you about. She staggered down the street and I was next to her, certainly not sober, but blocks away from Alan's notorious intersection. She staggered and then she fell.

Fell hard.

Right on her face.

Too blotto to bring her arms up.

She'd knocked out a couple teeth and badly chipped another. The blood seeped from her lips and she asked, "What happened?" and I wasn't sure how honest to be with her. I'd seen war movies in which one soldier, having just stepped on a land mine and missing both legs, asked another, "What happened?" and they said, "It's nothing serious; you're going to be fine."

I wanted to comfort my friend. V and I waited tables together at this glorified diner and she was one of my favorites. At the end of our shifts, we had to put money in envelopes to tip the bussers, the bar, the hostess, and sometimes we even left little envelopes for ourselves so we didn't drink all the day's take.

She'd know the next morning how serious her injuries were. No reason to rile her up now.

"You're okay," I said to her. "We need to get you home."

Hailing a cab with a bleeding six-foot-tall woman under your arm wasn't easy. Several whizzed by us, and it became clear that I was going to have to work out alternative transportation. I threw V over my shoulder in a fireman-carry. Like I said, she was a tall woman, really skinny, but still, she was heavy and I had a pretty good swerve going and periodically I needed to rest, keeping her over my shoulder but leaning on parked cars to give my legs a breather.

"Get off my ride," a guy said, coming toward us.

I understood his stance. I wouldn't have been happy either, seeing two heads on my car, but I was sure that if I explained it to him he'd calm down.

So I explained.

Yet he didn't calm down, didn't feel any human empathy, only saying, "I don't care . . . I don't care . . . I don't care . . . get off my fucking car!"

Notice how levelheaded I had been until this moment. This moment in which my friend was badly hurt. This moment in which I was only trying to get her home. This moment in which no cabs had the decency to help us. This moment in which I needed to rest my legs for like thirty seconds leaning on this guy's bumper and now he was screaming at me?

I folded V up on the guy's hood and squared up in front of him: "Here are your choices," I said. "I kick your ass all down the street or you give us a ride to my friend's house."

"Just get off my car, man," he said, moving back a couple strides.

"We're past that."

"Well, where do you need to go?"

During that car ride, he despised me but was trapped, seeing no other option but to play nice with his alcoholic carjacker. V nodded off in the backseat and came to every thirty seconds or so totally discombobulated and would start swearing at this guy out of nowhere, something like, "What the fuck is this fucker doing?"

"Shut up," I said. "He's helping us."

"He's a fucking fucker."

"Go to sleep."

"What happened?" she asked.

Then she'd pass out and the driver and I would look at each other, shake our heads. We had an apprehensive camaraderie brewing. I mean, he was only chauffeuring us because I threatened him, which is a precarious way for a relationship to begin. V would blip awake again, start with the whole spiel over: "What the fuck is this fucker doing?" and so on and we would have the same conversation, leaving me thinking that this was what it must be like to drink with that guy from *Memento*.

When we got to V's apartment, our driver peeled away, not helping me get her inside. I wondered what version of the story he was going to tell his friends when he got to the next spot. Would he change things? Make himself the hero? How he picked up a couple train wrecks stranded at the corner of Columbus and Columbus and basically saved their lives driving them home? Or would he exaggerate it the other way—that I was going to hurt him, that he met me, his near-death experience, a psycho ready to tear into him for no real reason?

I mean, I might have.

There's no telling.

There's only conjecture—his story and mine—and I'm in the mood tonight to give myself the benefit of the doubt, something that doesn't happen too often around these parts. Tonight, as I puke this story up like I've got alcohol poisoning, and in a way I still do, I look back at these things and can say that I wasn't going to hurt the man.

And I mean it.

I scoop Ava up and meet the paramedics outside our building. I hold her while they check her out, bending limbs, checking eyes for a concussion, head for lumps or cuts, and one of them jabs me with questions. He is a kind man, fiftyish with a white mustache with flecks of red, like pepper jack cheese. He is a parent as well, three kids, and says to me, "We've all been there. Don't beat yourself up," but with Ava bawling in my arms surrounded by emergency workers summoned solely because of my spectacular incompetence, it's impossible *not* to beat myself up, though I don't tell him that, I only avert my eyes and kiss Ava on the head and say, "This is almost over," and their initial checks on her body reveal no obvious damage. They recommend that we go to the emergency room anyway, better safe than sorry and the like, loading the two of us in the back of the ambulance, me sitting on the gurney, Ava on my lap.

I take it as a good sign that they do not throw on the lights and siren, instead following the rules of the road like everyone else, and one of the EMTs gives Ava a brown teddy bear wearing scrubs, a mask covering up its mouth, and Ava finally stops crying. She smiles at the bear. She smiles at me.

I say, "What's its name?" and she says, "Bear."

We do not know this at the time, but this bear will turn into one of Ava's favorite stuffed animals. She will carry it around for weeks, and it becomes some furry indictment, a denunciation in scrubs. Every time I see that bear, I live that day, those harsh pants pushing out of her as she goes down.

Because she's so young, the emergency room is on full alert, rushing Ava into an exam room with an army of doctors. I hold her on my lap as they give her a more precise checkup. Slowly, they determine she's fine, and docs fly away until there's only one left. There's also a woman with a clipboard, who is here to verify/rate the verity of my story.

And she believes me. She even says that as a mother herself, she knows full well how these things happen.

I had called Lelo from the ambulance and now she comes into our exam room, very calm. Ava plays with Bear on my lap.

"Mommy!" she says, happy as can be.

"Hey, girl," says Lelo, picking her up into a big hug. "Are you okay?" Lelo says to me.

"I'm so sorry," I say, knowing they're better off without me. I can't be trusted. I'll try to do the right thing, but I'll botch our life.

Lelo places Ava back on my lap, then she gives me a big hug herself: "Josh, it's okay, she's okay. Look at her!"

Ava bounces Bear around my stomach and chest.

"We're fine," Lclo says.

"Who's that?" I say, knocking Bear on top of its head and faking a smile.

"Bear," says Ava.

"Sorry we didn't make it to the Peek-a-Boo Factory."

"Bear," she says again.

Once I got V into her apartment, I contemplated putting her in the shower, but since she could barely stand up, why risk her falling again? So I stripped her naked and wiped her bloody mouth one last time and turned the lights out and she was in bed mumbling and cooing.

I stood by her bedroom door, eavesdropping while she talked to god. Stood there thinking about how much of our lives we can dent and have no idea. No sense of the consequences till later. There was nothing really wrong in V's life yet. Not until she awoke the next morning. Not until she realized what had happened in her mouth. She'd stir and sense something was off. Something ached. Something was no good. And that was when she'd understand people like us made our own destruction. We suicide-bombed our own lives.

In that moment I wanted to curl up on her floor and be there the next day, to spare her sorting through the inchoate facts alone. So why didn't I? Don't know exactly—don't have a very good excuse—except to say it felt like an intrusion. Like I was barging into her consciousness, jumping on her brain's bed. It was her mouth and I had no right to trespass.

I still wonder about the specifics of the next morning. I've never asked her, don't want to make her hop in that agonizing time machine. She's someone I love unconditionally, and if it would have made it easier on you if I'd stayed, I apologize, V. I'm so sorry if I let you down.

We could have cooed to god together and maybe he would have taken mercy, a miracle happening before the sun came up. The tooth fairy coming not to collect your lost teeth, but to give them back to you, spackle them into your gums so we remained beautiful forever.

3

When I think of my wedding day with Blue, the first memory that pops in my head has nothing to do with her. I don't mean that in a disrespectful way. She was a gorgeous bride. But the first person I think of is my father.

He was a Lutheran minister and he performed our wedding.

Eight weeks later, he was dead. Stage four lung cancer.

So when most couples are in the honeymoon phase of a new marriage, I was grieving. I was grieving and drinking, making things so much harder than they needed to be.

Of course, I didn't know anything about that on my actual wedding day. I knew he was sick. Knew his condition was getting worse. But I tried keeping all that reality barricaded away. The things we didn't talk about, him never asking about my drinking and drugging though he had to know. I showed up at his house all the time with only a couple hours' sleep, the sleaze of the night before smeared all over me.

I remember one Yuletide disaster, in which I was Christmas shopping on Christmas Eve, with Jordan, a marine. The day turning into a shroom bender in the Upper Haight, drinking Bloody Marys at the Trophy Room, the Reverend Horton Heat screaming at us from the jukebox like a drill sergeant. Challenging us and we couldn't let him down. This was what happened when your heroes were train wrecks. You raced to board that same train and steer it into a tree.

Tequila shots? Sure.

You don't steer trains, stupid.

Jordan's voice getting louder. The shrooms getting louder. Me disappearing inside myself. Shouldn't someone buy a goddamn Christmas gift?

There were tourists at the Trophy Room. From Australia. They explained Boxing Day and I didn't dig their accents. That was the Reverend Horton Heat and they should have stopped interrupting him.

A bourbon now? Sure.

I had to be at my dad and stepmom's house at seven the next morning. Over in the East Bay. I had young sisters who wanted to get the whole presents thing under way as soon as possible.

The ice in my Bloody Mary tasted like blood. Was that true? Shit, my tongue was bleeding. Bleeding because I bit it. Blame the Australians. Blame Boxing Day.

Chilled vodka shot? Sure.

Sisters didn't want to hear any excuses about a presents-dearth, especially if it was shrooms. I said something to Jordan about buying gifts—*we should be buying them now!*—and he laughed. Marines weren't known for their emotions. And the bartender said if I played that record again he was cutting me off. I couldn't imagine walking in my dad's house, seeing him and my stepmom and sisters without presents. What would their faces look like? Goddamn Australians had an extra twenty-four hours to shop. I'd changed my mind about them.

So should we do a Fernet? Yup.

My tongue healing quickly. The lights in the bar flipping on. Me squinting and shielding my eyes. Unfit to feel such illumination. And soon we were coming down at my apartment. The shrooms getting softer. But Jordan staying too shrill.

I couldn't bear hearing him utter another syllable so I called 911. Dialing it and saying, "You have to get him out of here," and they said, "Who?" and I hung up, and half an hour later two cops at the door asking if everything was okay. Which it was not. Jordan still yapping. Me, eighteen inches tall, with a swollen tongue and disappointed sisters. The cops didn't want any part of this once they realized there was no real danger, telling me to stay put for the night and don't call them again.

Jordan going bananas once they bolted: "You called them on me?"

"I did."

"I'm leaving."

"Good."

"You're an asshole."

"Yes."

And there were things much worse than a bitten tongue. Such as a sucker punch in the gut. Such as a marine sucker punching you. Crumpling to the floor. Hunting every inch of my lungs for something to survive on but coming up with nothing. Emitting this wheeze and the shrooms weren't helping and the sisters weren't helping and Boxing Day was salt in a wound and Jordan storming out the front door and days later, years later, my lungs finally functioning again.

Breathe in, breathe out.

Surveying the scene.

Still on floor.

But laughing for some reason. I was alone in my room, and it was Christmas Eve. No. Not anymore. After midnight. It was

Christmas morning. Without gifts. Panic. Ran around wrapping up things found in my apartment. Olive oil. A bottle of wine. A Black Sabbath shirt that had obviously been worn.

When I arrived half an hour late, no one said anything. That was our deal. I showed up cooked out of my head and they never called me on it. Maybe that was the real gift they gave me. Or it was the worst thing.

Standing by a fake tree, faking gifts, faking feelings. Hell, even the fire was fake. The TV tuned to a station playing fire.

I had a headache and was sweaty and clammy, still pulsing with mushroom dust driving in my veins. I sat by the fake fire and the sisters, Jessie and Katy, ten and four respectively, kept saying things like "Josh, what do you think this one is?" while pointing to or shaking a particular gift, and I saw how excited they were to open presents from me, their dented prince, their absentee playmate having too much fun in San Francisco to travel home, even though they only lived twenty miles away. Even though I loved them. Even though I resented their happiness. Even though love and resentment didn't dilute.

I loved my sisters more than anything, but they were a flesh-and-blood reminder of the fact my dad didn't want to be around me when I was their age. He didn't love me enough. Or he didn't love me like he loved them. They were who he picked to live in his stable household.

"What is this?" my four-year-old sister, Katy, said. She shook the gift I brought her back and forth.

Me shrugging my shoulders.

"Can I open this one from Josh first?" asked Katy.

My parents saying okay. Her tearing through the wrapping paper. Which was really just newspaper. Me cringing. Her pulling out that faded Black Sabbath shirt. Her holding it up. Overjoyed. She loved the shirt. Loved it! Because it was from me.

I could have given her a blanket sullied with smallpox.

Katy draped herself in the shirt's ill-fitting form and waddled over to me, the black thing hanging past her knees, and she hugged me and she said, "Thanks!" and I said, "Okay," and she said, "This is perfect!" and I said, "Okay," and my sister smiling and my parents frowning, and my heart blackening in a real fire.

This would take all day, opening gifts and bonding and chewing chalky turkey and hucking a Frisbee and yet it would end the same way. It would end back in the Mission District. In a dive bar. Plans already hatched to roll. Snorting lines of E, then popping pills, too. For good measure. Better safe than sober.

And yet there were hours to endure still. Hours of happiness. Hours of resentment. Whole logs of time to burn. Feeling every bit of warmth emanating from a televised blaze.

But we were talking about my wedding day with Blue, and here's what I remember: An hour or so before the ceremony, helping my father get dressed. We were alone, the two of us putting on rented tuxedos, and his hands shook so badly from the chemo, the radiation, the steroids, all the terrible experimental treatments he put his body through so he could watch my sisters grow up.

He wanted to live long enough, he told me, to know them as adults. "Like you," he said. "Like how I know you."

He stood in the dressing room with his shirt unbuttoned, so frustrated with his shaking hands and too stubborn to ask for help. I said, "Let me" and started with his bottom button and worked my way to his thin throat, and he said, "Sorry," and I said, "Don't be," and he said, "It's embarrassing," and I said, "It's only us," and he said, "I love you," and I said, "I love you too," and he said, "Proud of you."

He meant it, of course. He was my father and he loved me, and I was his son and I loved him. I watched those stupid shaking hands of his as he said that he felt proud—proud of me?—why and how and what for, and I hate that during the ceremony I stood in front of him, pledging that I'd do my best to make that marriage work, for better and worse. Because I didn't. I couldn't. I lied to him, to Blue, to every witness.

Yet there were a few seconds before the wedding, before my lies. A few minutes, a pure and shining and sincere moment between father and son. I'll always have that image of his frail frame barely filling out a rented tuxedo. Not a hair left on his head. A complexion like a raw prawn.

And truthfully, I probably wouldn't have ever proposed marriage if my father hadn't been so sick. He was at the end, and he knew it. One time, we were in the Mission together, sitting in his minivan after eating a meal, and he said, "You should get married."

"I'm twenty-five."

"So what?"

"What if I'm not ready?"

"I'm dying," he said, "and I want to officiate your wedding."

I knew he'd die soon, thought I didn't know that he'd only live another eight weeks after our wedding. But I knew that I wasn't strong enough to refuse him. "You're right, Dad. I'll propose."

"Why wait?" he said. "You love her?"

"Yes."

"Don't wait."

"I won't."

"I want to perform your wedding," he said. "I really want that before I die."

Then a few months later, he called me and asked me to meet him at Noah's Bagels. The night before, I'd been teaching a creative writing class at UC Berkeley's art studio, lecturing about characterization. I got a cocaine nosebleed in front of my students. I ran to the bathroom, balling up a square of toilet paper and jamming the pellet in my nostril. The bottom of it was white and I watched the mirror, the blood slowly soaking down, the whole clump going red. I pulled a drenched pellet and squashed a new one up. I must have done this twenty times.

I loved teaching and wanted to do right by my students, but I loved drugs and wanted to do right by them, too. These aren't contradictions. They're positive and negative charges existing together, like in an atom.

Once my nose stopped bleeding, I made my way back to the classroom. The students all sat there eyeballing me, and I said, "Where was I?" knowing I should offer some useless excuse— *allergies? altitude? humidity?*—and no one answered me, so I said, "What was the last thing I told you?"

They shuffled through their notes. Someone said, "Our main character has to be the story's hero *and* its villain," and someone else said, "They have to be both good and bad."

I wiped my nose another time. No new blood. Saying to them, "Yes, we are our own antagonists."

So that had been my headspace when I rolled into Noah's Bagels to meet my dad. Now, because it was a Saturday morning, the place swarmed with kids, all wearing grass-stained soccer uniforms. There must've been at least fifty of them, all hopped up on post-game hysteria, running around and yelling at one another.

My dad met me out front of the fracas, standing by the door. His cancer had been in remission about a year, but he still looked sick. Only wisps of hair on his head, so skinny and sallow and slow. He'd lost the feeling in his feet from the chemo, making driving almost impossible, never knowing how hard he pressed the brake or gas. The thing he hated the most were the birds—"I hear birds in my head sometimes," he told me, from his brain tumor, that wrecking ball.

"Welcome to the zoo," he said, motioning to a gang of soccer kids motoring by.

"We can walk somewhere else," I said, "if the kids are bugging you." Noise had bothered him since starting one of the experimental treatments. My sisters called him Decadron Man, after a steroid that hindered his ability to sleep, making him mean. But I didn't live with my dad when he had cancer; I didn't see the day-to-day, didn't know how cruel these pills and tumors and infusions had made him. My sisters did. And Dad always put on a brave face when I came around. "I'm fine," he'd say. "I'm getting better."

We all knew that was impossible—we all knew that stage four lung cancer with an inoperable metastasis in his brain was a death sentence. Just don't bother telling him that. And maybe that stubbornness was necessary staring down a diagnosis so dire. Maybe you needed to convince yourself that you were the exception and fuck the rule.

"No," he said to me, "let's just stay here. I need to talk to you."

"This sounds serious."

"It is serious."

We opened the front door and waded into the grass-stained chaos. We ordered drinks. I asked if he was hungry, though he hadn't been in years. Finally, we took a seat at a small table.

"My remission is over," he said. "I have eleven new tumors."

He never talked emotionally about his cancer, sticking to the facts—at least until the very end, when the cells of his rage kept dividing and dividing. When he was incensed that his pious occupation wasn't pardoning him from an early death. He must've thought that there was a sort of interstellar ledger, that the god he preached every Sunday morning kept a tally and rewarded good deeds. That this wasn't the sort of planet where malice was rewarded. That this wasn't the place where the worst of us often succeed. So because of all that, my dad would die embittered, cursing his thankless faith, spitting on it like the soldiers dousing Jesus in saliva as he carried their cross.

But this trip to Noah's wasn't close enough to his death for that last burst of heresy. Not yet. No, this was still the Time of Facts.

"Did you say *eleven*?!" I said. "How is that number even possible?"

"These are the facts," he said. "I wanted you to know."

"What do we do?" I said to him, such a stupid question.

"What do we do with what?"

The soccer children ran around us, chirping their eternal confident calls.

"With this news," I said. "What can we do to help?"

He just shook his head—at me, at his god, at this repugnant news. The world was done with him.

For my dad, that morning among all those shiny soccer players, rubbing our bloody noses in their long lives, it was only Noah's Bagels, not Noah's ark—and nothing was coming to keep him from dying. He wouldn't float above the fray. He wouldn't watch from the safety of the ark's deck as everyone else drowned.

Then he did die, and I had this stampeding grief, had this stash of unused love for him—where were we supposed to put that love once they'd gone?—and it wanted to travel, wanted to gallop and guzzle trouble. It wanted to race off so I could waterboard my feelings with booze.

Driving on acid is underrated. Not as dangerous as you're thinking. You float down the road. Granted, it's hard not to speed. And staying in your lane is almost impossible. It's a cross between a luge and a magic carpet ride.

Okay, it's probably as dangerous as you're thinking.

I scored some acid with three of my dirtbag friends, and we drove off. Okay, I drove to Reno. On acid. They drank beers and sang along to the radio. We had it on a godawful station that played things like Kenny Loggins's "Footloose" and that became our anthem for the trip.

Downtown Reno was a super sad stash of diners, casinos, strip clubs, and cowboy bars. Nobody had any fun there. The strippers practically used nicotine patches for pasties.

Our first night was your typical hard-drinking, hard-drugging, take-no-prisoners bender. It's what we expected the whole weekend to be like, but Anthony got arrested early the next morning. I've never been exactly clear on why, and I don't think he is either. One theory was that he was sleeping in the hallway of a motel we weren't staying at. They frown on such behavior.

So we were killing time the next morning—Jabiz, Ben, and

me—waiting for Anthony to be freed from the tank. It was before noon, say ten or thereabouts, and we were at a strip club that had a "renowned" buffet so we figured we could kill two birds with one bad idea: see naked ladies and eat at the same time.

It didn't seem to bother Jabiz or Ben, chewing their food while smiling at these working women. But I couldn't do it: the acid gave me a weird vein of morality, making it tasteless to eat food in front of the girls. I actually sat in the back of the club, facing away from the stage, chewing my food like a good little boy, then joining my friends once I could ogle without worrying if I had prime rib in my teeth.

At a certain point while getting a lap dance, I asked a stripper, "Can you help us get some blow?"

"Sure."

"Here?"

"No," she said, "after my shift."

"When's that?"

"Two hours. I can't leave with a customer or I'll get fired. I'll pick you up around the corner."

I reported the good news to Jabiz and Ben. This was the thing to turn the day around. I mean, don't get me wrong, the buffet was top-notch, but some yayo would make sure we made it through the entire weekend with drinks in our hands.

"We should see if the DJ can play 'Footloose' while the next woman strips," I said.

Both Ben and Jabiz thought that was a stellar idea.

Unfortunately, the DJ didn't have the track. Instead, as a Kenny Loggins consolation, he offered "Danger Zone" from the *Top Gun* soundtrack. You should have seen this woman dance to "Danger Zone." It was a wonderful sight.

Jabiz, Ben, and I killed the next two hours with watered-down drinks. Then the stripper—I can't remember her name so let's call her Quinn—said I should meet her in ten minutes up the block.

She drove me to one of those prefab complexes out on the edge of town. All the condos washed in beige stucco, front yards just tan gravel. We walked into her house and she vanished into the bedroom, told me to grab a beer and sit in the living room. I heard voices in the back and for the first time I got scared. I didn't know her. I could very easily get robbed. Not that their take would be worth the effort. But still, no one wants to get rolled in Reno.

Soon, she returned carrying a baby. A little boy with bright red hair. The same shade that I had as a youngster.

"This is Bobby," she said.

"Who were you talking to?"

She motioned to the baby.

"Where's the sitter?" I said.

"Yeah, yeah, anyway, you watch him for a few minutes and I'll go get the blow," Quinn said, handing him over before I had the chance to say anything back. Then she disappeared into the backyard, through the sliding glass door.

It was Bobby and me. We stared at each other. I bounced him on my knee and said, "I'm a friend of your mom's."

I held that little boy and thought about all the strange men my mom had left me with over the years, once my dad bolted for California. There was this one crazy cat, Tim. I don't know much about him, really. He was the handyman at the company where my mom was the secretary. He had a hair trigger. I once saw him wing his coffee cup at a car's windshield because the guy cut him off in traffic.

One day in his truck he chomped a cigar and said to me, "You tough?"

I was about ten years old. "Yeah, I'm tough."

"Let's see about that." He told me to place my forearm down on the armrest between us. He placed his forearm right next to mine so they touched. Then he took his lit cigar and laid it down on us, so it was burning both our arms.

"First one to move is soft as a baby's ass," said Tim.

Without any dad around I wanted to impress Tim. I wanted him to say, "Holy shit, kid, you're chiseled out of rock." But I wasn't tough. I was a ten-year-old faking it. I held my arm there, smelling the burn of his arm hair, our skin. I tried to be as tough as possible but pretty soon I jerked my arm away and rubbed the spot where the cherry had kissed it.

"Toughest in all the land," Tim said, retrieving his cigar and taking some celebratory puffs.

I bet my mom had no idea about the day Tim burned my arm. I probably didn't mention it to her. Truth was I liked spending time with Tim, even if he scared me. He was a man, a tough man, and no matter how dumb it sounds now, I enjoyed being around him. Yes, he was dangerous but he gave me lots of attention. And if you spend enough time being ignored, a burning cigar on your skin isn't so bad.

"Your mom loves you," I said to Bobby, bouncing him some more. "So does your dad. They are trying their best."

Because of my sisters, I was good with babies. But Quinn didn't know that. She didn't care, needed her cut of the money from selling me an eight ball. She wasn't getting rich working the morning shift at the club.

I don't want to say apathy. Don't want to say malice. Don't want to believe Bobby was left with men like me often. Men looking to score drugs. Score anything Quinn was willing to hock. I don't want to ponder all the Tims that might have sat on this same sofa, whipping out their burning cigars or worse. I don't want to say any of that because Bobby deserves better.

Quinn was back in about twenty minutes, offered me a ride to town and I said I'd rather walk.

"It's eight miles," she said.

"I'll call a taxi."

"They don't come here."

"Why?"

"Just let me drive you," she said.

"Can Bobby come?"

"Of course," Quinn said. "I can't leave him here by himself, right?"

She smirked at me, and I pretended that I didn't know what her face meant. The image of Bobby left there alone, scared and crying, clammy with a dirty diaper, while Quinn worked her morning shift at the club made me want to impale my heart, let its juice drip down and coagulate on the floor—what was the point in even having a heart when babies needed help and we wouldn't ease their suffering?

It wasn't my fault per se, but I was there.

"Want a bump for the road?" Quinn said. It was a wretched suggestion, but I couldn't say no.

Bobby played on his blanket while we sniffed brutal eight-inch lines that almost required a running start.

The car ride back to town was quiet, Quinn and I not talking much, Bobby gurgling in the backseat. That red hair of his—of ours—I stared at it in the rearview, knowing that in a couple minutes I'd never see the boy again. He'd live his life and I'd live mine but in this wicked world our paths would never converge.

Sometimes, toward a movie's conclusion a couple quick sentences hit the screen telling the audience where this man or woman ended up down the line. And I'd like to do the same thing for Bobby. I'd like to cook up a future for him.

First, his mom gets clean.

Second, they get out of Reno.

Third, she falls in love with a good man and Bobby has a father figure. Someone who's never even smoked a cigar.

Fourth, this father raises Bobby as his own, teaching him to be kind, to be a hard worker, to honor his commitments, and this father never dies. This father lives forever.

Fifth, I want Bobby to never even try booze and drugs, swear off them just because he knows the havoc they wreaked in his mom's life before she got sober.

Sixth, Bobby is safe and solid. He is a safe and solid man with a safe and solid life.

That's what I want so badly for that innocent boy. And who knows? Maybe that's what happened.

All I can tell you for sure is that they drove off. I was alone in the motel parking lot with the blow and my dad's ghost. Anthony was probably out of jail by then. Jabiz and Ben were antsy to get high. Bobby was gone, leaving all us Tims in the rearview.

My childhood wasn't always lacquered in some monochrome gloom. You need to know that. We had good times too, my mom and me. She was an amazing pianist, but because she had rheumatoid arthritis in her wrists, it hurt her to play. She drank and drugged in part so she could fight through the pain and play piano. There were other reasons she partied, but don't worry about those right now.

Just worry about the boy under her piano bench.

There he is, lying on his stomach, beneath her, listening to her play. He presses one of the piano's pedals. His mom knows what he's doing, of course. This is a game they play. She strikes some tune and pretends that she has no idea that he's hiding beneath her bench and he sends a hand out, mashing one pedal down, making each note ring on and on, and she asks, "Why does my music sound like that?" and the boy muffles a laugh, moving his hand from one pedal to another and pressing that one now, and the mother says, "I don't understand what's happening!" and the boy can barely stand it, maybe a chuckle slips out, and he sends his hand to his favorite pedal, the one that severs each note she plays, making the song sound so staccato, and he is beside himself, anticipating what will happen next, and before he knows it the music stops, the mother slowly sliding the bench back a bit and peering down at him and saying, "What are you doing down there, silly?" and he says, "Gotcha!" and she says, "Gotcha back!" and tickles him, first on the ribs, then the armpits, then cracking up herself and saying, "Will you please let me practice?" and the boy saying, "Okay," and she says, "I'm serious this time," and he says, "Okay," already smiling, and so she slides her piano bench back into position and picks the tune up where she left off and ten, twenty seconds later—however long the excited boy can endure waiting—he sends his hand out and presses the first pedal again and their routine starts over and they are so happy.

4

Of course, you can only relapse if you've gotten clean, and you can only get clean if there are things you promise yourself that you're never going to do, and you saw each of these promises in half like magicians' assistants, this litany of lines you will never cross, coded beliefs that are sanctified and unimpeachable, maybe a moral compass that will always point in the other direction from certain degradations, certain bad ideas, but you trample these demarcations.

After the Peek-a-Boo Factory fiasco, I can't tell what's *true*. Am I being honest about how devastated I am after seeing Ava fall, or am I hunting for a reason to relapse? Am I manufacturing motive? She wasn't even hurt, so why am I making it sound so grave?

If I zero in on my life, if I scour and skewer and stew on any aspect, I'll always locate some benign reason to give up. To fail and flee. So the question becomes, is that what I want? Do I want to end up alone and alcoholic?

No, of course not.

Yes, of course.

There's this secret thing about relapse: You want there to be a reason. You crave cause and effect. You want some tragedy, a trigger, something that directly leads you to a bar or a dealer's house or a corner. You want it to be easily explainable to people after the fact. You want them to hear your reason and you want them to pity you. You want this captive audience to hear your ordeal and think to themselves, wow, in a similar circumstance, I would have behaved the same way.

If you have that, if they gift you that, then maybe there's a small chance you can stomach living because I'll tell you what, the shame—the electric shame—that accompanies a relapse is something to behold.

I had thirteen months clean the first time I relapsed. Thirteen months, gone, given away on a day bulging with ordinariness. No glorious incident, no lethal news, no reason.

This was before Ava, before Lelo and I were married. We lived in the Mission District, at the corner of 20th and Valencia. Coincidentally, we were right across the street from where I used to live with Blue, but I tried not to take that as a sign for a lack of progress. Signs, I rationalized, weren't that on the nose.

It had been a normal morning, Lelo and I showering and swigging coffee and going to work. A morning with meetings, emails, a morning that can't be separated from any of a hundred just like it. Conjoined mornings. All anonymous and bland.

A morning with a bagel and carrot juice, where my boss was distracted and so I wrote at my desk. I was pretty deep into my third novel, *Damascus*, and one of the reasons I tolerated this shitty start-up job was that I had huge chunks of unsupervised time. My boss was a failed musician and he dug that I wrote books. He knew I scribbled on the clock and maybe it made him feel like a patron of the arts. I have no idea what that sad cat was all about, but he's a part of this story. In a couple hours, he'll invite me to lunch. I'll go. He'll order a scotch. So will I.

I won't mention rehab, won't utter one peep about trying to be a better person.

It was 2010; it was a Monday or Thursday or Friday; it was winter or spring or summer; I was content or feeling stifled; it was another reconstituted morning until I ruined everything.

I don't remember consciously thinking about this then, but as I look back, I wonder if I was simply bored, learning to live quietly. Before rehab, I had a life flush with chaos, and now there was routine, carrot juice and conjoined mornings and whatnot, and perhaps this inflamed some tacit impatience, some ammunition I didn't know was live until it was too late.

Maybe I didn't want to ruin everything that day; maybe I just needed a splash of anarchy.

Thirteen months sober felt like a long time to me. So when that sad start-up boss, Neal, invited me out for lunch, I saw no reason to say no. I could nurse a soda water while Neal drank his lunch. He was notorious around the office for getting loaded over a mid-day snack. First thing in the morning, he lurched toward his desk, head down, all tousled and dejected, that slow chain-gang shuffle, knowing he'd spend his day slamming rocks with his sledge-hammer and belting out spirituals. But his whole demeanor was different when he returned to the office from lunch, after throwing back a bunch of cocktails. He was giddy, smiling and peppy, like a kid at Disneyland taking his picture with Goofy.

I didn't know this at the time, but my thirteen months off booze and drugs didn't mean shit if I was too afraid to tell people I was sober. I hated saying that, admitting it.

I'd always hated sober people. I spent my twenties tending bar and sober people were the enemy. I spent my twenties and early thirties as a drunk and an addict and sober people were the enemy on that front, too. They were teetotaling cowards. They were scared to live recklessly. They were cautious and safe and timid, all things I never wanted to be.

So during that first thirteen months of my sobriety, I never told anyone I was clean. Nobody except my dearest friends, say five or six heads. I harbored that detail like a diagnosis.

"Dewar's and a beer back," Neal said to the bartender, a few blocks from our office.

"That sounds good," I said, knowing that ordering a drink didn't mean I had to put the liquid in my mouth. I didn't have to swallow. There was nothing that said I had to gulp the whole shot down.

"I'll join you guys," said the bartender. He poured us three huge shots of scotch, triples. That was one nice thing about drinking during the day with a thirsty bartender: he wanted playmates, so his generosity knew no bounds.

They snatched theirs and looked at me; I grabbed mine and stared back.

Soon, all three of us held our scotches in the air.

Soon, all three of us drank them.

The other thing no one tells you about relapse is that you think you can drink as much as you could before you quit. I was out of practice but didn't care. Tossing back scotches round for round with Neal.

We laughed and told war stories and lied and thumped our chests and our bravado blew up like helium balloons floating over our heads.

And for a couple hours, this was fun. I was having fun. Drunk enough that I didn't care what I was dismantling. I was hours away from that.

But I did think about Kae. That's something I clearly remember. I went to take a leak and after washing my hands, I thrust them under the automatic hand dryer. Feeling that warm breath, thinking about his donut shop essay, the life he gave away being busted back. I swear the whole bathroom smelled like car exhaust. Fumes filling my lungs with polluted beauty.

For a few seconds, Kae was with me.

At a certain point I blacked out. Last thing I remember was Neal and me doing another scotch and the bartender telling me to stop yelling. He had no idea who he was dealing with. I never stopped.

Never in a million years did I want to sober up. This was how I wanted to feel forever. So cooked I couldn't stand, couldn't do much of anything, except drink and sit and yell, drink and sit and yell. This was a perfect way to spend your life.

And then I was being zipped in a body bag, the whole world

disappearing. I'd known that feeling since elementary school. Liquor had been "helping" me for a long time.

When a fifth grader drinks it's often alone. It's often alone because he's often alone.

This is after the fifth grader's dad leaves. So the mother works two jobs, one as a secretary, the other as a music director at a church. Which means she works way more than forty hours a week.

He's what they call a latchkey kid. Or that's what they were called in the '80s. Mom leaves money for pizzas. He orders Domino's because they have to deliver in half an hour or less or the pizza is free.

When the fifth grader is not drinking alone, he drinks with his best friend, Brenty, who has his own story for why he likes to drink in elementary school but that's not for me to tell.

The fifth grader gulps fuzzy navels or box wine. Depending on what's left over. It's easy for him to swipe box wine because the box isn't see-through. The mother has no idea the quantity, no idea how much she's had. The fuzzy navels are out of a blender. That's how she likes to drink them. Blended. Orange juice and peach schnapps. It makes sense to drink blended drinks in the desert because it's so hot. She'll always leave some in the blender. Sometimes it's just the dregs. Sometimes, it's half full. Regardless, the fifth grader always finishes the sad slush. Finishes it and feels silly. He feels—if this makes any sense—important.

And when Brenty's over it's like New Year's Eve. They blast MTV. They sing along, dance, play air guitar. They watch basketball; they play basketball. They call girls. They swim in the pool. They play Nintendo. They call getting drunk getting *juiced*.

"I'm so juiced," one will say.

"We're juiced!" says the other.

And this isn't just about a fifth grader. It's about a fourth grader. A sixth grader. There's so much box wine back then. So many blender-dregs that the boy can fill that swimming pool in the backyard.

Sometimes feeling important lasts for hours, drink after drink, the fifth grader having the time of his life. He likes being drunk. Likes being dizzy and clumsy and silly and slurring his words. One night, Brenty watches the fifth grader shit his pants, and this important fifth grader just stands there laughing about it, laughing his head off, and his eyes cry 'cause this is funny, so fucking funny, the fifth grader feeling happy with shit in his pants.

It only happens once, but he does get a free pizza. It takes the delivery guy something like thirty-three minutes to get there. The boy can hear him screech up out front and slam the car's door and run over the gravel in the front yard and ring the bell and the boy enjoys the sounds of somebody rushing to be with him.

"Sorry, I'm late," the delivery man says. "The pizza's on the house."

"It's cool," says the fifth grader, drunk and important.

◻

Dreams were freebies, our brains vacationing in squalor. Going back to old lifestyles. Popping bottles or pills or plunging needles into veins or muscles.

One counselor in rehab told me to enjoy these inebriated fantasies. "Like a sex dream," she said. "Fun with no consequences."

So for a shot glass full of seconds, I thought that whole afternoon session with Neal was fake, a fever dream for my subconscious, some imaginary debacle and I would wake up refreshed. Freaked out but refreshed.

Coming to the next morning, one thing was obvious: my nose was broken.

A couple other immediately obvious things: I was at my apartment but had no recollection of getting there. I wore only underwear, which meant someone must have helped me out of my clothes. Another obvious thing was that I was alone in the bedroom. That was when this popped in my sick head: *Did I get caught?* Because if Lelo didn't know, maybe I could lie about it. For a drunk, that whole thing about a tree falling in the forest—and did it make a sound if no one heard?—it worked for relapse, too. Meaning I might not have made a sound when I fell. And if the only people who knew I'd gone on a quick run were Neal and the bartender, I could live with that. Just never go back to that job, that bar. Just pretend that yesterday never happened.

"Are you okay?"

I hoped that was my broken nose talking, but it sounded like Lelo.

"I've never seen someone get so sick," she said.

"What happened?"

She told me I came home early last night, about seven. My face had dried blood all over it. I got sick right away and every half an hour after. She thought about taking me to the emergency room, but I talked her out of it between retches.

"Yeah, but what happened?" I said.

"You tell me, Josh."

"I've ruined it . . ."

"I'll go get you a Gatorade."

"Thanks for taking care of me," I said.

She looked at me with what I assumed was mauling disappointment. She was sad, tired. She'd been up all night doting on a useless drunkard. What really ripped my heart out was how I'd tricked her, teasing her with these thirteen months and then one day our clean life was gone. And for no reason. I didn't like scotch, I didn't like Neal, I didn't like drinking in some snooty tapas joint, I didn't like my mysterious broken nose. There was nothing I could blame this on except myself.

How was Lelo supposed to forgive me and why should she? And how should she ever believe me after? If I'd relapsed once, why wouldn't it happen again and again and again?

Lelo had been my girl four years when I finally went to rehab. She'd seen the caveman, seen a lot of the stupidity firsthand. "Thanks for the Gatorade," I said. "That's nice of you."

She left our apartment and I could hear her heels clacking down the front stairs, could hear the huge weighted front door of our apartment building slam behind her. "Please come back," I whispered.

The clock said it was 7:41 in the morning. I staggered to the bathroom and threw up. Flushed the toilet and crashed on the bathroom floor. There were streaks of vomit everywhere. No wonder the muscles in my sides ached. I must have gotten sick thirty times.

I lay down. Why go back to bed only to be summoned here to dry heave? I threw myself into the tub and cranked up the cold. It dribbled from our hopeless showerhead.

Thirteen months, busted just like my nose.

Lelo was leaving me. She had to. I'd made it impossible for her to stay. That Gatorade was a parting gift, a concession. I drove her away, like I did with Blue.

"Either you go to rehab or move out," said Blue. This was in July 2005, four years before I tried getting sober for the first time. It was the morning of my birthday. It might sound malicious on Blue's part to threaten me like this on my birthday, and it probably was, but in her defense, I deserved it, staying out the whole night before and not calling, crawling in about 8:00 a.m. with a coke nosebleed.

"I'm sorry," I said.

"I care less and less with every apology," she said. Then she went to work, telling me we'd talk more about it when she got home. She was disgusted, and I couldn't blame her, and it made me nostalgic for the days when she dug bedlam. And she used to be a card-carrying nutcase. Like the night we went to see Beckett's *Waiting for Godot*. I bought us kickass seats, way up front, and we decided to dress in our best Beckettian costumes. All black, of course. Eyeliner smeared in great ovals around our eyes. Hair teased up and pasted in weird gravity-defying geometries.

And we cocktailed starting three hours before the show and even shared a bottle of champagne in the car on our way to the theater. For most heads, drinking and driving was a two-step process but not in my life: I loved to drink while driving. Something I used to do all the time and even sometimes now I get the itch behind the wheel, reaching for a bottle like an amputee scratching a phantom limb.

Anyway, on this night we imbibed a bit too much, and Blue was asleep in her seat midway through the first act. That would have probably been fine if she didn't start snoring. Really snoring. Beckett himself would have *loved* this, a beautiful woman conked out at his show and cranking up her snore like it was running through

Marshall stacks. But the people around us did not dig Blue's music, and I shook her a few times, saying, "You okay?" and she said, "I want to go home," and I said, "Really?" and she said, "Will you carry me?"

Will I carry her? Of course, I'll carry her.

I swooped Blue up in my arms and kicked my way to the aisle, trudging away from the actors, the audience, feeling proud of her, the scene she was making. It was a perfect night.

But it wasn't, I guess. Eventually, she wanted to stay awake, see the show. Our lifestyle wore on her until she quit the restaurant biz to be an acupuncture assistant. Blue binged still but only on tinctures, tilting cocktails of herbal extracts and water. We had a huge shelf in our kitchen that was dedicated to all her murky herbs.

The drunker my lifestyle became, hers swirled with healing beverages. No more coffee in the morning but a shot of Siberian ginseng. No pills to sleep but valerian root.

Sometimes when home alone, I'd cut lines of blow or heroin out on her special herbal shelf, thinking I was proving a point, but what would that even prove? That I was petty?

Blue was evolving into something new and vibrant and better, and I stayed one species behind.

Even if I knew she was right on my birthday, I wasn't going to rehab. I was under the influence of something else: being *obstinate*. Every junkie knows it well, all our friends telling us to get some help, get our shit together, but hell no, we're holding out. This ain't closing time, Jack. This ain't the bottom. This life can get much worse and we'll show you, thank you very much.

So once Blue left for the acupuncture clinic that morning, I packed my favorite clothes, which were all dirty, fishing them from the hamper and filling a yellow duffel bag and bolting. Went straight to the dive bars on 16th Street, hell-bent on celebrating my birthday with or without Blue.

Years later, she told me she didn't think we were splitting up for good that day—thought we were only having a fight, that she issued an ultimatum but only to scare me, to get me to come to my senses.

She said, "I cracked the door and you ran through it."

That was the end of our three-year marriage.

Being a drunk demands that of you: vanishing from all kinds of required life.

I plopped my yellow duffel bag down on the stool next to me, like a drinking buddy. Let's call her Josephine because I needed some female companionship, even if she was chock-full of stinky argyle socks and plaid pants.

She and I had picked the Kilowatt for our first stop because it was easy to get drugs there in the afternoon. Any bar would have access to narcotics once the sun dipped down, but at the Kilowatt, you could see people from noon on with cocaine rimming their noses like salt on margarita glasses.

Since this was a birthday bash, Josephine and I decided to get an eight ball. Spare no expense! We needed an ample supply of party favors to do the job right.

The Kilowatt was a narrow room, a weird maze of tables and booths with spilled liquor smeared all over their tops. Rock and roll always piped, and dogs scurried between tables looking for handouts.

Really, we were all looking for handouts at the Kilowatt.

On that day, the bar was all men—a bunch of testosterone pouches hunched over one spirit or another, in various stages of spoil. We could have been lined up for a time-lapse educational video on the ruin of alcoholism. There was a young, skinny, speedy punk sitting at the bar, tapping both his feet and talking mach syllables, his Mohawk pasted to such jagged tips it could have been a throwing star, and there was me, around thirty, still handsome but carrying that doughy drunkard's weight in his face and neck, and at a table was a couple fortyish fellas reeking of alimony, botched rehabs, kids not bothering to text dear old dad on his birthday, and finally our crown jewel, our destiny, a raving broken pathos machine, somewhere in his sixties, nose a mosaic of fissured veins.

Josephine and I didn't want to be around them anymore so we had a couple shots, a couple beers, and decided to troll. Went to Delirium next, the joint with my favorite sign in the city—the one behind the bar that said SERVICE FOR THE SICK—and again, not much in the department of the fairer sex, so Josephine and I made our way to Zeitgeist, sitting at a picnic table out back on the patio with a pitcher of wheat beer, sneaking bumps of coke off my (former) apartment key when no one was looking.

There were groups of other people like me—tattooed hipsters, artists—congregated at other picnic tables. Social D played. I was the only one alone, the only one snuggling up to a duffel bag. I needed to fix that and fast.

"Listen," I said to Josephine, "I like you, but I need to find an actual person to hang out with today."

My friends, who had started growing increasingly absent when I went on a binge, even Shany, all had plans when I called and told them that Blue kicked me out on my birthday and I needed their assistance to bender properly.

They knew what was coming and excuses sprouted like a rash.

Root canals.

Tax audits.

Vasectomies.

Boob jobs.

Anything so they didn't have to meet me and watch what they knew was going to happen. I brought the duffel bag closer to my mouth. "The plan," I said to her, "is to find somebody to go to dinner with me tonight. I want to keep that reservation."

Earlier in the week, Blue and I had made plans to go to a fancy seafood restaurant. I was going to go there that night and eat overpriced fish and drink overpriced champagne and I was going to blow out a candle stuck in an overpriced dessert and I was going to have a great fucking birthday.

"Where should we go next?" I said to Josephine.

Her name was Sadie. I met her at . . . well, I don't actually remember where I met her. Maybe Bender's. Maybe the 500 Club or Doc's Clock or Mission Bar or the Attic. Could be the Lone Palm. Josephine and I were thorough explorers that day. All I know is that I saw the lovely Sadie sitting at a bar by herself. She was black Irish, and I was a sucker for that mix of dark hair and blue eyes. She sipped whiskey on the rocks by herself.

I slid Josephine under my barstool and sat a couple down from Sadie.

I knew how to seduce her because I'd done this many times. I wouldn't talk to her directly at first, chatting with the bartender so Sadie could hear. I'd be funny, charming, and when Sadie finally initiated eye contact, I'd offer to buy her a drink, and anybody nipping whiskey by herself in the late afternoon would accept, and that was exactly what happened.

"It's my birthday," I said.

"Bullshit," she said, "that's just a line."

"I wouldn't lie to you."

"Show me your ID."

I did. She spent thirty seconds analyzing the information.

"Should you really be an organ donor?" Sadie asked.

"I'm in tip-top shape."

"You're old, too."

"I'm twenty-nine."

"That's old."

"Would you like a bump?"

Pretty soon, we huddled in the little girls' room, in a stall, and I cut a couple rips on the back of the toilet, handing her a rolled-up dollar and saying, "Ladies first."

"Prince Charming, huh?"

I waited until we were good and loaded and told Sadie the truth: Blue kicked me out, and I had a dinner reservation that I wanted to keep. "No strings attached," I said. "Come to dinner with me. Let's drink champagne and then you go your way and I'll go mine."

"Don't you want to take someone who actually knows you?"

How could I tell her that people who knew me hated me? How could I tell her that she was my only chance? "That's the last thing I want," I said to Sadie.

"Why?"

"Are you hungry or not?"

"Of course I'm not hungry," she said, "and neither are you. We did a gram of blow. But I'll come to your weird birthday party."

We walked in the restaurant and I told the hostess my last name. She didn't know my wife threw me out. Didn't know that my dirty laundry was crammed in the yellow duffel bag over my shoulder. All she knew was that a bleary-eyed guy showed up in the company of a gorgeous young woman, and there was nothing wrong with that.

I ordered a $75 appetizer, a tower of shellfish and oysters and Dungeness crab and lobster. Of course, I couldn't stop blowing lines, so each expensive bite tasted terrible—a cocktail of saltwater brine and cocaine drip—but that wasn't going to stop me. I choked down every gluttonous forkful.

Sadie sat across from me swigging champagne and shaking her head. "I've seen drunks do oddball shit," she said, watching me cracking meat from a crab claw, "but you are your own animal."

"I'm not my own enemy."

"I said animal."

I accidentally kicked Josephine under the table. "Oh."

"And you can't argue with that, can you?" she said. "Aren't you an animal?"

These weren't the things I wanted to be talking about. This was a birthday party, and I was the guest of honor. Sadie called me an animal, so I meowed—the nerdiest, girliest meow I could muster, channeling my inner eight-year-old and getting a good one right in Sadie's face.

Meow!

We laughed. We made a toast: *To kitties the world over.* We kissed. And for a moment, it worked. I completely forgot who I was.

"I want you to fuck me," said Sadie.

"I'd like that."

"Now," she said, "I want you to fuck me now."

○

We moved toward the back where the restaurant had two unisex bathrooms. Both were locked, but we were the only ones in line so we kissed. A woman walked out of one of them, startled by how we were going at it, but we couldn't care about that.

Once the door was locked, Sadie ripped off her jeans and panties and hopped on the sink, balancing herself, holding up her shirt to play with her nipples. I still stood by the door and pulled my cock out, and I stared in between Sadie's spread legs, her pubic hair cut to a buzz, and I licked my lips, salivating, slowly moved toward her, only two more strides and I'd be there, with her, I'd be there with her and I'd be far away from all my mistakes and far away from my conscience and far away from anything or anyone who could judge me, two strides and I'd fall to my knees and taste her.

But I never made it.

I couldn't make it because everything changed.

One minute she sat on the sink with her pretty pale legs spread wide, and the next minute the sink ripped from the wall, water spraying everywhere, Sadie landing amid the shattered porcelain.

We looked at each other, and Sadie laughed like crazy, lying on the floor. It was a small miracle that she didn't cut up her ass, but thankfully she was fine. I put my dick away and helped her up, knew that the sink had made a crazy-loud noise and soon workers from the restaurant would be there wanting to know what had happened, what had I done now, what was the latest thing I busted?

After giving my phone and driver's license numbers to the manager of the restaurant—"You're going to pay for the damage! You're going to pay for what you did!"—Sadie, Josephine, and I went back to the Mission District dive bars. Back home. We didn't belong in that posh place.

The cocaine had been the pre-dinner drug of choice, but now it was time to go down, getting some pills to finish the job, finish this birthday boy off. And that was what must have happened because next thing I knew I startled myself awake in the morning. I was so thirsty, having no idea where I was, whole body throbbing for some sugar.

Sadie was passed out next to me, and I snuck out of her room with Josephine. Found a bottle of beer in her kitchen, brought it into the bathroom, turned on the shower. The room filled with steam while I stood there naked, sipping that beer.

I closed the toilet lid and set Josephine there, unzipped her to change my clothes. The waft that escaped her maw, the stench of my dirty laundry, was a sucker punch and I retched.

Then I leaned over and stuck my head right inside Josephine's guts, shaking my face around in there, burrowing as deep as I could.

I was a nude homeless drunkard hiding in a duffel bag.

And then years later I was a nude relapsed drunkard hiding in a cold shower. Fresh off a relapse. A mysterious broken nose. The good life, given away. Probably losing Lelo.

I made myself a promise lying in the cold running water.

Promised I'd go to a meeting and tell a roomful of people what I'd done, promised I'd at least try to build on these last thirteen months, maybe find wisdom in that old cliché "Relapse is part of recovery."

Because though I hated myself for drinking again, at least I didn't enjoy it. I was throwing up and my nose had looked better. It could have gone the other way. I could have loved going back out. It could have been some seedy reconciliation, seeing an old flame and kissing her passionately, pledging devotion, eloping, living out our time in splendid squalor.

Maybe I was lucky that didn't happen so my relapse could stop at one day. A lot of people aren't that lucky, and they shack up with that mistress.

One thing was certain: I wasn't going to keep my sobriety a secret anymore. I'd scream it in Kae's tailpipe like it was a microphone.

Something amazing happened once I finally peeled myself out of the shower. Lelo came back. She had that Gatorade and a breakfast bagel. She hugged me. She said, "Let's lie down together."

She and I had started dating right after Blue and I had split up back in 2005. She knew I was an alcoholic, and she was there when things went from bad to worse to suicidal. She stayed through all that nonsense and it looked like she was going to stay through my relapse, too.

I want to say something here about the nature of love—how it's hard as a diamond and can't be scratched, no matter what. But I don't believe that. Many loves end; hell, most of them do. That doesn't mean they're any less *love*. Diamonds might be hard but they can be lost. Anything, everyone, can be lost.

I loved Blue and it ended.

I love Lelo and, thankfully, she's in the next room right now. It doesn't make any sense to me why she stayed. What was in it for Lelo back then?

We were out walking with Ava yesterday, and I said, "I don't understand why you didn't leave me."

"What do you mean?"

"I was liquored up all the time."

"You were a good boyfriend," she said. "Generous. You were nice and funny and charming, just like you are now."

I didn't like this answer because I feel different. I like to separate myself from that caveman as much as possible. I'm a better person. He's gone. I'm here.

"Don't make yourself the bad guy," she said.

She meant in this book. Meant don't punish myself page after page, but how can I do anything else? This book is my barrel of blame, and I'm going to guzzle the stuff.

"Just make sure and tell the truth," she said. "Tell everyone that I'm an angel."

She was joking, but I agreed with her. I couldn't find any other answer. I don't deserve anyone's loyalty, anyone's open heart. So she's an angel.

She must be.

5

Once you're clean, there are no merit badges for being around booze. No bonus points if you stay up late, sitting with the animals, watching them gobble pills. I had too much confidence that day with Neal, or maybe it wasn't actual confidence but a masquerade: It might have just been my hibernating junkie tricking me. It might have been his way of luring me into dangerous situations, knowing eventually I'd collapse to the occasion.

That afternoon drinking with Neal happened because of something a few months prior, when I was fresh from rehab. I was in treatment most of January and the beginning of February 2009, and my first novel was published that June. I had to go on book tour without drinking, something I knew was going to be challenging. I even mentioned it to one of the drug counselors before leaving rehab and she said, "Listen, drugs don't care if you're from Yale or jail, Josh. Maybe don't go on tour."

I didn't have the heart to tell her that I went to a state college. "I have to go," I said.

"You have to stay sober."

"I will."

"Be careful."

I was nervous but was doing it anyway. Maybe that's called

overconfidence, or it's the tunnel vision that happens when your greatest dream in life is coming true, and the thing I wanted more than anything was to be a published author.

I had worked relentlessly on my writing for years, though I found it accidentally. My initial creative love back in my teens and early twenties was playing music, singing and slamming out power chords on a '71 Strat, even strapped on a bass in one outfit. I dug writing songs, gigging out. But what I hated about it was I needed other people to express myself. There was always some asshole in the band who was a flake or a diva or a drunk. Granted, that asshole was me, but I was tired of the whole hive thing. I was an avid reader even then, especially when I was hungover. Those mornings, I loved sipping six-packs in bed and reading Burroughs, Selby, Céline, Acker, Plath, Braverman—anyone who abused themselves.

So after another band's breakup, I decided to write. All I needed were some stories, and I had plenty of those.

My ghostwriters were drugs. I sat down around midnight armed with booze and coke, sometimes opiates. I wrote and wrote and pretty soon the Jameson bottle dwindled and I'd black out but keep writing till the next morning.

Looking back now, I'm reminded of the Brothers Grimm. They told a story about a cobbler who needed help making his inventory and by some wondrous chance a couple of elves showed up in the middle of the night and built him some kickass shoes.

I worked the same way with alcohol and drugs, and my whiskey elves never disappointed. I mean, they didn't always write the prettiest prose—cocaine isn't known to instill poetry—but they usually unearthed interesting images, haunting motifs. It was completely sub-/unconscious writing, with me having no idea what I'd done until I read the pages the next day.

Writing became an obsession and soon I couldn't go a day without scribbling.

And apparently, I was okay at it. Flung some short stories at a couple lit mags and they got accepted right away. No money, but a little literary gasoline in my tank, cranking up my imagination and work ethic to get back at it. I fell in love with the form, the solitude. Fell in love with creating characters, worlds from scratch, bringing consciousnesses to life.

Blue was on board. We weren't married yet, but were dating seriously. She was a poet, and she wanted us to be wild writers together, wanted sensuous, filthy adventures.

"You be my Henry Miller," she'd say, "and I'll be your Anaïs Nin."

Who was I to argue with such an opulent arrangement?

I'd met her one day at a restaurant where I tended bar. Suddenly, there was this stunning brunette, a new hire, polishing silverware. She was half Chinese, half Irish, super skinny.

I unpacked wine boxes, and the owner sat at the bar reading the newspaper. I pointed to the brunette. "Who's that?"

"New server. Named Blue."

"You should call her 'Josh-will-have-me-in-the-sack-in-six-weeks.'"

"I'm not participating in this conversation anymore," he said. "I don't like lawsuits."

And it was a bit longer than six weeks, but Blue and I were having sex soon after. We'd drink and write and sniff E and read to each other. It was that age where you can imagine yourself changing the world with your words. That age where there was a wick of creative madness burning inside, and life was a laboratory, each day an experiment to become a better writer. Nothing was more important than splattering sentences on paper.

We were completely immersed in our art. With no other practical concerns. Before babies or mortgages or careers. Before stock options or car payments. This was when booze and drugs were there, but they hadn't yet staged their coup.

The best example of this newfound dedication to writing was how I actually generated material. I worked with all the lights in the apartment off, the only illumination coming from my computer—the ecosystem of my book being like the moon in an empty sky.

There was nothing else alive.

In order to become the best writer I could, I decided to get an MFA. College was never my bag, but learning to be a writer felt different. I cared about my craft so much that I could be a good student, I was sure of it.

There was a crappy old TV show called *Quantum Leap* and every episode started with the main character, a scientist/time traveler, beamed into someone else's body and he didn't know who he was or where he was in space-time, had to figure all those things out on the fly. That described my first night of graduate school: I was Alcoholic Quantum Leaping.

Which meant I got too drunk before school and blacked out.

Which meant I came out of it sitting in a classroom, having no idea how I got there or what I'd been saying or doing.

Ten people talking books. A professor pontificating. And blacked-out me.

Not the first impression I hoped to make.

My day had started off in an excited manner. I couldn't wait for grad school. Hanging out with other nerds who dug words the way I did.

A new friend had invited me to a baseball game that afternoon before school and I figured no sweat, catch a Giants game, then go to USF.

Simple, right?

But as we walked to our seats we passed too many beer stands for me not to get thirsty and offer to buy a round, seeing as how it was only 1:00 p.m. and school didn't start for five hours so it was no big deal, just one harmless cup of suds, and Scott was too much of a gentleman not to reciprocate a round of beers by the second inning, and I was raised right and knew to meet his kindness with a sky-scraping consideration of my own, buying not just beers this time but also whiskey shots, and Scott didn't come of age in a wolves' den and knew about etiquette and brought the same combo back, and we ping-ponged rounds until we decided to ditch that dumb game and hunker down in a dive bar and I lost contact with the world.

One time, I went scuba diving in Cozumel and down there, they drift dive: people sinking to a hundred feet in the ocean and get-ting swept up in the current, moving through the water without swimming at all. Floating, weightless. The boat follows your trail of bubbles, picking you up, say, forty minutes later in an entirely different spot from where you went under.

That's what blacking out is like. Submerged. Zero gravity. A specter in the world's current, slithering and gliding like seaweed. Until the minute you are pulled back in the boat, back to your life.

In the case of my first night of grad school, that happened when someone said, "What do you think, Josh?" and unfortunately that somebody happened to be the professor, and I didn't say anything back at first, looking around at the other people sitting at this table, looking at them looking at me, knowing I must have stunk like stale spirits and spongy saliva, knowing that I'd probably shot my mouth off and made a fool out of myself already and aborted this whole opportunity before it even got a chance to succeed.

I should've run out of there because I couldn't do a thing right, couldn't stay sober for one goddamn afternoon, couldn't take care of the things that mattered to me. I tried to stay calm, plastering on a poker face and saying to the professor, "Can you come back to me?"

"Who else wants to go?" he said.

Someone volunteered. I surveyed my surroundings. None of my classmates eyeballed me. I knew those gazes, the sideways double takes, the periphery sneak-a-peek when I'd made a fool of myself, tossing a garbage can at a window for no reason other than it was Cinco de Mayo, pulling my cock out in public, throwing up under a bar and ordering another drink, any of a hundred dim things that seemed to happen.

I stayed quiet the remaining hour of class. Still loaded at the end. The teacher didn't say he and I needed to talk privately; either I'd gotten away with it or it had been such a nightmare that he planned on telling his superiors and I'd be heaved from the program tomorrow.

I didn't know and I didn't care.

Or I did care.

But there was nothing to do about it.

I searched my pockets and found a gram of cocaine, slipped in the school's bathroom to blow a rip, cutting one humungous drift on the back of the toilet.

That was when I wondered how I got to school.

I probably drove. I was a serial drunk driver. But I called Scott, hoping he might tell me I did the responsible thing, hailing a cab. Unfortunately not. Scott said I sped away from the bar, blaring the Clash.

There was nothing to do except wander the streets around campus until I found my ride.

That was the thing about quantum leaping: all the particulars were lost to you. You had a body, atoms and molecules and shame, but anything requiring context couldn't be grasped.

I didn't have a jacket and strolled the roads, up and down, for what felt like a hundred years but was probably less than half an hour. Then another student who I had met at the orientation a couple weeks prior, Randy, stopped his car and asked if I needed a lift.

I got in and he smiled at me, saying, "Where to?" and I told him I couldn't remember where I'd parked and he took a closer look, a closer smell, and asked, "Are you okay?"

I did the only respectable thing: I lied.

"I'm diabetic," I said. "My sugar's not so good and I can't re-member where I parked."

"Let's get you something to eat."

"No, I need to get home."

"Where's your car?"

I should have stopped talking there, but the cocaine was like a coach, coaxing me to make this lie the most convincing, surely Oscar-nominated clod that could fall from my mouth, and it clanked out of me, a whole spiel about how I'd had diabetes since elementary school and I normally was good at keeping my sugar balanced, but I'd gone to the Giants game earlier and my only options were junk food at the stadium and had to go straight to class and forgot to pack a protein-rich dinner in Tupperware and _____. Who cared what else oozed from my lips?

Point was I'd blacked out and came to in the middle of class and my car was MIA and poor Randy had to listen to me blather until we finally found it. I smiled and pointed at my car like we'd discovered America.

"Thanks," I said, opening the door.

"Should you be driving?" Randy asked.

It was right there, in his eyes.

"I'll be fine," I said.

"I'm happy to drive you home."

"No thanks."

"Be safe," he said.

Still drunk, still coked up, still the best drunk driver in town, I made it home unscathed. Blue was zonked on the couch, watching reruns of a terrible sitcom. I tried sneaking by her to the shower, but she muted the TV and asked, "How was your first night?"

I barely said three words before she interrupted me.

"Are you loaded?" she said.

Everything came uncorked, blurting the whole day out to her and crashing in her lap, kicking and wailing.

I said, "Why can't I . . ."

"Why can't you what?" she said.

"Why can't I . . . do better?"

She didn't answer, spent her energy consoling me, letting me writhe around, letting me gnash my teeth, purge until I pulled it together enough to say, "I think I got away with it."

If sympathy and empathy could evaporate, Blue's was gone in an instant.

"What?" she said.

"The teacher didn't say anything to me after."

"You've been looking forward to writing school forever."

"I know."

"So you didn't get away with anything," she said.

"You know what I mean."

"I don't know what you mean, Josh. No one does."

She threw me out of her lap, un-muting the TV and staring at the sitcom.

She watched her show, and I lived mine, making my way to the shower, holding my head under the water, hoping that this episode of *Quantum Leap* was almost over and as the next one kicked off, I'd come to in a life unlike anything I'd ever known.

◻

There were no consequences for my quantum leap. The teacher never mentioned it, nor did the other students, not even Randy. My graduate classes were every Tuesday and Wednesday nights, and I never screwed up like that again for the whole two-and-a-half-year program. In fact, I swore off going out with my peers. They all went drinking after every class, but I never tagged along, didn't trust myself.

During the summer between the first and second years of the program, I had a one-on-one thesis instruction with a professor, Karl. I had to give him roughly a hundred pages over the summer, and we'd get together a few times and talk about the material. We met in coffee shops, in the Mission or the Castro.

Karl was a fantastic reader, and I learned a lot that summer. For our last meeting, I turned in a short story called "Vulgar Transmissions from an Awful Galaxy." It was about a cocaine aficionado who worked in a restaurant, having trouble balancing his habit and being congenial to the customers. It was a solid story, the best one I'd ever written, and Karl agreed.

"I don't have any notes," he said. "This one was a gift from the muse."

It was exactly what I needed to hear. The night before had been a rough one, slugging Fernet half the night, then switching to tequila, which was always a hazardous combination. Fequila could kill you.

So being praised was a great salve, a hangover cure. It was the future I wanted so badly.

"Should I send it out to mags?" I said to Karl.

"Why not?"

My nose started bleeding. I don't remember whether it erupted right after he said that, or three minutes later, nine? But it bled and I brought my hands up to catch the drips, excused myself to the bathroom, and never wanted to go back out and face him. I wanted him to know me only as an artist, one with talent. Wanted him to know me on Tuesdays and Wednesdays, not who I was the rest of the week.

Coincidentally, in my story "Vulgar Transmissions from an Awful Galaxy," the main character kept running into the bathroom to check his nose (and of course enjoy another bump). Each new trip brought increased anxiety for him, the horror of being found out.

I was on the cusp of being discovered for my drug problem that morning with Karl. Without any guidance to help me improve my writing, I'd tend bar for thirty years, till I found out about a cirrhotic liver, my dreams pickled right along with my organs. I'd ignore the doctor's warnings to shirk booze and keep swigging spirits and eventually I'd drop dead at work, keeling down on the bar mat. The customers wouldn't even care, once they realized no one was going to stop them from filling up their own glasses.

Everything was on the house when the bartender died.

I was never able to publish "Vulgar Transmissions from an Awful Galaxy," even though I sent it to a ton of mags. Guess it wasn't a gift from the muse after all. One common theme from editors' criticism was this: *Why should I care about some drug addict?*

Here was what I wanted to email back: *Because he's me. Because, despite all evidence to the contrary, he's trying. He just doesn't know how to stop and shouldn't that elicit some goddamn empathy? What makes you such a calloused and ruthless reader?*

We all use the word *empathy*, but do we think it means the same thing? To me, empathy is being chummed by the blood of somebody else's mistakes and betrayals, baptized by these blunders and never offering condemnation or judgment. All you do is wipe the chum from your face and kiss them.

That's empathy.

That's how we are the most humane, covered in one another's blood.

But, of course, I couldn't explain that to these magazines, so I sent this instead: *Thanks for taking the time to read my work.*

I split from the bathroom, so scared to see Karl. But luckily, he was cool about it. Not like there was much to say, really. I wasn't going to cook up any lavish excuses like that night with Randy. I'd just tell Karl the truth if he asked. I had a cocaine nosebleed. What's the big deal?

◙

My last semester in grad school was when Blue threw me out, the summer I packed my dirty laundry in Josephine. The summer of couch surfing. A plaid couch, one of corduroy. Stripes. One with cigarette burns. One so white and spotless that I couldn't get comfortable, knowing I'd leave some streak. A couch that had punk rock stickers on its armrests. There's the couch that smelled like cats, and there were the cats themselves, crawling on me all night, an intruder in their den. The cats kept me up. Sure, I felt like shit the next day. But their fur and their faces and their paws and their purrs, it was nice to be walked on like that.

I didn't so much surf these couches as I clutched them like pieces of driftwood.

I was at Matty's house. Or Rick's. Or Molly's, Mike's, Heidi's, Johnny's, Cat's, Jessica's, Nicole's, Erin's, Joge's, Sharbel's, Rob's, Tim's, Ross's. I spent a couple at Shany's. Buffy and Kevin let me spend a few nights on their thrashed couch, just so there was someone around to curb their fighting.

I had to bring Josephine to my final thesis meeting, along with the manuscript that would become my first novel, *Some Things That Meant the World to Me*. I was working with Kate that summer. She was hard on me, demanding rigorous revisions, which might seem impossible considering all the couches I clung to during that nomadic summer, might seem like I'd be too scattered, too volatile, but the opposite was true: I found sanctuary in the novel. It was the only place where I wasn't lost.

Kate sat across from me, having no idea that my whole life was in that yellow duffel bag.

"Do you think I can publish this?" I said.

"When it's ready," she said.

It was a fair, measured response, though it wasn't what I wanted. Kate, unbeknownst to her, had become my surrogate mother over the summer. Except I wasn't her child. I was a grown man with a duffel bag.

"You know what you have to do, right?" said Kate.

She meant with the book. She was asking if I understood the plan we'd put together to make improvements. She was trying to verify if I felt prepared to tackle the remix over the next few months. Kate would leave me behind and have a whole new batch of students to worry about.

"Yeah, I do," I said, "and thanks. Thanks for teaching me so much."

"I can't wait to see what you do with the book," she said.

I wanted it to be like a movie, the mentor bidding an emotional adieu to a promising student. Here was the woman who was emblematic of my education, of my honing a passion that will course through me till my dying day. I wanted us to have a last cinematic interchange, directed by a sentimental ham like Spielberg: the violins swell, the shot goes grainy, a final talk freighted-up with canned poignancy.

But nothing else was said. After a quick hug, we were done. The safety of my Tuesdays and Wednesdays was gone.

A swanky literary agent said she'd sell my novel in three weeks. I'd queried ten agents, give or take, and I got lucky: on the same exact day I got interest from one at ICM and another at William Morris, the two biggest talent hubs. I talked to both on the phone and decided to go with the woman from ICM—let's call her Liz—who was very maternal and warm over the phone, and I was a sucker for that.

"Three weeks, really?" I said.

"It's that good," she said. Liz was a legend in the business. She had a bunch of heavy-hitter clients, and I felt honored to be on her roster.

About a month later, I flew to Manhattan to make her acquaintance, to have meetings with prospective editors. I was to meet Liz at a restaurant on a Friday evening.

"What do you look like?" she had asked earlier in the week. "So I recognize you."

"I have a bleached Mohawk and a broken hand," I said. The

hand was a casualty of a late-night stupor-turned-tantrum that ended with me punching a kitchen cupboard.

"You really look like that?" she said.

"Yup."

"They'll love it."

Before I left to meet her, I got to thinking about Liz's assurance about how quickly she'd sell the project to a publishing house, so I did the only levelheaded thing I could think of: I quit my job.

I thought, *Three weeks is nothing. I've got some savings. I can quit and in less than a month I'll strike it rich with a lucrative publishing contract, my working days are over, things are finally breaking my way!*

My meeting with Random House was promising. The editor there really dug the book, but had editorial suggestions that she'd need me to implement before her higher-ups would let her bid on it. I liked her and the idea of a first novel coming out with RH was every author's dream, so I said, "I'll see what Liz thinks, and if she's cool with it, let's do a draft together."

Liz said, "It's a win-win for you. Either Random House buys the book, which is great. Or you get to do a rewrite with one of their editors, and we can take it with us as we hunt."

I ended up signing an exclusivity deal with RH to do this draft. I had about two months. The editor sent me ten bullet points to work on during the rewrite. Six of them were fantastic suggestions, and I knew exactly how to implement them. Two were okay, and by that I mean, yes, she was identifying problems in the book, but her ways of tackling them weren't right. The final two bullet points were only *bullets*. She wanted me to take them and blow my book's brains out, lobotomizing the thing.

I told her I couldn't live with myself making changes I didn't believe in. Then she refused to buy it. Once Random House passed, very quickly every other publisher passed, and Liz, who knew she'd be able to pimp it in three weeks, threw her hands up: "Oh well," she said. "We tried."

Oh well?!

We tried?!

"What now?" I said.

"Write another book," said Liz.

I did, but she didn't dig the new novel I wrote. In her defense, *Termite Parade* is a pretty angry story. I wrote it quickly in an amphetamine fit. I can feel the cocaine coursing through every page.

"I'm not the one to champion you going forward," said Liz.

"Huh?"

"You need a true believer to champion your work and foster the audience you deserve."

Champion should never be a verb, by the way, unless you're a serious asshole.

And that was how she fired me, with those glitzy euphemisms.

I sulked for a day, a week, a month—I can't remember exactly, but I assume I milked this setback for all its boozy worth. Finally, a friend from graduate school who worked for a local lit agent in the Bay Area asked me to send both novels. The agent went out to a cluster of houses, including an indie shop called Two Dollar Radio. I signed a two-book deal.

So five months sober on my first book tour, and that antagonist, *confidence*, crackling propaganda, telling me that I'll be fine, I can handle it, just go enjoy traveling around and talking about books, go ahead and sit around people cocktailing and you'll be all right.

I hadn't factored being around other authors I'd long admired. Like Joe Meno. He wrote *Hairstyles of the Damned* and was an indie-lit rock star. He and I were scheduled to read together at Powell's Books in Portland. A magazine had asked me to interview Meno about his new novel so he and I decided to have dinner before the event to chat.

So I was anxious and excited, which really meant fidgety and sweaty.

It was one of those bistro pubs, all mahogany and burgundy and brass, like what I imagine dining on the Titanic would have been like.

Joe and I took a seat, and a server said, "Can I start you with cocktails?"

"Maker's and soda," said Meno.

"Me too," I said.

Wait.

What?

It had slipped from my mouth effortlessly, an actor reciting a line well into a show's run, tongue trained in muscle memory to enunciate so every seat could hear.

Me. Too.

All I did for the next few minutes was loop that decision.

"Maker's and soda," he said, and I said, "Me too."

"Maker's and soda. Me too."

maker's and soda me too.

maker'sandsodametoo.

The server returned. Joe picked up his drink and said, "Cheers," and I held mine and said the same and we let our squat glasses touch and he had a taste of his and I excused myself to the bathroom.

Don't be stupid, proud, naïve. Just tell him you don't drink.

But I wanted to taste that bourbon, wanted to sip an army of drinks, would have drank the spills and sludge from one of the bar's floor mats if I could. There I was in the City of Roses with a beast made of bourbon waiting on my bistro table and me trying to pull it together in the bathroom because I had to be back out there soon, couldn't hide forever, no chance, I had to go fight that beast, because that was what happened at the end of fairy tales, heroes fought their enemies, heroes bested their adversaries. None of those tales ended with a hero hiding in the john dodging the showdown.

So:

"Or you could take that drink," something said to me.

It was one of my ghostwriters talking, my whiskey elves. They were in that pub's bathroom with me, perched one on each of my shoulders as I leaned down to splash water on my face. Their heavy claws digging into my skin. Their rabid jaws snapping as they made a terrible mewling noise. All the shrill squawks morphed into syllables and the beasts started making sense, telling me that this ridiculous sobriety of mine could be over, thank the lord, we could get back to doing what we knew how to do, stop pretending that we were something we were not, we could lie on the floor like ecstatic roadkill, forgotten and splattered and dead.

"Doesn't that sound nice?"

"I want to stay sober," I said.

"We wouldn't be here if you did," they said.

They snarled again, mewled again, and I buckled. It wouldn't be so bad having a drink. It wouldn't be the end. I could stop at one. I could stop at one like a normal person.

They steered me back to the table like the worst designated drivers in the world, and Meno said, "You all good?" and I said, "My stomach," and he made a face like *that sucks*, and I was in my chair and I looked at the table and saw that bourbon and soda and picked it up. A glass of fire in my hand. Under my nose. The smell of Maker's, that peanut-and-caramel scent. The smell of sanctuary. A quick tip of the wrist and I would be all right again.

One of the beasts said, "Down the hatch!"

And Meno said, "Should we start the interview?"

And I just sat there.

And the other beast said, "Down the hatch is code for drink your drink."

And I just sat there.

And Meno said, "We have to be at Powell's in about an hour."

And I just sat there; and I just died there.

That there could be a future without booze felt impossible.

That I could do the right thing felt impossible.

That I could amount to anything more than a drunk felt impossible.

That I should expect anything other than relapse felt ridiculous.

That I could clutch a glass of bourbon.

That I could keep this stupid secret rather than just saying, "Joe, I don't drink."

That I felt so ashamed of being sober.

So uncool.

So un-whatever.

That I was willing to risk it all. That there was any hope that my *once upon a time* could lead anywhere but back to the bottom. That there was any hope with a drink in my hand. That there was any hope.

But I could put the drink down. I could put the drink down and turn on the Dictaphone. I could put the drink down, turn on the Dictaphone, ask Joe questions.

I could live, not live happily ever after, but the first word. Just *live*.

ırbon back on the table and said to Meno, "Where
?"

○

I checked my Dictaphone, and the interview with Meno is still on
there. I listened to the whole thing right now. About forty-five minutes of conversation. Two writers talking shop, bullshitting about
books. Normal. Not sure what I was expecting, some horror movie
soundtrack? Shrieks. Pleadings. The terrible mewling of my beasts,
clues of how close I came to screwing up my life, but the tape held
no evidence.

Just questions. Answers. Even some jokes. There were no noises
of my almost-relapse. You couldn't hear any of the night's true
chaos, because it all happened in my skull. It reminds me of when
someone in rehab said, "The biggest battles of my life have been
fought in my mind. Fought with myself."

And what does that sound like on a Dictaphone?

Nothing. Dead air. The sound of deep space. A lonely hiss. No
one hears the wars in your head. Except you. So you keep that Dictaphone recording. You listen to it because you know what's really
there. Because you know that your beasts live inside the hiss.

○

I wonder if this book emits its own hiss.

What happens when you hold it to your ear?

Can you make out my scorched music?

6

For the few weeks after the Peek-a-Boo fiasco I carry around all sorts of selfish fantasies about copping and drinking, and because the world's rising oceans are polluted with irony, something unbelievable happens: I *have* to relapse.

I need surgery that will require opiate sedation.

In the junkie community, it's called a freelapse. You relapse, but it's okay. You get a free pass. You're supposed to get high, just following the doctor's orders.

I'd been praying for drugs and alcohol since seeing Ava fall, and a wicked god heard me, granting my wish with one malicious twist.

Which brings us back to where we started: Six in the morning, New Year's Day, me retrieving Ava from the crib and bringing her back to bed, the three of us lying like a happy family, then the numbness starting, no feeling on the right side of my body, from shoulder to toes, and me saying to Lelo, "911," and me saying to Lelo, "It's happening again," and she says, "What?" and Ava crawling all over me, yelling, "Hop on Pop! Hop on Pop!"

The night before, we'd been on a nearly empty New Year's Eve flight from Seattle to SF and I said to Lelo, "I hope 2015 is better than 2014."

"Me too," she said.

"It has to be, right?"

But eight hours after the flight, I'm numb and Lelo snatches the phone fast, propelled into action with desperate tunnel vision because we have some unfortunate experience in situations like these: Three years earlier, we went south from our home in San Francisco for the *Los Angeles Times* Festival of Books. I was scheduled to sit on a panel with some other indie press novelists and heard a popping noise in my head and lost the ability to talk, ended up at a Hollywood emergency room on a Sunday morning. After a CT scan, a chest x-ray, and an MRI, we were told the terrible news. I'd had a stroke. I was thirty-five years old.

And actually, I hadn't just had one stroke. The MRI showed a lesion on my brain, a scar from a stroke in my past. When I mentioned my enthusiastic drug history to the neurologist, she said I probably had the first stroke when I was loaded and might not have known. I imagined myself sitting at a dive bar, coked up and twisted on whiskey, and stroking right there, surrounded by other sorrow machines, me speaking in tongues, brain curdling, and no one noticing, including me.

Once Lelo and I traveled back north from Hollywood, over the next few months my neurologist would run a gamut of tests and eventually shrug her shoulders. She'd note a ubiquitous heart defect called a patent foramen ovale, or PFO, say it's nothing to worry about, it's found in 20 percent of the population. She'd say, "The stroke seems to be an anomaly. Take a baby aspirin every day and hope for the best."

I didn't know this at the time, but it wasn't an anomaly, nor did I have a PFO.

Years before: It was Christmas morning and someone was dead. A suicide on the tracks. I was stuck in the BART station, and service was stopped. Till the body was collected. Eleven in the morning and I had another cocaine hangover.

"The delay will be at least half an hour," someone said over the intercom.

I was on my way out to my stepmom's house. My sisters were already there. My dad wasn't. We were trying to celebrate without him. He'd been dead two years and it wasn't getting any easier. I didn't go to his grave anymore. Felt some obligation to schlep up there for the first few months after he passed. I'd sit and pick weeds from his headstone, try to talk to him but everything coming out of me was bullshit.

I was so sick that morning in the BART station that I couldn't sit. I had to pace, do laps around the underground platform, keep moving or die.

"Cleanup crews are working hard to rectify the situation," said the intercom.

The night before, Shany and I had gotten two grams for Christmas Eve. She was a Jew so the date was meaningless. Plus, Michael had just dumped her, screwing a bartender at one of our favorite watering holes.

I'd known Shany since the tender age of nineteen, when we both got jobs as bussers at this waterfront restaurant. It was an instantaneous friendship and we were roommates for years. Recently, we'd started talking about the nineteen-year-old us. How simple and easy we had it back then.

That Christmas Eve, I was on my own for a few days, Lelo was up in Seattle visiting her family. I had my own reasons for wanting to get high: namely, I didn't want to go out to Sarah's, didn't want to be there, around my dad's absence.

All night, Shany and I shot pool and did rips. Talking about that bastard Michael. Talking about how everything got worse with time. Wishing we were those nineteen-year-old fools again, new to San Francisco, so obliviously happy.

"What happened to them?" Shany said.

"Yeah, where'd we go?" I said.

We did another line, ordered another round of whiskeys.

I remember that we couldn't think of a single thing to cheers about. We held our shots up, racking our brains for something to say. Finally, we just drank.

In the BART station, all I could do was walk in circles on the underground platform and wait for every piece of that dead body to be collected off the tracks. Truthfully, jumping in front of a train wasn't the worst way to go out. You wait till it's almost on top of you. Then you dive.

You don't get high on Christmas Eve.

I didn't want to be en route to the dead man's house because I didn't want to be around people who loved me. I couldn't kiss my sisters or Sarah, couldn't feel their affection. I didn't even have Christmas presents.

It was good that other trains weren't running right then because that coked-up Christmas morning was the first time I actually thought about suicide.

"Service should be restored in another half an hour," the intercom said.

I kept circling, staggering around the platform, wishing I had that ill-fitting and faded Black Sabbath shirt from that other Yuletide disaster. It was better than turning up empty-handed.

Lelo summons emergency services, and it's not the same ambulance, not the same EMTs, and no one gives me a bear in scrubs, but nevertheless we speed to the hospital and my symptoms get worse, affecting my vision, my speech, and the guy asks me questions in the back and I'm having trouble talking, producing these horrible moaning noises that don't mean anything and he averts his eyes, tells me not to worry about it, and then we are at the admittance desk at the hospital and I'm being asked the same batch of questions, along with some forms that I'm supposed to fill out, clipboard thrust at me as I lie on the rolling gurney, I'm supposed to start by writing my name and address and the like but my brain is broken, the pen won't work—I try to spell J-O-S-H, knowing full fucking well that the second letter of my name is O, so why did I write down a W? why can't I remember how to make an H? and the nurse takes pity and says she'll write these things down for me if I tell her the info, though my speech is still distorted, garbled, the words "San Francisco" take forever to fall out of my mouth and the nurse taps her pen.

After that Christmas morning in the BART station, I started to tell time differently.

Eight in the morning, and Lelo left for work, and I was unsupervised till six. Ten hours alone, idle in the Mission with all the bars.

Best-case scenario was I wouldn't have a drink till she got home, and then I'd whisk her away to happy hour somewhere, say the Latin American Club or the Lone Palm or the Attic, and we'd talk about her day and I'd lie about mine and she'd nurse one or two drinks while I tossed twelve, a look on her face like someone stranded in the rain without an umbrella.

Keep in mind that those days were the best-case scenario; I was steadfast, resolute—no booze till she got home. Distractions: going to the gym, sparring with some guys, running miles, writing. These were sober days I felt proud of, and truthfully, I have no idea why I was able to stay clean on these mornings, these afternoons. What made Monday a sober one, while Tuesday was a blackout? I'm not sure, but I do know that drinking with Lelo always felt like celebrating, awash and kept warm in her smile's light, while the cocktails I had by myself hit my mouth like spoiled milk.

But those *other* days, the soured ones in which I didn't make it till she got home—during these, there was a vulgar clock that told time by vices. Lelo leaving at 8:00 a.m. Me drinking a beer. Loved drinking in the shower. Pop a tall boy and stand there with the lights out; that contrast between a cold beer and the scalding stream was heavenly.

By nine, those mornings were all rock and roll, doing lines by myself if I felt like going up, or throwing back a pill if I wanted to get that opiate thrum going, the buzz starting in my feet and slowly swelling up around me, like living inside an electric toothbrush.

By ten, it was time to socialize. These outings always began at Clooney's. Back then, the neon sign outside had a malfunctioning C. So it said LOONEY's. Our insane asylum. What can I tell you about that bar? It's nicer now, but back then being there in the morning was like the emergency room on a Saturday night. An utter shit show. A pageant of debasement. Everyone in various states of injury, defiantly celebrating their damages with drinks. People in wheelchairs, with walkers, on crutches. Casts, splints, bandages, eye patches, you name it. Drinks were so cheap that it attracted the worst of us. I met an African man one morning who had these weeping sores all over his face and I half expected a bumblebee to land on his cheek, sucking nectar from those sick blossoms.

Behind the bar an old-timer worked the early shift. Often, I had a lined denim jacket with me, balled up in my arms because the morning beer made me sweat during the walk over. One time the bartender smiled at it, the wool of the jacket exposed, bringing over a little cookie and asking me, "Does your wee doggy fancy a biscuit?"

He wore crazy-thick glasses, a prescription that might have matched his needs back in the sixties, but over the last half century, his eyes required more help.

"My what?" I asked.

"Your wee doggy," he said, nodding at the wool on my coat.

"That's a jacket."

His enthusiasm buckled. He dropped the cookie on the floor and retreated back to his post. When I sat down on a stool, he pretended like we hadn't been conversing about my jacket-doggy thirty seconds earlier. "What can I get you?" he said.

By noon, it was time to have lunch so I'd meander to one of the Irish bars, maybe Liberties or the Phoenix, eating a burger and drinking wheat beers. I'd tended bar in the Mission for so long that I knew everyone in the business. These day-drunks weren't expensive, never putting a dollar in the till, just tipping my friends.

At three, I'd walk to Mission Bar where Ross worked the afternoon shift. I'd sit there before it opened, drinking Tecate from a can, the two of us bullshitting while he stocked liquor and cut up citrus. Every ten minutes or so, we'd have a shot, me hoisting Fernet, Ross doing rum. He was the only bartender I'd ever met who willingly put rum in his mouth.

Getting near five o'clock, the day would end one of two

ways—either I'd brown-bag it, getting a twenty-two of Pabst and sitting in Dolores Park, people-watching, resenting how easy they made life seem while pushing babies on swings.

Or I'd go to Bi-Rite, the local market on 18th and Guerrero, buying supplies to surprise Lelo with a meal. I loved to cook; it made me feel better about myself, doting on her as best I could. Sure, I was wasted all day, but I could cook for her. I could sear a scallop. I could perfectly grill a rare steak. I could present these meals to her and think: *I am a dependable and caring person.*

By the time I change out of my clothes, get some preliminary tests done, my physical symptoms have all subsided. No numbness. My speech is normal.

The on-call neurologist is a young guy. Too young. Younger than me. I want gray hairs. I want crazy wrinkles. I want his eyes to say *I've seen it all.*

He orders a batch of tests, imaging to make sure my brain isn't still bleeding, which it's not but the pictures do confirm that I've had another stroke.

I say, "That's three."

And he gives me the same pitying face as the admittance nurse.

I am wheeled up from emergency a few hours later, loaded into the stroke ward. It's me and a bunch of eighty-year-olds, and each new hospital worker, every orderly and nurse and doctor, all say the same thing upon seeing me for the first time: "You're so young."

It becomes a chorus, and they don't mean it in a cruel way, but that's how I'm hearing it. *You're so young, you must really deserve this, that's the only reason you'd be here.*

At least I don't have a roommate. It's in the afternoon, and because it's New Year's Day, there are a bunch of college football games on and I try to watch but my head hurts and I nap, fading in and out.

My stepmom relieves Lelo of any Ava duties at home so my wife can spend time with me, bring me supplies, a pillow, a blanket, some books. Things to make this room feel less, well, like this room feels: a place where eighty-year-olds have strokes and die.

We watch football and try *not* to talk. We are both scared. Lelo is worried about becoming a widow. I am terrified that I'm going to have the *big one* any minute now, and Ava will have no idea who I am—or was.

My daughter and I have had so many moments together, so many milestones, that afternoon her feet first felt the ocean, a bite of pizza, hearing Jimi Hendrix on vinyl. Her inaugural sunrise— the two of us bundled up on our apartment's roof, after I'd just gotten home from a red-eye—and we watched the sky spill color, hugging the whole time. The two of us singing "Frère Jacques." Playing princess, taking baths, tea parties, boiling macaroni, putting stick-on tattoos on her arms so she looks like Daddy.

All these vignettes will die along with me. I don't remember anything from being eighteen months old. She won't have access to our cache of memories; I'll be a figment, a fleck of useless history.

Lelo and I stare at some stupid college football game, trying to hide our fear but it's not working. We gaze at the screen like it's broadcasting the cause of my strokes and how to fix the problem.

My mind retreats to a memory, a Thanksgiving before Ava was born. Lelo and I got a cabin in the foothills and spent four days barricaded away, working relentlessly on our books. On the way up, we ate holiday-inspired turkey sandwiches in the car, but besides that, the weekend was dedicated to scribbling.

And so much laughter!

The ground had a fresh dusting of snow and each morning we'd play Frisbee out front of the cabin, holding steaming mugs of coffee while winging the disk back and forth. We talked about our novels. I loved how important literature was to her. Loved how *possible* it felt to someday succeed as an author around that infectious hope of hers.

As I sit in the hospital bed, the memory is clearer than any football game. I can see her standing on the snow, smiling as the Frisbee made its way to her, catching it, winding up, tossing it back, the plastic cutting its arc through the thin mountain air.

I would give anything to be back there.

Another nurse comes in to draw more blood. "You're so young," she says, sticking me.

I get a roommate late that night, Mr. Zhao arriving about 2:00 a.m. Lelo is long gone. It's been only me tossing and turning in this hospital bed, periodic visits from the nurse to check my blood pressure, my heart rate, temperature, etc.

Mr. Zhao doesn't speak English and any time a doctor, nurse, or physical therapist needs to talk to him, a translator is called on the phone and these translations are broadcast over speakers in our room and seeing how the only "wall" that separates us is a curtain, I am hearing the translator's loud voice as much as Zhao.

At first, this pisses me off. Haven't I gone through enough today? Do I really need to listen to Mandarin?

Quickly, though, my feelings on my new roomie change. I realize that we're the same.

Somebody please whisper that this will all be over soon. For god's sake, say Ava will know me!

We are separated by a thin curtain. Zhao and his stroke on one side, me and mine on the other.

When our room clears out again, I speak to him: "I want to live. I really want to this time."

We sit in our flimsy gowns with our beeping machines and our damaged brains in a room reeking of death.

In January 2009, not long after the BART suicide, after I stopped telling time by the clock, only cocktails, I made a pilgrimage to Columbus and Columbus.

At Vesuvio, my favorite North Beach bar.

Seven in the morning, and I was finishing myself off from the night before. Or starting the next binge. I had no idea what I was doing, but I was partying alone again. That was happening more often: people not wanting to spend time with me.

Alone, meaning there was nobody on the barstool next to me. There were a few other masochists drinking in the morning. A couple had briefcases and wore suits, on their way to the office, stopping in for a quickie to tide them till lunch. The other guy was like me, keeping his bender above water, drinking whiskey and ginger ale. I ignored him until I heard a noise like a rattlesnake, realizing he was shaking a bottle of pills back and forth and smiling at me. He was four stools down.

"Are you in need of medication?" he said, sliding slowly toward me, going from one stool to the next like a stoned frog hopping lily pads.

He was in his forties. Or twenties. It's hard to tell people's ages when they're boozing in the morning.

"What's in there?" I said.

Still rattling all those pills.

"Do you really fucking care?" he said.

The Rattler had me. I would have taken anything. He was a doctor and a priest and an angel and a mother.

He opened the bottle and dumped two pills in my hand. Then he tilted the bottle to his mouth and munched a couple. "Bottoms up," he said, slamming most of his beer.

"Bottom . . ."

But I stopped myself there. This had to be it. I'd been hoping to get here for a while.

The Rattler rattled his pills again. "It's going to get nuts soon, brother," he said.

I bought the next round, both of us switching to Bloody Marys, making the obvious jokes about tomato juice and vitamins. We made the kind of small talk you do while waiting to be nailed to your cross.

And I'd love to tell you what happened next. Love to tell you some adventure I went on with the Rattler. But the truth is I can't tell you anything else. One minute I was sitting at Vesuvio nursing a Fernet shot, choking down a terrible Bloody Mary that tasted like aluminum. One minute, it was Friday morning and the next thing I knew it was Sunday.

Most of the weekend gone.

Lost.

I've thought a lot about that vanished Saturday, and this is what I think happened, what I'd like to think happened. This is my make-believe Saturday: The Rattler was wrong about the pills. They weren't nuts. In fact, they weren't even drugs. They were soul salve. You ingested a couple and suddenly all the things that made you ache dissipated.

I couldn't stop smiling and it was one of those contagious smiles that only certain people are lucky enough to have (Lelo has one) and all these people that I loved were with me. We were on a cruise ship, which was odd seeing as how I'd never been on a cruise, but that doesn't matter, not on a make-believe day.

My dad was back from the dead, looking handsome like he did before the chemo and radiation, a full head of black hair. My two moms were there—biological and step—and not only were they getting along, they were dancing, dancing together! And singing a silly song, something like "You Are My Sunshine," and my two sisters were there and they had this look in their eyes like I'd never let them down, never blown them off at the last minute because I was too hungover to see them or too ashamed to crawl out of bed, and Lelo was there with that Frisbee from our Thanksgiving trip, ready to play catch with a look in her eyes that said I might amount to something if only I'd get out of my own way, and all the friends that stopped returning my calls once my drugging got out of hand, all these wonderful people from my past were on this cruise ship. Shany and V and Kerrie and Michael and Marc and Sara and Watch and Jabiz and Anthony and Rick and Johnny and Calder and Loperena and Ben and Barrett and even Blue and a bunch of other hammerheads, and yes, we all had dreadful dance moves but it didn't matter, no way, we were out at sea, under a disco ball, under a full moon, under every star in the history of the world, we were dancing on the open ocean and we were alive and we loved one another.

But Sunday morning rolled around. Because no fantasy lasts

forever. Let me tell you about that Sunday morning—the day I almost died—before going to rehab.

I had the Rattler's pills. There were still twenty or so left. Did I steal them? Did he give them to me? Did I hurt him?

I don't know.

Never will.

I certainly couldn't have afforded to buy all of them. All I know is that they were in my possession.

Or I was in theirs.

Someone was somebody's.

I was in a hotel room. I was alone. I was naked. I was crying. I walked over to the door. There was a sign on the back of it. That said CHECK OUT TIME. Under it was supposed to be written a specific number. Ten or eleven. Noon maybe. Instructions for when you had to get out of the room. But there was nothing.

And I was bleeding. From my asshole. A steady leak. The bathroom destroyed. Towels soaked and strewn on the floor. Towels died pink with water and blood.

I hadn't been raped. I'd have been able to feel that. No, this trickle of blood was from something inside. Something was wrong in my guts. Something was breaking or already broken and a body could only process so much before quitting.

Check Out Time.

Looked at my nude, disgusting, bloody body in the bathroom mirror and it was like being in a Francis Bacon painting, and I needed to get out, thought to myself: *Let's get on with this, no more benders, I have about twenty of the Rattler's pills left and am probably about to bleed to death anyway so why not pop all the pills and float away from all this lacerating sadness?*

Well, why not?

There was a warm beer on the bathroom counter. In fact, there were half-finished beers and various bottles of booze all over the room. I popped six of the Rattler's pills and drank straight from a bottle of whiskey and then finished three of the open, flat, warm beers and then went back into the bathroom to look in the mirror, spreading my legs so I could see every trickle of blood, and for a couple minutes everything felt right, I was going to be free, going to make it out of this, going to survive this life in another way entirely, survive it by leaving it, and those calm moments were righteous moments, but they didn't last.

I got this feeling like a fish first pulled into the boat. That fish flopping on the ground, gills going crazy, panicking and puckering my little fish mouth because I wanted back in the water to live and the only way I could shake this fish feeling was to fall down to my knees in front of the toilet and make myself throw up the Rattler's pills and that was exactly what I did, giving all those narcotics back, shooting them up my throat and there was blood in that too, and I kept kneeling there and got embarrassed that I couldn't follow through with this—what was I holding on to, why was I resisting giving up on such a hollow existence?—and these questions sent me back to the Rattler's bottle to take another handful of pills and wash them down with more open, flat, warm beers and I got to enjoy another batch of calm, righteous moments before the fish feeling returned and I dropped down to puke again, and I did the same thing a couple more times, until all the Rattler's merchandise had been ingested and spit back up, swimming in the toilet with so much of my blood and so much of my heart, and that was when this naked crying person capsized.

PART II

THE FREELAPSE

(OR: DO ADDICTS DREAM OF ELECTRIC SHAME?)

7

Tests. More tests. Even a spinal tap, though they don't call it that anymore, now it's the euphemized *lumbar puncture*. It still means that I lie on my side as they attempt to drain fluid from my spine, an agonizing experience because the doctor keeps "hitting the spaghetti."

"I don't know what that means," I tell him.

"Nerve endings hang down and look like spaghetti noodles," he says. "I'm brushing up against them."

"Can you not hit them?"

"I'm trying." He works the long needle into the base of my spine, like he's trying to pick a lock. I'm getting the sense he's not a gifted burglar.

"I thought you said this wasn't going to hurt."

"I'm getting past the spaghetti."

"Have you done this before?"

No answer.

"You haven't!" I say.

Just the needle sliding in and out of my spinal cord roughly. Every time he "brushes the spaghetti," my legs kick involuntarily. When I had my elbow tattooed, there was something similar, sending showers of sparks hurtling to my feet. But this is a hundred times worse and I worry I might pass out.

"Almost in," he says.

But he's not. I'll endure his stumblings for ten more minutes. He does finally penetrate the spinal cord, the fluid slowly dripping out. He holds a small vial of it up for me to see. "It's clear blood," he says, though I see a shot of gin. "This will hopefully tell us why you're having strokes in your thirties."

Because I decided not to die in that motel room, I called Sarah, my stepmom, and told her I needed help. I took the subway to her house in the East Bay and crashed. Waking up the next morning, her dog's snout was inches from my face, deadly breath blasting from his open mouth, as he scrutinized me like a shrink. I didn't like how Boots studied me, so I lashed out: "You're going to die soon. That smell coming up from your insides is horrible."

"You'll die too," said the dog. I hadn't had any booze or drugs in twenty-four hours and the withdrawal was starting to rewire the rules of the world. Boots kept on me: "I mean, aren't you tired of this life?"

"I'm getting my shit together," I said, sitting up on the air mattress.

"Uh-huh," he said, smirking, limping away to scratch at the huge tumor on his side. It looked like a saddlebag thrown over a horse.

Boots was a retriever mutt, fur the color of bourbon. He stood at the back door, waiting for me to let him outside. I thought about ignoring him, but realized if he relieved himself inside, I'd have to clean it up.

It was a little after seven in the morning.

I was set to start to rehab in an hour.

I opened the back door and he waddled outside, off-balance from the massive growth. I followed him out. The patio was beautiful. A rose garden. A trellis with blooming bougainvillea. This was the suburbs, and after living my adult life in San Francisco's fog, it felt good to see the sun so early in the morning.

Boots nosed around some rose bushes and, after raising his leg, found a patch of dirt near the fence. He started digging. Not digging like I'm-tunneling-out-of-this-prison. Digging what looked like a shallow grave.

"I knew it," I called over to him.

If dogs could thrust up their middle fingers, I would have seen his right then. Instead, Boots worked his paws in the dirt, moving more from his plot.

Sarah joined me on the deck, handing me a coffee.

"Is that his grave?" I said.

"I should put him down, but after losing your dad, I can't do it."

"How long has he been digging it?"

"A few months."

"Months?!"

"We need to leave soon," she said, shuffling back inside, and I watched Boots dig.

Okay, as the docs go through all their tests, they finally find the culprit causing all these strokes, my congenital defect. My heart is missing a wall.

I have an eight-millimeter hole (a dime is about one millimeter thick, so imagine a stack of eight dimes). There should be a wall separating the two upper chambers of the heart. This partition prevents blood from flowing the wrong way, so if in fact you have a blood clot, it will hit this wall and be filtered through the lungs, hopefully dissolve on its own; that's the way it should work. But without this wall, there is an open border, a highway for clots to travel up to the brain.

A neurovascular surgeon will build a wall in my heart.

I will be under anesthesia, a lovely opiate called fentanyl.

I wanted to get high, so here's the universe honoring my request. That's the thing about lobbing vague prayers—what if they're answered by a sadist?

There is only one surgeon who does these types of heart procedures, called ASD closures, and he won't be able to operate on me for two months. What that means is that I will have to pump an intense, outrageous, and hideous combination of meds to keep me safe until the surgery, each pill keeping my blood "slippery." This is one of the doctors' buzzwords. Slippery. They mean thin, something that can't clot, can't turn to ice, blood like vodka in the freezer.

Keeping my blood so slippery, of course, comes with its own risks. Such as bleeding to death. I am given a list of things I should not do on all these meds, and this list, this crazy list, makes me fear everything. Don't drive a car, says the list. In fact, don't ride in a car. Don't shave. Don't use knives. Don't exercise. Don't have sex. Don't floss your teeth. Don't cut your nails. Don't pick up the baby. Don't be alone with the baby. Don't sit for longer than an hour. Don't take a multivitamin. Don't eat kale or spinach—too much vitamin K.

Don't go outside, if it can be avoided.

These meds have a lot of side effects and I stumble around my life, top-heavy, my head feeling like an old parking meter full of quarters. The worst is the diarrhea. I lose twenty-five pounds in three weeks.

Sarah and I drove to a town deeper in the East Bay that started with a V. Vacaville? Vallejo? All strip malls and stucco and fast-food shops. There was a liquor store across the street from the rehab facility.

Since this was an outpatient program, Sarah told me she'd be back to get me at five. She was being very nice, driving me around, letting me crash on her floor, blowing up that embarrassing air mattress. I was in my thirties but it felt like she was dropping me off at elementary school.

Sarah was the person you wanted around if something went wrong. Not a lot of people would have shown me mercy at that point. But Sarah didn't even flinch.

"Say cheese," said the nurse, whipping out a Polaroid and snapping a pic of my face. This was in 2009, and I didn't know anyone still used Polaroids. She gave the picture a good shake.

"Why did you do that?" I said, annoyed that we'd just spent twenty minutes filling out forms, her asking all the gruesome details. I even told her about how much blood I'd lost over the last couple days. She wanted specifics, but all I could do was blame a blackout, that familiar feeling of a coffin lid closing over me.

"We take everyone's picture when they first get here," she said. "Then we show it to them later on. You won't believe how terrible you look."

"Thanks."

"We all went through this," she said, shaking my out-of-focus face in front of my eyes.

"Why is there a liquor store across the street?" I asked.

She smiled, nodding at me. "I don't know. Why?"

"No, I'm asking you."

"Oh, I thought you were telling a joke."

"No."

"Baby, there's always a liquor store across the street," she said, then held the picture up for me to examine. "So what do you think of this guy?"

"I'm not a fan."

Leading up to the heart surgery, I'm saying all the right things publicly. These doctors are the best! The surgeon has done over six hundred of these procedures! They are going to knock this out of the park!

Can't you see all my enthusiastic exclamation marks!!!

But there's a different discourse happening in my skull, various voices expressing a fundamental chorus: *I don't want to die.*

I try to assuage this fixation by learning all I can about the procedure and the man who invented it, Dr. Werner Forssmann. He invented this technique in the 1920s and couldn't get funding or any grants for research so he actually did this *to himself,* running a urinary catheter through the vein in his arm all the way into his heart.

Imagine that reckless conviction, that suicidal ambition. Imagine believing in something so much that you risk your own life. Forssmann must have known that, despite his hypotheses, there was the chance his heart would give out as the catheter bumped through the vein and into the organ. And it wasn't enough to simply do the crazy thing. No, it had to be documented, which meant that he had to walk down a flight of stairs with the catheter wedged in his arm and pushing all the way to his heart—so he could get an x-ray, an image to prove that he was right: a picture showing the world what could be done, a catheter running sixty centimeters, from his arm and ending up in his right atrium.

When I think back on that night in the hotel room, my *Check Out Time*, I wasn't risking everything to make the world a better place. I was trying to turn something off, a sieve of indifference. Forssmann did this crazy and brave and unthinkable act in his midtwenties, would win the Nobel Prize much later in life for this advancement. I can't think of my heart without thinking of his.

He's obviously to be praised for pioneering this procedure, yet he was also a member of the Nazi Party, one of their doctors during World War II. Here is a man who, for one shining and transcendent moment, changed the way we operate on the human heart, paving the way for pacemakers, angioplasty, valve repair, saving countless lives.

But he was a Nazi.

I've told you terrible things about myself in this book, and while I'm not a Nazi doctor, I do question my own worth. Ask any rational adult, she'll admit such moments of cataloging positive versus negative contributions in life, and nothing makes you ponder your own identity, its value, your role in the human condition more than a health scare.

I start to talk to Forssmann. Why? Well, it makes me feel better. He is my angel, my tarnished and shameful angel. I feel if I speak to him, he'll watch my back, keep me safe.

One morning, I'm at the stove, frying an egg, watching it twitch and flop in the pan, hearing its hiss, but my mind is focused on the surgery. I've already burned the toast, tossing it in the garbage, the room reeking of bitter char. My goal had been an over-easy egg, though that's lost. Maybe I can salvage over-medium?

"You should have cooked it with a blowtorch," someone says, though I'm home alone. I turn around, and there he is, my savior, Dr. Forssmann. He's been dead since 1979, but it's his young self that visits me, a handsome, dark-haired twenty-something. He stands there wearing a white lab coat and says, "Give me the spatula." I hand it over, and he gently pushes past me. "Tell me, what did this poor egg ever do to you, Josh?"

"I can't imagine seeing you is a good sign," I say.

"I can't imagine how gummy this yolk will taste. Go sit down." He carries the pan to the sink and scrapes out the egg, then puts a heap of butter in, cracks another into the pan's center with a sizzle.

I walk to the kitchen table. "I'm not even hungry."

"You need your strength."

"Will I survive the surgery?"

Forssmann flips the egg over. "Do you know why I did it?"

"What?"

"Watch this." Using the spatula, he jimmies the egg from the pan to a plate and slides it in front of me. Then Forssmann sits across the table and rolls the sleeve up on his white coat. From his pocket, he produces a knife and a catheter connected to a long tube. "Are you squeamish around blood?" he asks, not waiting for an answer. I'd noted a similar pattern with the neurovascular surgeon who would be doing my procedure, during our initial consultation: he lobbed queries about my meds, my sleep, my state of mind, never hearing my responses out before barking his next inquiry. Surgeons, I guess, hold scalpels, not hands.

With the knife, Forssmann cuts himself on the elbow crease,

accessing the vein, a few red trickles leak onto the table, too close to my eggs. "Eat up," he says, using the knife to point at the plate.

"You shouldn't bleed all over someone else's kitchen."

Then he feeds the catheter into the incision site, slowly snaking the tubing up his arm, across his shoulder, and into his heart, periodically grimacing but calm. Finally, Forssmann leans back in his chair, wipes sweat from his brow.

"I've done bad things," I say. "I deserve to die."

"Surgery is simple," says Forssmann. "Living with yourself is the brutal aspect of being human. Trust me on this: I have a Nobel in medicine, but I also have one in remorse."

"Your bedside manner leaves a lot to be desired."

"Bed? We are in a kitchen," he says, ripping the catheter from his arm and bunching it in his coat pocket, a slow red stain blooming through the fabric. He ambles away, leaving me alone at my bloody table.

I was one of two people coming into rehab that day. The other guy was a kid basically. Barely twenty. Call him Trevor. He had this odd bleach job, uneven, bits of stark white mixed with brown hair, like somebody was peeling a potato and quit halfway through.

The first thing we went to was acupuncture. To help with withdrawal. We entered a darkened room with about thirty people sitting in a big circle. We took seats on the outside of the circle, next to each other, and waited for the acupuncture guy to get to us, to push pins in our ears. Then we all sat in darkness for forty-five minutes.

Maybe we were supposed to be meditating. I had no idea. I sat there thinking about Lelo—what this meant for us, would she wait for me, should she? Like Boots, I'd been digging my own grave and maybe the best thing to do was let Lelo leave so she didn't get sucked in, too. Sucked down with me. Some graves have gravity, and she deserved much better. Blue had met a nice guy since we split and started a family. Lelo should have that same opportunity.

When the lights finally went on, the circle all stared at Trevor and me, waiting for Acupuncture to pull the pins from our ears. A little guy with blue hair pointed at us and said, "Welcome to the shit show, newbies!"

Then a bunch of us drove to a taco truck for lunch. To win everyone over, I paid for all the tacos. "Next best thing to buying a round of whiskey shots," I said, holding my taco up like a shot glass.

They hollered and smiled; we cheers'd with our tacos.

The surgery is scheduled for the mid-afternoon. I sit in the hospital bed, trying to watch TV. I post this on Twitter: *I'm having heart surgery & as the procedure approaches, I'm getting scared. Please send some good thoughts/prayers/healing vibes.*

The outpouring of support is crazy. The indie literature community is tight-knit, but I don't expect so many notes. I refresh my feed and read through so many wonderful comments and they act as a salve.

Soon, a nurse comes over and asks if I'd like to walk upstairs to the operating room or be wheeled. I walk. I make small talk with him. A couple hours earlier, he had to shave my crotch, as the doctors will need to access the artery in my upper thigh.

"Thanks for being such a gentleman," I say in the elevator. "I usually don't go that far on a first date."

"My pleasure," he says.

Because I'd told the rehab admittance nurse about the anal bleeding from the day before, I had to go to the emergency room to get it checked out. Three IV bags of fluid to hydrate later, I lay in a bed, waiting for the doctor to tell me I was dying. Hep C or AIDS from sharing needles. All the unprotected sex. Cancer from crappy genes.

I didn't know what was wrong with me, but I expected him to come in wearing an executioner's mask. When he finally came by—maybe an hour later—he had a disinterested look on his face. He must have hated alcoholics. All the men and women hammering their bodies like piñatas. Except instead of prizes falling out of us, it was our organs, and we ended up here, on one of his beds, asking him to stitch our damage back up.

"You need to quit drinking," he said.

"That's the idea."

"No, your digestive tract can't take it anymore."

"Okay."

"Your GI is a mess, son. You have to stop."

"I am."

He looked at me like I was lying. Like he'd given this same advice to a thousand other piñatas who were back in a month or two.

"Know this is serious," he said.

And like that he was gone.

Forssmann holds the door open for me and the crotch-shaving nurse when we walk into the operating room. "Moment of truth," says Forssmann.

What's he doing mentioning *truth*? What am I supposed to do with truth so close to the surgery and the freelapse? I'll be okay. I'll survive. I'll just get high this once and that's it, back to being a husband, a father, a professor, a writer. This one needle going into this one arm one time doesn't mean anything other than that I'm following the surgery's protocols.

"Can I change?" I ask Forssmann.

"This life can be a misunderstanding."

"I'm not who I used to be."

"Maybe you are, though."

"I'm sober," I say.

"For another couple minutes, yes."

"I have to get high for the surgery."

"We are all Nazi doctors in one way or another."

I don't agree. Or I don't want to. People can learn, can grow. I have been fighting off a relapse for Ava and that's the key detail: I am trying to do the right thing.

But today, I have to do drugs to save my life.

Forssmann would point out the existential dilution, the good and the bad swirling through us, how in one life you can change the world by inventing cardiac catheterization and then align yourself with a fanatical, murderous empire. He'd say it's the filthy order of the human condition, our strengths and weaknesses tangling together to spell our names, pump blood through our defective hearts.

The door slowly closes, separating us. I'm on the side with the operating table, the surgeons, the support staff, my future. Forssmann is on the other side, with its history and precedence, with his confusion and murder of memory.

As I waited in front of the rehab facility, Sarah's text only said this: *late*.

It was already ten after, and everybody bolted right at five. I thought there would be more people waiting for rides, smoking, complaining, withdrawing, but I was by myself.

I was staring at that goddamn liquor store across the street. A beer—one simple cold beer—would do wonders right now. My head ached, my feet buzzed like they were asleep, I had that jet lag feeling. My body was tired of being deprived of all the liquor it was used to running on. Just one simple cold beer would take the edge off. And if I was going to do something stupid, why would I stop at one? Buy a twelve-pack and a fifth of whiskey and disappear.

"What's the good word?" said Boots, suddenly sitting right next to me, scratching at his huge tumor.

I nodded toward the liquor store. "I'm pretty thirsty."

The dog looked appalled. "Jesus, you're giving up after one day?"

"Mind your own business." Then I walked across the street, walked into the store, walked down an aisle, walked to the coolers, and just stared at all the beer behind the frosty glass.

I put my hand on the outside of the fogged window. It felt electric.

"Thing is you'll hate yourself," said Boots, now lying next to me on the linoleum, gnawing at his saddlebag.

Seeing him sprawled on the floor reminded me that I was sprawled on the floor too, sleeping on that air mattress in Sarah's dining room. I was thirty-three and pretty much broke and pretty much broken and pretty much screwing up with Lelo and I'd gutted out my first day in rehab and the withdrawal sounded like basketball sneakers squeaking in my brain, and I was arguing with a dying dog in a liquor store.

"There's no reason for me to try," I said.

"This is my tumor," Boots said, glancing over his shoulder, "those beers in there, those are yours."

I opened the cooler and grabbed a six-pack of tall boys. Thought about cracking one right there so the basketball shoes would stop squealing, but there wasn't time. Sarah would be there any second and I needed to split before she showed up.

I barely had any money, fifteen bucks left after paying for all the tacos, so I'd need to break into someone's car or someone's pocket or someone's house . . . But then the harsh shame of pondering robbery made me want to crash down on the floor, use my fingernails like Boots used his paws, to tear up the linoleum and tear through the concrete underneath and tear up the building's foundation until I felt dirt, burying my body so everything would stop hurting.

I marched halfway down the aisle and stopped. I couldn't do it. Jammed that sixer into a shelf of tortilla chips. Then I ran back to the rehab facility, sitting on the curb, panting.

"I'm going to screw this up," I said to Boots.

"You don't know that."

"It seems likely."

"I'm a dog," he said.

"Yeah, I know."

"You're lucky," said Boots, nudging my hand with his muzzle until I scratched his head. "You can put your tumors back. I have to ride mine all the way home."

We both saw Sarah's car approaching from a couple blocks away. She pulled in and smiled at me through an open window. "So how was your first day?" she said.

I got up off the curb and said to her, "One day done."

"Do you want to talk about it?"

I looked in the rearview mirror and Boots nodded his dog head—*yes*—from the backseat, letting me know his thoughts on the subject. There would always be a liquor store across the street, but I didn't have to go inside.

"What do you want to know?" I said to Sarah.

"Start with your favorite parts," she said, "and work your way to what scared the shit out of you."

And that was what I did all the way home.

On the operating table, I orient and calm myself by looking around at various lights, computer monitors, nurses. The anesthesiologist runs a line into the artery in my wrist. His needle, like an umbilical cord, pumps my favorite food.

This is it. I am relapsing. I am probably about to die. The surgery is minutes away. I've seen Lelo and Ava for the final time. My sisters. My moms. I've written my last sentence. These are the last moments of my life, lying here and looking up at the eyes of grumbling strangers, their mouths concealed behind masks.

"This first shot will be like drinking a beer," the anesthesiologist says, doing his merciful work. His needle brings the fentanyl. This is like seeing a long-lost friend.

Time loses its math, and everything gets heavy, oozy with smudged hues.

I am high again.

I am home.

8

We huddled around a wrecked man, getting as close to him as we could. This was in men's group, sometime during my first week in rehab. All of us—say eleven or twelve withdrawal machines—surrounded Mort as he whispered his syllables, straining to hear everything. Mort had crashed his car a couple weeks back without a seat belt on and had crushed his larynx on the steering wheel. He could only speak in whispers now.

There was talk about a surgery in a few months to fix his throat, but Mort was thinking about not doing it, living like this forever.

"I deserve it," whispered Mort.

"Why do you think you deserve it?" the counselor said.

"Because it's my birthday, and my kids won't talk to me."

Then he wept. No one knew what to say to Mort. Probably because there were no honest words to soothe him. Most likely his kids had good reasons for not speaking with him. Instead, we consoled Mort with our body heat, staying as close to him as we could.

For the first time since starting rehab, I was okay with being there. Okay spending all day sitting in circles, okay spending all night sleeping next to Boots on the air mattress. Okay with being away from my Mission District life with Lelo. Despite the agony of withdrawal, despite the anxiety for what a life without substances might mean, I moved with the other men toward Mort, our whispering sun.

A few days later, we were to write a poem telling our story, and the only thing I could think of was bed-wetting. I know, not particularly poetic or pretty, but the counselor only gave us ten minutes so if that was where my mind wanted to go, bed-wetting it was.

I was a serial bed-wetter. Blackout drinkers were known to darken the sheets because we never remembered to piss on our way to pass-out. So each bed in each apartment with each new woman, this was how I could tell my life story:

I wet the bed. I am twenty years old. I am alone. I am too drunk to care. I roll out of the soaked part, curl up on the edge, clammy, too useless to feel shame.

I wet the bed again and this time it's everywhere. I take a blanket and sleep on the hardwood floor. The next morning I don't remember doing it. I wake and think: Now what the hell am I doing down here?

I wet the bed and somebody screams at me and I have no idea who she is, watch her dress in a hurry and head out so I shrug and settle back in. I couldn't care less about some piss. I'm going to shower in the morning anyway. What's the big deal?

I wet the bed and don't know it and Blue shakes me and says, "Jesus, you did it again," and I say, "Huh?" and she says, "Go to the couch," and I stumble down the hall. The next morning, she comes out and asks, "Are you still alive?"

I wet the bed again. I am alone again. I lie right in it and shiver. I should roll over, roll out of it. I should get up. Should crawl to the floor or the couch or the shower or the phone to beg for help. But I'm okay with lying in it. Why on earth am I okay with this?

I got the whole poem out in one burst and sat in my chair. There was still six minutes left to write, but that was all it took me, four scrawny minutes to sum up the last decade-plus of my life.

Ten years doused in urine.

I should've written a stanza about Lelo; she had felt me sully a sheet or two. But there was no way I could include her. I was hoping our stanza wasn't over.

We were told to tell a story of doing something nice. Just saying that word—*nice*—to a bunch of addicts brought out the eye rolls and one-liners. Ask us to catalog the nefarious and we could trade war stories all day, but saying something kind? About ourselves?

Despite our objections, we had to go around our circle and share. The counselor waited for one of us to volunteer to go first.

I thought of Jessa, a woman I had an affair with back before Blue. On our first date we drank margaritas at the Latin American Club and she said, "I'm pregnant." We waited tables together. She had an outstanding sense of humor and a lewd mouth. And she was strong. She swam out to Alcatraz on the regular.

"Who's the father?" I said.

She told me about this guy she'd been with—Chris?—and how it had ended badly a couple weeks back. He gave her money for the abortion. "But he won't come to the clinic with me," she said.

"I will."

The day of the procedure, I sat out in the waiting room. I thought there would be a swarm of uncomfortable men, pacing about like caged animals, but it was only me.

Eventually, the nurse led me back to Jessa. She reclined on a small bed, sucking a small can of apple juice. That look in her eyes. How can I describe that look? Jessa was ten years older than me, and I couldn't comprehend what an abortion meant to a woman. To me, it was some clean decision: you don't want to have a kid. I was too young to understand the churning complexities.

Anyway, that look: Her eyes were teary and distant. She was here and a hundred other places. She was happy and unhappy and taking care of herself and not taking care of herself and she was sure this was the right thing to do and regretting her decision.

The only sounds in the room were the sips from her apple juice can.

Then I took Jessa to her apartment, got her in bed to nap. I asked if I should lie down with her, but she said it would be better if she were alone.

"But don't leave," she said. "Just be in the other room."

"That's fine," I said. And it was. An hour ago, she was pregnant. Now she wasn't. I sat in the kitchen with a pot of coffee and a Kesey novel, *Sometimes a Great Notion*.

"Will you get me some McDonald's cheeseburgers?" she said a while later. "I know that's gross, but it reminds me of being a little girl. Comfort food."

"It's not gross at all."

"Yes, it is."

"Okay, maybe a little."

She lived in the Upper Haight and there was a McDonald's about six blocks away. Once I'd gotten the bag of cheeseburgers, I hurried back. Feeling all empowered, all important. I couldn't wait to hand that greasy sack to her. I stormed into her room, holding the bag over my head, held it up like it housed the cure that would save her. Sure, those burgers didn't really mean much, but it was what she needed from me and I wouldn't let her down.

"Your comfort food, my lady," I said.

I hadn't thought about that day in years, but it seemed nice. I didn't want to go first, but the counselor waited for one of us to raise our hand. She needed me, like Jessa, and being needed was part of being human. That was why I was in rehab: to turn human again.

So I raised my hand.

She asked me to stand and share. I told them all about Jessa and the cheeseburgers, and a crazy thing happened: they gave me a standing ovation, my own comfort food.

A couple days after that, we were told to take out our phones and delete every contact. People weren't having it. "I need these numbers," they said.

The counselor was prepared for our incredulity. Every new crop of addicts must have reacted the same way. He countered our protestations with "Most of those people in your phone don't care about you. Delete everyone and make them earn their way back in. If they're good to you, reprogram their numbers. Otherwise, never talk to them again."

"Delete our parents?" someone said.

"Even them."

"My husband?"

"Yes."

"What about the Chinese delivery guy?"

"He'll understand," said the counselor.

I had over two hundred contacts in my phone. Maybe some cells allow you to bundle and delete a bunch at once; I had this crappy old phone, which would only delete numbers one at a time. A bunch of the numbers were people I didn't even know, probably plugged in at last call, promises to drink together again. Others were restaurant and bartending buddies. Some belonged to old one-night stands from the days before I met Lelo, programmed not with their names but clues about their identities—*Diner, Green Eyes, Platforms, Pizza Place, Pig Tails, Vodka, Young.*

I deleted all these people.

It was harder to erase my family, of course—my mom, my step-mom, my sisters—but I wanted to get rid of everything that day. If it was possible I would have deleted myself. I was experiencing a grieving process in rehab, saying goodbye to the caveman.

I even deleted Lelo, hoping she'd call back so I could add her again. I wasn't confident, though. She was saying all the right things—*I love you and want to support you through this* and *I'll be here when you're ready.* But why would she wait? Why should she?

"Addition by subtraction by disaster," I said to myself, nixing another number, Watch's. Thinking about what we did that night, how we made the world a worse place.

Watch and I were chaos junkies. I'd once sucked his cock on Baker Beach, in front of a bunch of our friends, but mostly we were interested in mayhem, not sex.

The night I need to tell you about happened years before I got into rehab. I'd love to say otherwise—that this horrendous act with

Watch made me wise up, sober up—that it made me want to be a better person. But this was years before.

Watch and I popped pills and shot pool in North Beach. It was game seven of the NBA finals. A stranger walked up to us, saying, "Next round is on me. I just won five hundred dollars on the game." He pointed to a TV behind the bar where one basketball team was hugging and pouring champagne on each other while the other team hugged and cried with no champagne.

"Winner winner, chicken dinner," I said to him.

"Huh?" he said, looking around the bar. He was white, in his thirties, dressed in ill-fitting and bland Costco clothes. "Chickens? Where?"

"It's an expression," I said.

"I don't think chickens belong in pubs," he said, pulling his cash from his front pocket. It was in his hand for a few seconds before thudding to the floor. The bills scattered down there. We could see a few hundreds and a wad of small stuff. He wobbled down to collect them. The guy was annihilated, standing back up and staggering a bit as he checked his six for rogue chickens. Watch and I smiled at each other, seeing someone who might subsidize the next couple hours of our cocktailing with his winnings.

It seemed important to agree with his anti-chicken stance in order to form a friendship. Watch and I both tended bar and knew the importance of indulging alcoholics their preoccupation du jour.

"I concur that liquor and poultry should be kept separate at all times," I said to him.

The guy nodded, then eyed Watch, awaiting confirmation of his allegiance as well. "Yeah, fuck chickens," said Watch.

This guy erupted into applause. "Now what would you fellas like to drink?"

We ordered three whiskey shots with bottles of PBR. The

bartender carried the whiskeys, balancing them in one palm. He carried our beers in his other hand, his fingers lodged in the necks of the bottles, bowling ball style. It was that kind of bar. You slipped your beer off the bartender's fat fingers and thanked him for it. Hoping, simply hoping, that he washed his hands after pissing.

"To winning all our bets!" the guy said right before we took our shots. "To being huge winners!"

Every session in rehab started with us going around the circle and introducing ourselves by our first names, saying what our drug of choice had been. Trevor always said, "I'm Trevor, and my drug of choice is MORE."

We laughed and clapped after he choked his catchphrase out, so imagine our letdown the day Trevor was called out by one of the nurses before the introductions. I was called out, too. Once in the hallway, she ushered us to a back corridor I'd never seen. "I need a urine sample," she said.

"Why are we being singled out?" I said.

"Everybody does it during their second week. I'll be right back with your cups."

We sat down in the hallway. Trevor looked worried, so I said, "What's wrong?"

"Will wine show up?" Trevor whispered.

"You drank wine?"

"What about weed?"

"Of course weed shows up."

"But weed stays in your system for like a month," said Trevor. "I could have smoked it before I got here. How would they know when I got high, right?"

"Have you gotten stoned since we started?"

Trevor gave me a smile, a condescending one, and said, "My name's Trevor, and my drug of choice is MORE."

I was angry, almost felt betrayed. We were in this together. We were withdrawing together, opening up during group. We were prescribed Suboxone and trazodone. We smoked cigarettes. We were friends. That's what sticks out to me now—how much I liked Trevor after only knowing him a couple weeks. He was a good kid, and I was jealous of him, wishing I'd gotten in treatment at twenty years old, avoiding all that aching.

But maybe he hadn't lost enough yet. That was the problem with being young in rehab. He hadn't sacrificed enough people, hadn't dismembered every promise he made, hadn't doctored and botched his dreams, leaving them for dead. The rest of us had left no humiliation uninhabited.

He was also in my dual diagnosis group, populated by people who had drug problems, *and* something else. For me, it was the first time anyone brought up being bipolar. When they listed the symptoms, it sounded like my eulogy: Josh's manic energy swings high high high, low low low, and those pits are worth it if it means the highs soar to inspired altitudes, he can't sleep, insomnia is a superpower that brings on confidence that cruises at thirty thousand feet, who needs sleep, who wants sleep, I wanna stay up forever, I wanna feel this inspired forever, I wanna feel every thought crash together inside my skull like popcorn kernels exploding, dancing, rocketing as they change states.

Trevor can tell you about why he was in the dual diagnosis group in his own book. Point is, I spent a lot of time with him in rehab. I cared about him. And he was already fucking up.

Now I said to him, "Why are you smoking? We're here to get clean."

"I'm here for my parents."

"What if they kick you out of the program?"

But all he did was shrug. I can see him doing that gesture so clearly even today. Shrugging like, *Oh well*. Shrugging like, *What can you do?*

And if I could talk to him from here, I'd say this: We can do lots, Trevor. We can get our shit together. We can, for the first time in our lives, try to make things better. We can decide to live a good life, one with Lelo and Ava, instead of carousing with Watch.

Me and Watch and this guy—call him Wasted Winner—had played five or six games of cutthroat, killing a few hours. Wasted Winner could barely make contact with the cue ball. Watch and I were of the opinion that it might be simpler to cut out the middleman and absorb his funds.

Which is just a bullshit way of saying we were going to rob him.

I can say it only happened because I was drunk. Because of the pills. I can say that with a clear head, I would never have acted that way, but do you really care about my reasons?

"Would you like to get stoned?" I said to the Wasted Winner, who didn't even have to think about it, going ballistic like a dog seeing the leash in your hand, saying, "Should we smoke in the bathroom?"

"No, he lives around the corner," I said, pointing at Watch.

The Wasted Winner's tail kept wagging: "What are we waiting for?" Then he kept blathering about his luck while we walked out front of the bar. "A lot of gamblers don't touch the NBA, but I've plied my craft," he said. "I'm an expert."

It was about midnight. No one else was around. There are a

bunch of trees surrounding Coit Tower, so it was the perfect place. One thing you need to know about Watch and me: We'd soldered together the ugliest parts of ourselves—our hate and rage and regrets, the pulp of our broken hearts—into one gigantic fist. And once our fist formed, there was nothing we could do to stop it. To stop us.

"We can take a shortcut," said Watch, pointing up toward the Tower.

"You live up there?"

"No, I live right on the other side. This is a quicker way."

"Let's take a taxi," Wasted Winner said. "I am in no shape for cardiovascular activity." He looked around for a cab and, even though none were around, hoisted his arm and yelled, "Taxi!"

"There's a nice view up at the Tower, too," I said. "Winners should see this view."

He put his arm down. He smiled. He had no idea.

Maybe an hour after our piss test, I looked for Trevor. He was with a few heads outside, smoking cigarettes. "Are they kicking you out?" I said.

He ushered me away from the group. "They saw the weed, but I had it in my system when I got here. My plan worked. I'm all good."

"Why did you smoke last night?"

"I told you," he said, "I'm only here for my parents."

"Why?"

"Ask them yourself. They'll be here for family day."

"I'm not going to family day," I said, repulsed by the suggestion. Everyone in rehab had spent the past couple weeks splattering the walls with our secrets, telling all the shit we tried to keep from our families, and now these populations were going to mix? How? Why?

But that wasn't what I was scared of, not really. My real fear was that I'd ask Lelo to come and she'd refuse, too busy boxing my stuff up and leaving it on Valencia Street. Too busy finding a guy who could moderate his intake, who could come home when he said he would. She'd find a gentleman and they'd share a normal life, and she deserved it, deserved him.

That was one of the things I hoped to discover in rehab: Was it possible for someone like me to turn into *him*? And would Lelo wait?

"You have to go to it. They make you," said Trevor. "Any of your people coming?"

"No. Maybe. I don't know."

I asked and she said yes, and then there we were: Lelo and I in the parking lot, out front of the rehab facility. One of the old-timers, Paul, was out there too, all agitated, pacing around and kicking rocks and talking to himself. He'd been in about a week longer than me. My first day, he was withdrawing from oxy so bad that he was wrapped in a blanket, sweating and swearing and moaning.

"What's the matter?" I said to him.

"My wife, that's what," he said.

"This is my girl, Lelo," pointing at her, both Paul and I forgetting about this thing called manners. He didn't even look at Lelo, saying something about his wife skipping family day so she could go wine tasting in Napa.

"Wine tasting?" I said, all offended on his behalf.

"Well, she should hate me," he said, all offended on her behalf.
"I'm a shitty husband."

We were all shitty in one way or another in rehab. Shitty spouses
and lovers and friends and daughters and sons and siblings and
fathers and mothers and drinking buddies, and like Mort, we'll be
whispering our whole lives, gruff forlorn voices saying, *Sorry, so
sorry, I wish you'd never known me like this.*

○

A bunch of trees surrounding Coit Tower. Midnight. No one
around. Secluded. The perfect place. To hurt someone. To rob him.
To unload the fist we packed. So it can run rampant. Rampaging.
Releasing our fury. Watch and I walking up the hill. About ten feet
ahead of Wasted Winner. He was out of breath. He was staggering.
He was sweating. I was sweating. Watch was probably not sweating, thriving on violence. Conversation petering out. Just trudging,
panting men. The promise of getting high motivating each new step.
At least for one of them. The other two malevolently motivated. And
I liked punishment. Punishing others. Punishing myself. Didn't really need a reason back then. Punished myself because I was there.

Thinking about that TV back at the bar. The basketball players
celebrating. Pouring champagne over one another's heads. Guz-
zling the stuff. Spanking every ass in the room. Their huge smiles.
The whirling way they moved through the locker room. Hugging
and frolicking and howling, "We won. World champs, baby!" I
couldn't stop thinking about the champagne. How that must feel.
How it must feel to have someone celebrate you. Your accomplish-
ments. Your role. Your hard work. Your being on the planet. What
must it feel like to have championship champagne drizzle down
your face?

My only drizzling was adrenaline. Maybe a squeak from a run-down conscience. Some fear. Getting caught and going to jail. And for what? A couple hundred dollars? That's the thing—we didn't need the money. We weren't doing this for that. No. Trudges and pants. Three men moving. Toward emergency. Toward an anger apex. There's no such thing as divine intervention. No such thing as celestial protectors. Nobody intervenes. We are left to cripple ourselves. Mangle ourselves. Left to our own devices, we crumble to the occasion.

Nearing Coit Tower.

I said to Watch, "Now?" and he looked around one last time and not seeing any witnesses out there said, "Now," and Watch turned and hit the man, who tried to say something but these syllables were muffled and busted, and he didn't fall down after the first blow so I hit him too and he went to the sidewalk with more muffled and busted syllables and we kicked him a few times and rifled his pockets for what was left of his winnings, ripping that cash away, and whatever we gained that night, say $200 split between us, doing all that damage for a hundred bucks each, what we took with us as we left that guy lying there had nothing to do with money. What we took was a stash of disgrace. Wounds only we could see. Ones that wouldn't lighten with time like old tattoos. Remaining visceral and wicked and profound. Colorful and ornate and raw. Ones with fists of their own.

And there we were on family day, three weeks into the program. Us, the addicts. Them, the intruders. I don't mean to make it sound ad-versarial. But I sort of do. Because that's what it felt like: We'd been in a womb and now this was the first stirrings of labor, proof that we'd be birthed back into the world, and there was the chance that I could know life without being a caveman.

The worst part of having them there was how little they knew us now, assuming we stayed clean. They knew us as drunks, IV drug users, people who smoked speed using broken lightbulbs as pipes, people who mangled promises, people who burned money like wicks, people who hit their loved ones, couldn't hold down a job, couldn't stay out of jail, couldn't love their kids. They knew our crimes and our lows and because they'd seen us at our worst, how were they supposed to give us the benefit of the doubt? And how were we supposed to give ourselves the benefit of the doubt with them around?

When it was just us, trying to make sense of a future without drugs or booze, that was one thing. But sitting among all the people whose hearts we'd gouged out—what gave us the right to expect better from ourselves, expect anything other than relapse?

We couldn't feel empowered sitting with these eyewitnesses to all our sins; like a suspect lineup, they could finger every last one of us. With them there, we were hopeless. Doomed. Preternaturally stupid. We'd never stay clean. Never amount to anything. We were swollen livers, shaking hands. We were DUIs, abscesses. We were violent nights with Watch.

Everybody sat in these neat little rows of seats set up in one of the conference rooms. If you didn't know better, you'd think we were there for a real estate seminar. Trevor and his parents were in the front row. I pointed him out to Lelo and said, "That's my friend."

"What's with that guy outside?" she said.

But I didn't want to talk about Paul or his wine-tasting wife. "See that kid up front? That's Trevor. Those are his parents."

"They look so normal," said Lelo.

She was right. If this was a real estate seminar, these responsible parents had taken their precocious kid here to learn the intricacies of flipping properties. They had no idea that he wasn't listening. They had no idea he wasn't interested in real estate or sobriety. He was only interested in MORE.

The guy running family day had a tragic ponytail running all the way to his ass. First thing he said was, "Does anyone know where the word *addiction* actually comes from? It's Latin. From the word *addictus*. Meaning to devote yourself entirely. To worship."

To worship!

Think about that for a second. Think about this congregation of junkies and drunks falling to their knees and praying for their god's love, knowing that their deity required more than mere prayer, and so if you wanted to belong here, with us, you needed to speak with actions, show your devotion to this contagious god through debauchery and debasement, needed to wreck everything you held dear, destroy everyone who had ever shown you kindness, and once you were alone and broken, only then would you be allowed to crawl in our coffin, our cathedral, and feel the thrill of worshipping pure despair.

Addictus.

To worship.

To be a worshipper.

I looked to Trevor, sitting with his family, them having no idea that he still secretly worshipped MORE, them hoping that his presence here meant that he was ready for a better life, but he wasn't. He'd be back in rehab, hopefully sooner rather than later. I looked back at Paul standing by himself, his family too incensed to show up. Looked at lowly Mort, whispering to himself. I so badly craved a future that wouldn't lead me back here.

I clutched Lelo's hand, maybe too hard, but I could barely

control my limbs. Here was my chance to never hurt anyone again. I leaned over and said to Lelo, "I love you."

"I love you too," she said.

"I can be a better person," I said. "I'll show you."

"I believe you."

And we listened to Ponytail talk for about an hour. Not me, the mess. Not her, the family-day intruder. There were no divisions between us. I was wrong about that. No, if she was brave enough to walk in the room, then she was a part of this thing. And if Lelo was that strong, maybe I could be, too.

The two of us, the entire room of us, listening together.

9

The fentanyl knocks me into a trance—how I've missed the feeling of a needle, of a drug pulling the bones from my body—and the next thing I know, I'm being awakened. The surgery takes about ninety minutes, though to me it feels like seconds. It is a success. My heart has the necessary wall, that eight-millimeter hole plugged up.

I'm groggy and still high as they wheel my bed downstairs. We are on our way to a test to make sure the procedure has worked. We stop by the waiting room so I can see Lelo. Very rarely in life do you know with certainty that you are in the middle of a profound moment while actually experiencing something. Usually, we assign value to these things in retrospect.

But not this time.

Not seeing Lelo.

Not watching the most beautiful smile I've ever seen erupt on her face. She runs over to me, leans down, and we have a hug, the most perfect one. All her worries about me dying, leaving her a young widow with a baby, all of these qualms mutate into pure affection. She is relieved, and I am relieved, which feels like too casual a word, though it's what we are.

They verify if the surgery is a success by "bubble test." They shoot saline bubbles into my heart and hopefully the bubbles hit their device, my new wall. If the bubbles can't get through to zoom around my heart's chambers, ambling this way and that like clouds, I'm fixed.

I lie there and watch the ultrasound machine. My heart is on the monitor, black-and-white, beating and repaired, and the bubbles hit the newly implanted wall. I know those are only bubbles made of saline, know that they are not in fact blood clots, yet that's what I see, a whole infantry of clots trying to cross through my heart and speed up to my brain, trying to take Lelo and Ava away, but they can't. They are blocked and I am all right.

I get to be a dad and a husband for a while longer. There are, obviously, no guarantees, but I'll make it till tomorrow. And if I'm lucky, I'll live long enough that we can walk through an entire garden of milestones, and I'll look back on a long life, one without another divorce or estrangement, one in which I bask in our luck: I survived three strokes in my thirties, survived an ill-formed heart, survived a procedure that saw surgeons entering and planting a device in my chest.

I say to the surgeon, "Everything's good?" and he says, "You're like everyone else now."

And he means it.

But he's wrong.

That opiate dose revives my caveman; I can feel his limbs stretch in me after a long hibernation, his stomach growling, famished for drugs.

The first time I shot Special K was back in my early twenties, at Becky's house. We worked at the same restaurant—her waiting tables, me behind the bar—and she'd been talking up K, saying how it was the best high in the world, and wouldn't I like to try it?

Of course. I tried everything.

After work, we went to her apartment, and she introduced me to her weird Nordic husband, Olaf. He had long blond hair, matted and flat, the bedhead of zombies fresh from crawling out of graves. Olaf was something of an amateur astrologer, sitting in front of a bank of computers. Right after shaking hands he peppered me with questions about my birth. What city and state? What time? What day of the week? What longitude and latitude?

"Your true horoscope needs to factor in the vernal equinox," he said.

"I was born in a taco truck," I said, "right outside the Vatican."

Olaf stopped pecking at his keyboard, shook his head. "This is your life. Take it seriously."

Then Becky walked back in the room with a plate that had three syringes on it.

K was a liquid horse tranquilizer. Club kids cooked it down, baking it in the oven to a powder so they could snort it. But some sickos shot it.

Immediately upon seeing her, Olaf stood up and dropped trou, pointing his pale butt at Becky. As opposed to heroin, which had to be shot in a vein, Special K went into muscle. Becky took one of the syringes and jammed it in his butt cheek.

After fastening his pants, Olaf took a syringe and stuck it in the back of Becky's arm, in the triceps. They looked lovingly at each other. It was actually a pretty romantic moment. They could have been new lovers sucking the same milkshake through two straws, foreheads almost touching, in some 1950s diner.

Becky said to me, "Where do you want yours?"

I swiveled my arm around, and she shot it in my triceps, too.

"Sit on the couch," she said. "You've got about thirty seconds till you can't move."

Being in a K-hole felt like falling from my consciousness, but not so fast that I was scared. The drug had a parachute, and I meandered through the clouds, the haze. I was in a warm sky.

Falling . . .

Yes, falling . . .

And then landing back in my life.

Back on Becky's couch. It was an hour later. Maybe more. They were watching *The Matrix*. They sat in a chair together, Becky curled on his lap, playing with that long zombie hair of his.

"How was it, Taco Truck?" said Olaf.

"More," I said, just like Trevor. "Let's do more."

After family day, after my few weeks of rehab were done, I was back in the Mission. Every night was movie night, and Lelo and I watched weird combinations of films. French New Wave with spaghetti westerns. Gangster flicks and satire. Slapstick mixed with surrealism. *Trading Places* with *Eraserhead*. Were we afraid of John Candy opening for Ingmar Bergman? Will Ferrell for Truffaut? No, we were not.

We embraced every fart joke, every banana peel, every time a fat person fell down. No matter how telegraphed these gags were, we laughed anyway, chomping on takeout food, watching from bed, wearing pajamas, sleeping on wonton crumbs.

We endured the most stilted and arcane scenes from the other end of the spectrum, too. The highbrow blowhards. The turgid. The cranks. Filmmakers who thought pacing was for the feebleminded and so they slogged on, one bulbous scene after the next.

Lelo quit drinking, too. Not that she was a drunkard, but she did it out of solidarity. It's the nicest thing anyone's ever done for me.

I'm probably not supposed to admit this, but I miss drinking with her. Not the hammerhead nights, but the ones where I impersonated a normal guy. I miss making her smile while we polished off a single bottle of wine and went to bed, though that didn't happen too often. I bet she misses that, too. Granted, she doesn't miss what comes with it, me staying out all night, seeing me punch some sap in the face as we toured Sonoma wineries, watching me expose myself to an old woman on the street, having to sit in the driver's seat while I spiderwebbed our windshield with a whiny fist—all the bullshit. No bottle of wine is worth bringing that back.

Lelo chose to date me even though I told her I had no intention of curtailing my partying. On our first date—the first official date—we had gone to see a Tennessee Williams play and stayed in a hotel downtown after. We were naked, drinking scotch. Lelo looked amazing, blond curls and blue eyes.

I was dazzled by her optimism. Here was a woman who saw *good* in the world. Here was a woman who made me want to see that, too.

I remember saying to her that night, "I party harder than you do."

"I know," she said.

"I'm not going to stop drinking."

"Okay."

I'd never done that before—been honest from the get-go. Usually, I downplayed my vices as I reeled in women. But the way things had imploded with Blue made me want to try this thing called honesty.

Of course, in that hotel room, we didn't know we'd make it.

We didn't know we'd date for seven years; I'd get clean; we'd get married; we'd have Ava.

On paper, there's no reason why Lelo and I made it, but we did. We're here.

For the first three months clean, we watched everything, going to the video store, Lost Weekend on Valencia, and feasting on all sections. No film was safe. Nothing was off-limits. We devoured three or four movies a day. One time there was some shitty action movie in the new release section that came with 3D glasses (this was 2009 so it seemed like a treasured anomaly). We nodded, knowing instantaneously that we had to do this. You would have thought we were stoned the way we laughed, wontonning our asses off, splattering our pajamas in dipping sauces. It was one of the worst movies ever. I mean, Brendan fucking Fraser was in it.

It barely looked 3D—2½D?—is that a thing?—but we couldn't pull our eyes from the screen. Not caring at all. Because 2½D was as close to real life as I was capable of right then.

For a few days after the surgery, I stay at my sister's place. Jess just lives a few blocks from us on Bernal Hill, and I need to take it easy. Specifically, I'm not supposed to pick up or play with Ava, which would be impossible for me if we're around each other.

So I'm in Jess's guest room, spending much of my day thinking about drugs. I had been offered a Vicodin script to help with the pain, but I passed. If I took those pills I would for-sure relapse. I might anyway, but I would have zero chance of making it with a pill bottle on the nightstand, rattling like that pick in my guitar.

When I had first gotten out of rehab, watching all those movies, hiding in 2½D, I felt sure that I wanted to get clean and stay that way. I felt steadfast, amped up on hope.

Yet after the freelapse, that's not true. That simple taste of an opiate supersedes everything else. It's what I think about, what I care about. Cravings like that aren't hints or whispers. They're pencils hitting palms. They're Nazi doctors saying, "It's impossible to do the right thing for a whole lifetime. It's not our nature."

I have the worst insomnia at my sister's and Forssmann won't shut up. I lie in her too-soft guest bed and sweat and squirm, too weak to do anything. Normally, with a mind barking like this, I'd get to the gym. Lift weights or spar. Run ten miles. Punish myself in a pure way.

But I'm feeble from surgery and so Forssmann stands over me, holds me captive in fantasies.

"I don't want to tear this life down," I say.

"Of course you do," he says, laughing at me.

I would like to be the kind of person who after successful heart surgery feels nothing but thankfulness. Someone who swells with grace, knowing how lucky I am for this opportunity to heal and live.

But it's not who I am.

I'm this skeleton stuck in his sister's guest room, angling to squander his life.

"Everyone will understand," says Forssmann. "No one will judge you. It's not your fault; it's the surgery's. Take advantage of this. Exaggerate the pain. Get that Vicodin script filled. Go on a run."

I don't sleep at all that night.

I get out of bed and make coffee about six in the morning, sit in my sister's empty, dark kitchen. Cardiology doesn't open until eight, and they'll issue the prescription. A dash to the pharmacy and I'm free.

Sip of coffee, check the clock.

Sip of coffee, check the clock.

6:27 a.m.

I can turn anything into a vice.

After that first shot at Becky's house, about six months passed in a K-hole. Each needle had a dream in it, and I fell into their worlds without the burdens of reality, rules, logic. Like living in my own little Dalí paintings.

If I wasn't at work or out at bars, I was locked in my room, shooting as much as I could. Spending every cent I had on vials. Sharing needles, cleaning them out with bleach, but who was that fooling?

I lived with Shany at the time, and she didn't like me using needles. "Not in our house. It's gross." She did so much cocaine you could have used all the powder to pot a plant. So coming from Shany, any debauchery regulations were a joke. The major thing in our flat was the *no shut up* rule. Which meant that no matter what the other person was doing or how loud, how annoying, how illegal, you couldn't tell them to be quiet. So when one person partied, even if you didn't feel like joining, you got out of bed, cracked a beer, rolled up a dollar.

All that made it hard for me to hear any ultimatum about needles.

"Look, I'm just experimenting," I said. "No big deal."

"You've been in your room for three days."

That seemed like an exaggeration.

I probably would have kept experimenting with K until it was all I did. No job or friends or future. Till experimenting was my whole life. Luckily, one day at work there was this brunette, a new hire, named Blue.

"I know you do K," Blue had said to me, "and if you want to date, no needles."

"Okay."

"I'm serious. That's the one rule: no needles."

"I promise."

"You won't be a writer if you're a junkie."

"I'm not a junkie."

"You can be Henry Miller, and I'm Anaïs Nin." That was the first time she had said that, mentioning them, mentioning us as them, the first of many.

"Nice to meet you, Anaïs," I said.

If you're a Nazi doctor, you do the drugs. You cop. You swallow. You drift away from your family. You choose the grim path. You choose to be alone. You choose to never be accountable. You choose to ache. No drug is strong enough to make you forget all the love that's spilled from your life.

And she'll track you down, despite you being a low-down Nazi doctor. Ava. When she's eighteen or twenty-three or thirty-one. She'll find your ramshackle world and enter your dirty perch. It will be her mission to see you, to tell you that she hates you, that she's fine without you, to plead for answers, in the same useless way you pleaded with your own parents. Ava will know it won't do any measurable good to confront a drunkard, but she'll be compelled to see this through.

If you're a Nazi doctor, you don't answer the door. You spy her through the peephole and hide. She's not buying it. Knocking and ringing the bell, knocking and ringing until you answer. She's persistent and poised. You are naked and frail. You feel yourself afire with shame. You feel a sense of regret that's been tamped out for years but she's gasoline, lighting you up.

"Was it worth it?" she says, eyeballing you, her magnificent disappointment.

"What?" you say, a sloshing cocktail in your hand.

"We had everything," she says. "I mean, we didn't have much money, and you and Mom had to work hard, and I slept in a glorified closet, and you were overtired and always behind and always feeling frazzled and questioning whether you were doing a good job, but so what? We had a happy life, Dad, and you left us. Why did you give us away?"

Anything you say will be useless and so you choose to say nothing. To shrug. To take a sip of that sloshing cocktail.

"You should have stayed," she says. "You should have known me."

At 8:00 a.m. I can't call cardiology.

I know how to work a phone. I have fingers to dial, a mouth, an ear.

But I also have a daughter.

Both my sisters take that day off work and hang out with me at Jess's. Katy brings over Jarmusch's *Only Lovers Left Alive*. It's a film about vampires, their alienation and disillusionment, citizens of a world that doesn't know they exist. They drive aimlessly around ruined Detroit. They wander the empty cobblestoned streets of Tangier. They need blood.

I don't tell my sisters about my confusion. I probably should. Keeping it a secret makes it worse, empowering these cravings, inflating their influence. I should be writing sonnets about rebirth! I should be rolling around in mud, praising Gaia for each and every creature on this striking, confusing planet!

Instead, I think only of the anesthesiologist running his needle into my artery, that brilliant shining bite from his fang.

Lelo and I get some time alone. We are at my sister's place, while Jess and Katy take Ava to a local park. We get to be husband and wife for a bit, before she goes home to do all the heavy lifting for our family while I sit around, lie around, recuperating and harboring an eight ball of guilt while talking to an imaginary Nazi doctor.

I want to be someone else, somebody better. Someone who's never conversed with a duffel bag or a dying dog or Forssmann. But this is my little life, the only one I get, and I'm not going to let relapse run rampant, razing happiness.

That's what I keep telling myself. As I lie in Jess's guest room. In the shower. On walks. I say, "You don't matter anymore. It's Ava; it's all Ava."

Lelo sits next to me on the couch. She is, I believe, just happy that I'm still here, with a patched up heart. I am, I believe, primed for a run and need to tell her the truth.

"I want to get loaded," I say to Lelo.

"Okay."

"I need to go to a meeting."

"Now?"

"Soon."

"What can I do?" she asks.

"It's all I'm thinking about and that makes me hate myself."

"Don't."

"It feels impossible that I won't relapse."

"You won't."

"I might."

"No," she says, "you're not allowed."

I laugh, which is what she's trying to do.

"Drugs and drink and strokes and heart surgery," I say, "you should've picked a better husband."

"Leave my husband alone," she says.

When I was still hiding in 2½D, say two months out of rehab, one night Lelo and I watched *The Deer Hunter*. She was awake as it started but she nodded off before De Niro and Walken were shipped to Vietnam.

If you've never seen it, these American POWs are forced to play Russian roulette, sitting at a small table, holding a revolver to their heads and pulling the trigger. A lot of them shot themselves. One of their VC captors loved seeing these soldiers blow their own brains out and when he didn't think they were pulling the trigger quickly enough, he'd slap them in the face and scream, *"Đi đi mau!"* which means something like "Hurry up!" and these broken POWs could only be smacked so many times and could only hear *"Đi đi mau!"* yelled inches from their ears before they'd do it, pulling that trigger, and some of them fell down dead and some of them survived—at least until their turn came again—and these men were terrified and wrecked but they didn't have a choice: at least if they played the game, there was the possibility that the gun's chamber would be empty, that the bullet wouldn't cut into their skulls, but if they refused to play, they had no hope.

And as I watched the movie, I cried. For all of us who played Russian roulette with booze and drugs. Those of us who pull the trigger and wonder whether the bullet will come. Those of us who hear *"Đi đi mau!"* all the time, not just from other people, and not just from ourselves, but from all sorts of inanimate objects. Bottles talking to us. Pipes, pills, needles. Every time we brave the outside world, we play a sadistic game of relapse roulette. But we don't have a choice, can't stay in 2½D forever. We have to hold that gun to our head and see what happens.

I haven't really told you much about the stroke three years prior: That morning, I had been in a Los Feliz bungalow, checking email, and was set to sit on a panel at the Los Angeles Times Festival of Books. This was before Ava was born. It was only Lelo and me. It had been an exhilarating weekend, filled with the camaraderie of other literary nerds, and shortly we were on our way to the festival.

A pop in my right temple, a noise like a match being extinguished in water. In some animal sense, I knew I was dying. I remember thinking: *This is the end of my life and what will I do with this final batch of seconds?*

I decided to spend them telling Lelo I loved her.

Wobbled into the bedroom where she was getting ready and tried to say "I love you," but my mouth didn't work, produced these macerated syllables that didn't mean anything, and she said, "Are you okay?" and I thought, *What a way to go out, being misunderstood when trying to tell a woman you love her.*

I do finally end up at the LA Times Festival of Books, better late than never, a month after the surgery. I'm still so weak but that doesn't matter. I sit onstage with a few other writers, Lelo and Ava not far away. During the panel, I talk about art and parenthood and teaching and learning.

There is a placard in front of me with my name.

There is a bottle of water.

There is a microphone.

And there is a roomful of people, the audience a hundred strong. It isn't a stadium full of screaming fans, and it doesn't have to be. It's a moment in which I am surrounded by others who love literature the same way that I do.

My heart is fixed, and it beats. And the three other writers onstage have beating hearts too, and everyone in the crowd has them.

We are all together.

10

Writing about relapse roulette reminds me of this time back in the late '90s, working at a French restaurant on Valencia Street that's since turned over a half dozen times, and after one shift or another, a bunch of us stayed to sit in the basement, drinking beers and blowing rails.

This happened at least once a month, sticking around from midnight to six or seven in the morning, staggering out into the sunshine with our stampeding cocaine hangovers, pulling these tiny pellet-scabs from our noses that looked like watermelon seeds.

There was a revolving crew who participated in these all-nighters, but a few of us had perfect attendance: a busser who we all called Angel who sold the drugs, the executive chef, and another guy who tended bar with me, who I'll call Shamus.

On this night, Angel brought along his cousin, who we were informed before he got there was Angel's supplier. He was coming to give away some product, say thanks for all the grams we'd been buying. His coke was good, and we were all excited to meet him, in the name of hitting it off and future price breaks on bindles. Of course, it never worked that way, but we held out hope.

There were eight of us, give or take, crowded in a small basement office. Angel's cousin shook all our hands upon arriving, a slick-looking Mayan who wore a designer suit while the rest of us sat around in dirty T-shirts, Ben Davis pants, combat boots—a clog of nappy dudes listening to Minor Threat and burning through a case of Shiner.

I can't remember our guest of honor's name so let's call him Javier. He pulled out two cue balls of cocaine. He distributed a few razor blades, and we chipped pieces off these cue balls, rowing them up, until the table looked like a Google Earth shot of a farm, crops lined up straight and immaculate and ripe, ready to feed people's hungers.

The next few hours we feasted on these crops, time a blur of beers and rips and bad jokes. Shamus blowing his nose into a bar napkin and saying, "There goes twenty bucks!" and all of us sitting in this circle, laughing, even Javier.

We played records by the Misfits, Op Ivy, Fang, Bad Brains, SLF, NoMeansNo, Neurosis, the DKs, and a hundred others. We opened another case of beer. The room was hotboxed by spliffs. A flask of whiskey magically appeared. It was a party and we were happy.

But by 4:00 a.m. we were all totaled, too gakked, too bent up to drive ahead, though none of us would admit that. When it was our turn for a new line, we feigned enthusiasm, sucking up another rip and hoping our hearts would keep working.

On Shamus's next turn, he said, "I'm passing."

This gave us a gust of energy. "You're passing?"

"I can't do any more."

"You're passing?"

"My nose isn't working."

"Passing is for suckers."

"I don't care what you guys say," he said, sitting there, folding his arms.

We were teasing was all. Everything coming from our mouths

was in good spirits. Like I said, we were all sideways wasted, but rules were rules and nobody bolted till we'd sucked up everything. That was how this worked.

But if he passed, that meant more for us.

Even if we didn't want more, we'd do it. That was how this worked, too.

So we'd all gotten our digs in on Shamus, and now we'd keep the circle going, each of us holding dollars to our noses and doing our lines, Shamus's lines.

Except Javier barked something at Angel in Spanish.

Angel barked back.

Javier's face going red.

The chef, a white dude, spoke Spanish too, and he followed the conversation with his eyes bouncing between them.

Javier rocketing to his feet, his chair falling over.

Angel, still sitting, hollering back at him.

The chef's eye popping between them.

Javier screaming, poking Angel in the shoulder.

Angel averting his eyes to the floor. Acquiescing.

Javier pacing back and forth. Screaming, still.

Us all sitting there. Not even ashing our cigarettes. Not even drinking our beers.

The chef saying to Shamus, "Do the line."

"I can't," said Shamus.

Javier said something else to Angel in Spanish, really calm this time, which made it even worse for us, even creepier, hearing Javier all collected.

Angel said something back. Angel said something that ended with *"Por favor,"* and we knew what that meant and we didn't understand how *please* belonged in this basement.

"Just do the line," the chef said to Shamus.

"I can't."

"You have to."

"Sorry," said Shamus, his arms still crossed.

Javier lost his shit again, pacing and yelling, and we just sat there with our rolled-up dollar bills. There might have been music playing at that point. It probably was. But I don't remember.

"What's up?" I said to Angel.

He waved me off. Angel and I were friends. We ate menudo and drank Dos Equis together before work sometimes, so when he didn't answer me I knew we were headed to hell.

"I'll do his," I said, pointing at Shamus. "I'll do it, Javier. *Está bien.*"

"No!" Javier said.

"*Está bien,*" I said again.

Mimicking my terrible Spanish accent, he said, "It's not *está* fucking *bien!*"

"I'm not trying to be a dick," Shamus said to Javier. "I'm wrecked, man."

That was when the gun came out. Javier stormed over to Shamus and put it right against his head.

Shamus shutting his eyes. Shamus's shoulders scrunching up. Shamus balling his hands and resting them on the table. Shamus gritting his teeth.

"Holy shit!" we said.

"What the fuck?" we said.

All of us looking at Angel. All of us expecting Angel to do something. But he just stared at his cousin, not saying anything.

Javier holding the gun to Shamus's temple.

Shamus's lips moving a bit. Probably praying.

"I give you free *bolsa,*" Javier said, so calm, "you do it all."

We knew the word *bolsa* because that was what Angel called his little plastic bags of coke. *Bolsa* didn't feel right for cue balls.

Javier bouncing the gun softly off Shamus's skin.

"Okay," Shamus said.

"I'm sorry," Shamus said.

"I'll do it," Shamus said.

The gun grazing his temple. Shamus leaned over and blew his bump. Javier put the gun back in his suit. Simple as that. He said, "There. Now *está bien.*"

He righted his chair and sat back down at the table. Smiling, making eye contact with the rest of us. A look like, *Let's go on as if nothing happened.* A look like, *Continue, friends.*

From there, the night became a race, trying to do the drugs as fast as we could. If all these lines were in fact crops, we had to eat everything in a hurry before it all went rotten, before everything spoiled.

I quit that job soon after, jumped ship to a new restaurant a couple blocks down, at the corner of 22nd and Valencia. I lost touch with that whole crew and hadn't thought of that night in years until the day Lelo and I took Ava to the zoo.

Ava loves birds and wakes us up about 5:30 in the morning, wanting to look across the street to a church, pigeons and tweeties perched on the steeple, some pacing back and forth. Ava watches them for twenty minutes without squirming on my lap, and sitting still for that long is unusual for her. I cherish these moments of snuggled stillness.

"What's in your mouth?" I ask her.

"Gum."

"Where'd you get gum?"

"My nose," she says.

It's the hardest she's ever made me laugh; I hug her, kiss the top of her head.

It scares me so much that she relies on me to survive. Relies on the dirty-laundry leper. The quantum leaper. The alcoholic carjacker. One of the Tims. The winner with his stolen money. The criminal. The caveman. The check-out-timer.

All those deranged, dislocated days. All those curious masks, living inside me like backwash in a bottle. And I'm in charge of keeping someone safe?

Because of her fondness for birds, Lelo and I take Ava to the zoo, thinking she'll love the African aviary, but she's not impressed, barely giving any of the exotic birds the once-over. She does giggle and coo at a pigeon playing in a dirty puddle by the monkeys. She lacks sophistication when it comes to birds.

We stand in line getting hot dogs at a concession stand, next to a crazy-big playground filled with ecstatic, shrieking kids. I notice the guy bussing tables. He looks familiar, though I can't place him right off.

His hair is gray. So is his skin. I keep double-, triple-taking him behind my sunglasses, and that's when I recognize Shamus.

He's not wearing these fifteen years well, rotund around the middle, more hunched than I remember him being. He has a rag in his hand and there are plenty of tables that need to be wiped down, but he ambles between them, not really doing much. He wasn't a very good bartender back in the day either, but he was always a great guy. I felt all right working extra hard doing a shift with Shamus because we laughed so much during the night.

"Don't look," I say to Lelo, "but that busboy used to be one of my drinking buddies."

Of course, she looks. He doesn't notice, surveying a dirty table before doing nothing about it and moving on to survey the next mess. The rag looks like a prop in his hand.

I feel bad for Shamus, feel embarrassed for him. If I was bussing tables at the goddamn zoo the last thing I'd want was some wiseass from my past waving his daughter and wife in my face.

"He was a good dude," I say to Lelo.

"He's not dead," she says.

While I pay for the hot dogs, while all those children writhe around the playground making their own animal noises, Lelo and Ava find a spot to sit.

Shamus still stands on the edge of all the dirty tables, hoping they might clean themselves. That rag is pristine.

I'm overthinking this. Just go say hi.

"Shamus," I say, walking up to him and tossing my hand out for a shake.

He looks at me like we don't know each other.

"Josh Mohr," I say.

He still has no idea.

"Josh Mohr," I say, "from Three Ring."

He moves the prop rag to his left hand and smiles at me. "Josh!"

"Shamus!"

Our handshake evolves into a monster hug.

Then we bullshit like it's the old days, fall into an easy rapport because why shouldn't we? There were hours, many hours, when it was just the two of us, before work or after, unloading the liquor delivery, counting the till, blowing bindles, shooting bourbon.

One night, he even warned me to stay away from needles,

knowing how much Special K I'd been shooting. "Be careful," he said. "That shit can cripple your life."

"I'm fine."

"You're fine until you're not," he said.

He was right. He is right. K can mash you.

But so can booze. And standing next to Shamus at the zoo, it's clear he's been going at it pretty hard. Not only can I smell the alcohol on him, I can see it, skin zombied out and plumped with water weight.

We talk about this person from Three Ring and that one, and did you hear about so and so? We laugh, talking about all the servers and food runners I screwed.

"I was always jealous of your conquests," he says, "but I got one, too. Tracey. Remember her?"

"I left one for you because I care."

"Glad to see you're still a dick."

"Hold on," I say, "I want to introduce you to somebody."

I run over and swipe Ava from Lelo, ask my wife to follow me. The throng of kids swarming that playground.

Animal noises in the distance.

Pretty soon, I thrust Ava at Shamus.

He puts his pristine rag up, blocking the baby. "I'm not good with kids."

"She's easy," I say.

"You keep her," says Shamus.

I do. It's a couple minutes of small talk, introducing my wife and daughter to him. We make phony claims to track each other down for coffee or lunch. We're both lying and both know it, but it doesn't matter.

I don't know if he felt uncomfortable or not. But I feel uncomfortable for him. I wonder if that rag could wipe away some of his decisions. Would he want that? Or is he happy living at a table still stacked with empty bottles?

I'm not saying any of this to make fun of Shamus. Far from it. Point is I could be Shamus and he could be me, or either of us could have gotten shot in that basement or died in any of a thousand asinine alcoholic ways.

One wrong fistfight, one wrong needle, one too many *bolsas*, a freelapse, one more lonely night than any human can handle and soon you're on the Golden Gate, sobbing and wondering if the answer's at the bottom of the ocean.

It's not, of course. But you endure too much electric shame and you'll imbibe any antidote. I'm not safe from that fate. In fact, I can relapse before you finish this page. That chance lurks in all our lives, though. A diagnosis. A car accident. Heart attacks. Lightning strikes. Whiskey shots. Whatever.

But so far, I haven't relapsed again.

And *so far* is all I've got.

PART III

THE HOOK IS
THE FISH

11

They were supposed to fix me. These doctors, their extraordinary surgeries. Every six months or so, I head back to the doctor's office for a routine ultrasound—to make sure my heart is fixed.

I lie on a gurney. They run a line into my vein, which will shoot saline bubbles into my heart. If the surgery is healing properly, the bubbles will only be able to wander through half of it, hitting the new wall. What's crazy is there's nothing holding this device in place, except my own tissue, as it grows around the wall, anchoring it. If the surgery hasn't worked, if my tissue hasn't secured all the leaky spots, the bubbles will flow through my whole heart, showing how susceptible I am to another blood clot chugging up to my brain.

There is an ultrasound monitor next to me, and the tech holds her wand on my nude chest. Both of us look at my heart in the center of the monitor's frame, wobbling its rhythmic shudders. The image of it is black-and-white, like some 1960s television signal, weak and wonky.

The tech hasn't yet shot the bubbles into me and so I wait, watch the blurry heart. It is lopsided—that's part of my condition: half of my heart has been working so hard my entire life to compensate for the congenital flaw that it's asymmetrical, looks like a deformed fruit.

Because the ultrasound machine resembles an old TV, I always think about god, some cranky creator watching some broadcast. I imagine god crashed on a rickety couch, remote control in hand, snack balanced on lap. Furiously flipping from channel to channel, from human heart to human heart, billions of beating disappointments.

"Here we go," says the tech. I haven't felt any anxiety because it hasn't occurred to me that the surgery might not have worked as well as the doctors had hoped.

She shoots the bubbles in, and my carbonated heart fizzes, a flourish of rushing bubbles. They enter one side, and the majority stop at my new wall, but some slip to the other chamber. She notices, and I notice—neither of us saying anything at first, watching these rogue bubbles bounce.

The only sounds in the room are the whirring of the ultrasound machine, the sticky slide and slop of the wand as she adjusts where it lies on my chest.

"That's not good," I say, pointing at the rogue bubbles.

"We'll need to wait for your surgeon and your neurologist to examine the results," she says.

"But it's not *good*."

The tech holsters her ultrasound wand and wipes my chest and stomach off with a paper towel. She has been avoiding eye contact and now she finally peers over, shrugs.

"Wait and see," she says.

Somewhere, a cranky creator watches the flurry of bubbles in my malfunctioning heart, sighs, and thinks: *It was a long shot anyway, fixing a man like him.*

We are having dinner with friends in Berkeley, Rio and Kyle. They are rich, and so we sit in a big backyard, on a lavish couch (that's what rich people do, I guess, have couches outside); we watch our kids run through the sprinklers. The rascals have even found a way to angle one of the sprinklers to douse a big slide, so they can speed down it, crash into the bright green grass, and look over at us, laughing and gasping for air.

"Did you see that, Daddy?" Ava asks.

I'm distracted, thinking about the rogue bubbles, but I snap into dad mode, telling her, "I bet you can go faster."

Then Kyle suddenly changes the topic of conversation to something grim. He's been drinking and apparently this information has been speeding around his head, like ghosts on their own wet slide, and so he burps a non sequitur: his friend has just committed suicide. Probably. It might have been an accidental overdose. But that's unlikely. I offer my condolences, but he keeps talking over me, over all of us, and he'll keep talking until this makes sense to him. He tells us that she only had one arm. She only had one arm because twenty years ago she shot up bug spray—Raid or Black Flag—sucked the poison up into a syringe and shot it into her arm. It did spectacular damage to her body and the only way they could save her was to amputate the toxic limb.

He is drinking red wine and he's not really looking at any of us as he spills this story. Kyle has the information in his head, but it's formless, like dry sand, and you can't make anything out of dry sand, and so he has this sliding pile of news about her overdose, and his mind can't make sense of any of it. My instinct is that nobody can make sense of this, unless you've tried to take your own life.

If you are in our disgusting club, you take that dry sand and add an angry liquid, and suddenly you can form anything you want of those sandy facts.

I know the motorcycle man, I want to say, and I'll tell you about him in a minute. *I know what it's like to swallow so many pills to escape this place, know what it's like to look around and only see despair. When your surroundings are polluted like that, you know beyond any doubt that your life will never get better. You know with absolute clarity that leaving has to be better than being here. So you find whatever supplies will midwife you away. You find a needle and poison to eradicate insects, and you shoot this solution into your system, and you wonder—well, if it kills the creepy-crawlies that infest the outside world, will it work its magic in me? Can it clean me? Can this poison purify?*

Her arm—I can imagine it—I can see it wilting—that gangrenous, oozing limb—a herald of the whole body if they hadn't hacked it away. I remember in the aftermath of my own suicide attempt feeling thrilled at my cowardice—how my whole being puked up those pills because once they landed in my stomach, waiting to kick in and kill me, that's when I realized how badly I wanted to survive. My face over the toilet. My mouth open. My pills leaving me. Landing with a splash. The smell of bile and tequila. The tears in my eyes making everything look shattered. The infamy of not following through with it. The futility of going on. At least like this.

And this woman's missing arm was invisible to everyone except her. I bet she saw it; yes, she saw it every day. Yes, she saw it and she felt it and she loved it. We mutilate ourselves not out of hate, but from a place of sanctuary. Because it feels good, because it's a relief, an antidote, either temporary or permanent. She needed to follow her arm's example and go. She needed to see this other world for herself. Hell, maybe the arm had been reporting back to her. Maybe the arm knew something incredible, a healing ecosystem awaits, yes, a lush garden of angels whose amputated arms flap around like beautiful birds and everyone is cured, and everyone is happy.

But these aren't the sorts of things we're supposed to lob into casual conversation, especially on a fancy outdoor couch, especially while our kids zoom down their makeshift waterslide and land on the bright green grass, laughing and laughing and laughing, angels in this strange noxious place.

Seeing as how you and me are grafting and growing together, diluting our senses—my heart becoming yours, my mind seducing your set of perceptions, holding them, well, not hostage exactly, as that makes it sound sort of adversarial, and we are the furthest thing from enemies, on the contrary, we are slowly becoming each other, which makes the whole hostage idea goddamn ridiculous, you can't hold yourself hostage, that's impossible, leave us alone, we are just two consenting adults dissolving any boundaries between our brains, watching them form a new murky world, wasabi melting in soy sauce, you dissolving in me, us a whole new vibrant animal, and so if I told you about my motorcycle-assisted suicide you wouldn't hold it against me, right?

No way. You couldn't.

You couldn't because you're me.

Because we're the same.

You can't schadenfreude yourself.

But before we had this melting moment—before we came together to share this beautiful and terrifying thing called Community, I was coming out of a blackout in Tahoe.

Now: Did my binge start in Tahoe?

No, it did not.

Did I have any idea how I got to Tahoe?

Not so much.

Coming out of a blackout while you're conscious is, well, disconcerting. That's the nicest way to put it. Normally, I'd black out and come to the next morning, in my bed or someone else's. The first thing I always did? Run my index finger over my front teeth, making sure I still had all my chompers.

In Tahoe, I came out of the blackout sitting at a bar. This wasn't the first time it had happened to me by any stretch, and I'd like to think I handled it like a trained professional, leaning over to the guy next to me and saying, "Excuse me, kind sir, can you please tell me where I might currently be located on this marvelous planet we call home?"

I doubt that, though.

I remember needing to throw up, remember seeing everyone's snow hats and snow jackets, and that the bar was scattered with everyone's gloves, which looked like dead bats lying there. I remember thinking: *Now that's strange—people in San Francisco wearing winter gear. Are we in some severe cold snap?*

The urge to throw up cranked to desperate retches so I ran out the bar's front door into a snowstorm and puked a fine puddle, landing like a Rorschach blot on the parking lot's white powder. The roads were empty, the whistle of wind the only noise. I peeked at the bar and its warmth, then up to its sign. That was how I solved one of the looming mysteries: the sign said something about being the place for Tahoe's locals.

It must have been a fairly impromptu decision to roll from San Francisco to the mountains because I wasn't dressed for the weather. I had on jeans and a hoodie, stood shivering next to the Rorschach puke, watching the snow fall on the near-empty parking lot.

And that was when I saw him drive out of the snowstorm. Actually, I heard his gruff engine first, then spotted the arc of white light in the distance, halos of wonder playing on the falling snow. His headlight felt like a search party, coming to rescue me.

Finally, I made out the motorcycle, emerging from the snow. He was obviously some snow-mirage, something from my shame-brain, bringing this motorcycle man to life to carry me away—to exorcise these galloping demons. He was a priest—I could tell; he could shuck my poison.

I hoped he would pass by close so I could feel his tenderness and love. Hoped he might shout some wise words as he sped by: "Life seems sadistic, brother, but happiness can swerve in at strange times, just like my headlight slicing through this snowfall!"

"Thank you," I'd say. "I'm lost."

"You were chosen—specifically chosen for this life," he'd scream and I'd hear every word as though his mouth was inches from my ear, despite the speed and snarl of his machine. "You were one sperm racing toward an egg, competing with millions of your brothers and sisters for this world—and here you are. Here you are, motherfucker, and aren't we all rancid miracles?"

○

The motorcycle man didn't just drive by; he parked in the lot and crunched up to the front door, right past me. He walked in and sat at the bar.

I watched him through the window. All of the windows had bars on them, but on their insides, there were neon beer signs. The one I looked through to see the motorcycle man had a different kind of mirage. This fantasy had a parrot, a palm tree, and, of course, a Corona.

I put my hand on the snowy barred window.

A beer, a bird, a shining day.

Paradise, behind bars, I thought.

I wondered if this was an accident, ending up in Tahoe. Had I sought this destination out? Or just hitched a ride with someone who made a road trip sound enticing? And who were they, where were they?

Truth was, however I'd ended up in the mountains, it was a solid decision. Back in SF, Blue had thrown me out, and I'd been couch surfing for weeks.

I wanted back in that barred paradise.

"You've returned," the bartender said to me, sighing.

I crawled up on my stool. The bar was about half full. Most of the stools were occupied, and they ran in a right angle around the bar. The rest of the floor was reserved for rickety tables, with old sugar packs jammed under table legs to steady the top, though that trick never worked for long. People were always spilling their drinks and blaming the table legs. But they never got up.

"I'm feeling better," I said to the bartender.

"Good to know," he said, "but you're still cut off."

"Oh . . . okay . . . I didn't realize that was the case."

"That's probably why I had to cut you off, right?"

"Fair enough."

"Want some water?"

"When I got here earlier, was I alone?"

"Yes."

So much for my drunkard noir, leads, clues, cracking the case. I decided to change the subject: "Can I buy him a drink?" motioning to the motorcycle man.

"You can buy anyone in here a drink. Except yourself."

The bartender put a pint of water in front of me, no ice, with a straw. I took the straw as a sarcastic barb, but maybe he was trying to be nice. Probably not.

"Do you have a sense of when I might be *un-cut* off?"

"Stop puking," he said, "and we'll start there."

Then he approached the motorcycle man, motioning to me while he explained the circumstances. The motorcycle man shrugged and ordered. The bartender poured him a shot of brown liquor and brought a beer in a bottle. Besides his shrug, the motorcycle man didn't acknowledge my gesture.

"Two bucks," said the bartender, coming back and refilling my water.

"That's all it cost? What did he order?"

"He gets a discount."

"Why?"

"Because I fucking said so."

"If I have another water, can I order a cocktail?"

"Two. Bucks."

I gave him a five, told him to keep the change, and gushed thanks over this new glass of water, made a big show of having another sip with the pomp and circumstance of wine tasting: "Just sublime. I'm getting all kinds of forest floor fruits in the finish."

"You're only making things worse."

"That's my forte."

"A beer," he said, shaking his head. "You can have *one* beer if you shut up."

"Deal," I said, "and thanks. I'd like to talk to the motorcycle man. What's his name?"

"I'm not gay," said the motorcycle man when I walked up.

"That's not what this is about."

"What's it about?"

"Your bike," I said. "I need a ride."

"I'm not a taxi."

"I can pay you."

"Only have one helmet."

"I don't want a helmet."

"It's snowing."

"I want to ride on the back of your motorcycle right now."

"Why?"

"I want to ride on the back of it without my shirt on."

"You'll freeze to death."

"I know that," I said.

The motorcycle man's mood was buckling. He didn't like me in the first place, and now we were talking about motorcycle-assisted suicide.

"You need to walk away," he said.

"What do you care?" I said. "Just drive. I'll be holding on to you and then I won't be. You'll barely feel me fall."

"You need," he said again, "to walk away."

I didn't understand. For the life of me, I couldn't conjure one reason to care. For both of us. For me and the motorcycle man. We needed to follow through and do this right.

Blue had just kicked me out, and I'd recently accepted the fact that I had a real deal drug problem. I'd always liked drugs, but now I wasn't driving. They were the original motorcycle man.

I'd been at the Latin American Club in the Mission, the last place I remember being before "waking up" in Tahoe. I'd had sex once in one of the two putrid bathrooms, and every time I went in there, I thought, *Wow, I screwed in here.* But this last time, I was in the other one, and that's where all my self-deceptions overdosed and died—and all that was left alive was the truth: I'd never stop doing drugs.

I had a gram of coke in my pocket and wanted terribly to dump it in the toilet. I begged myself to toss it in the water, but I couldn't do it, instead cutting the whole gram out and blowing two humungous lines, crying the whole time.

I needed a way to tell the motorcycle man that I wasn't strong enough to do it alone. I wouldn't be able to simply strip naked and walk into the woods and freeze to death. I'd chicken out. But not on the motorcycle. It would already be too late. All I needed was a ride.

As for the motorcycle man himself, he shouldn't care about me because I didn't matter. Not to him. Not to Blue. And living alone was ripping me up. I was temporarily crashing above some odd strip mall in the East Bay and having one-night stands with women in the mall, working my way around sequentially, starting with Peet's Coffee, then next door to Verizon, then Blockbuster, a taqueria, a pizza place. In four more storefronts, I'd be to the tanning salon, which would represent the crème de la crème in strip-mall sex.

And yes, I know how sexist that sounds, but that was where I was back then, literally and spiritually, and if the only thing to look forward to in your life is lying down with some orange lady in a tanning salon, falling off a motorcycle and freezing to death doesn't sound so bad.

Or it didn't at the time.

I wished I could just say this to him: "Please, pretty please, motorcycle man. Take me to where I need to go."

But begging wasn't going to get the job done. My last hope was money.

"How much would it cost me to hire you?" I asked him.

"Thanks for the drink," he said, standing and zipping up his jacket. "You should see a doctor. Tonight. Go see a shrink *tonight*."

"I'm fine."

He started toward the door. "Even the ER—just talk to someone."

"How about a hundred dollars?" I said, following him out of the paradise-behind-bars. My puke was gone, covered in fresh snow.

He hopped on his bike. "I don't want to punch you," he said.

"I can't fight," I said. "I've been drinking for a couple days."

"Get some sleep. Talk to a doctor."

"No one can help me."

"Have you asked?" he said. "Have you ever asked for help?"

"Not really."

He started the bike. "Just say 'help,'" he said. "Hit up the ER tonight and say that one syllable, 'help,' to the nurses and doctors."

I didn't want to think about the ER or help. I wanted to think about killing myself. I could see the whole thing perfectly, could see the motorcycle man say, "Climb on, friend," and so I did, sidling up to him, close and connected, my arms holding on to his hips. I'd rip my shirt off like it was a sweltering day and the snow would sprinkle on my bare shoulders, little crystals caressing me at first, though they'd soon feel like tiny predators. I'd say, "Let's go," and he'd say, "Where to?" and I'd say, "San Diego?" and he'd say, "That's too far," and I'd say, "Seattle?" and he'd start laughing, belly laughing, tossing his head back and saying again, "That's too far, too," and I'd say, "Fine, take me to your favorite place on earth," and he'd nod his head and say, "You won't believe this spot. You are in for a treat," pulling out of the parking lot and onto the snowy road and I wouldn't even shiver, not yet, only feeling the lavish love of a person helping me get to where I need to go.

He drove away, the motorcycle man. He left me. I needed his

help and he couldn't find any human kindness, any decency. He couldn't be bothered to rise to the occasion.

I stood in the falling snow.

That gruff engine of his, which had seemed such a harbinger of an angel's arrival, sounded completely different as he drove away from me.

Now the only thing I heard was abandonment. Neglect.

I heard a baby in a crib shrieking for his mother to console him. But the motorcycle man traveled back into the storm, without me, and I couldn't see him anymore.

12

He had an engine on his motorcycle, and I had a magical one on my bike when I was a boy. But in order for me to tell you about that, you need to know about a man I met at a police station when I was seven years old.

I don't know where he came from, don't know his name or how he was allowed to be milling about a police station, talking to kids who were there because their mother got a new DUI. All I know is that I was sitting in the waiting room alone, and suddenly there was this giant with glasses, his lenses looking like wet spiderwebs.

"Hey," he said, sitting right next to me in the waiting room, crashing in the chair like we were old pals.

"Hey."

"Would you like to see something nuts?"

"Okay."

"I'm gonna rip a urinal off the men's room wall."

"What?"

"Come on," he said, "let's go do it."

◻

Every once in a while, I got to ride an airplane to go visit my father. After my parents' divorce, he'd left the desert for the Bay Area, planting in Berkeley to pursue a PhD at Cal. Since this was the early '80s, ministers weren't allowed to get divorced, so he was reinventing himself. By the end of the decade, Lutheran clergy and divorce would be fast friends. He didn't know that at the time, though, and since he'd always enjoyed history, a transition to archaeology made sense to him.

It's only now, with the sadistic clout of retrospect, that the irony of a liar loving archaeology punches me. My dad had no respect for the past. In fact, he despised it. The past was a cemetery of fossils, bones buried, waiting to be dug. And those were the last things he ever wanted. He couldn't abide by excavation because that would mean he'd be uncovered, discovered. We would all witness his acrid secrets.

I can see that now, but back then, all I knew was that my dad was in school to become someone like Indiana Jones—and what kid didn't want Indiana fucking Jones as a father?—so I'd get to visit him and these were my favorite weekends, baseball games, jogging together, arcade games, air hockey, Frisbee. These were weekends of pizza and Burger King.

My favorite memory of these visits happened during a rainstorm. It was eight or nine at night and we'd been trapped inside all day and he said, "Should we go throw the Nerf football around?" and I said, "It's raining," and he said, "Who cares?"

I nodded my happy head—*who cares!*

We played in the street out front of his apartment. He lived a few blocks from UC Berkeley. We were out in the road, and the football soaked up more mass with every raindrop. It was like tossing a toaster. By the end, I could barely throw the sopping thing six yards.

We never talked about anything serious or of substance on these trips. He never really asked how I was doing. I don't think he wanted to know. If he asked, I'd have told him—and I'd like to think he never posed many questions because he loved me so much, loved me so intently that to hear of the travesties happening in Phoenix would destroy him.

And I didn't want to talk about those things, anyway. I lived them every day, didn't want to spend my vacation explicating them to Indiana Jones.

Leaving him was rough. Back then, flying as an unaccompanied minor, they'd stick me in the front. My father would stand by the window in the terminal, and I'd be sitting by the window on the plane, and we'd wave. There was never much physical affection between us, but I never felt more love coming from him than when I watched him wave at me.

I can still see him standing there—today—right now—like he's one of those nuclear shadows from Nagasaki, stained, effaced forever.

Except this shadow can wave its charred hand—can move its shadow-mitt back and forth, back and forth. It can tell its boy that he's wanted and valued.

I wanted to stay. I wanted him to want me to stay, to demand that I stay. I always hoped that he'd storm onto the jet at the last minute, insisting they let me off, he loves me too much to send me back to all that chaos, he's here to rescue me and don't get in his way.

"Enough of this," he'd say, "your mom is sick, and you should be with me."

But he never asked me to move.

This was before he'd met my stepmom. Before my two half

sisters were born. This was way before I turned twelve and I could pick which parent I wanted to live with. Way before he died at fifty-two.

He never took me to dive bars, didn't use me as a copilot to get free drinks, a prop, a sidekick, doing little tricks and gags for the other drunks so they bought him a round. He never pretended, as she did during the '84 Summer Olympics, to be the gymnast who fell off the balance beam and broke her wrist. She'd try it on all the bartenders—"I'm the gymnast who injured her wrist!"—and no one believed her, of course, but she'd get a couple gratis rounds for originality, while I sat next to her drinking 7 Up with a handful of rotting bar cherries.

I kept waving at my dad, and he waved back from his window, and a stewardess said, "Are you okay, sweetie?" and I said, "There's something in my eye," and she said, "Okay," and kept walking down the aisle.

And then the plane slowly backed away from the gate and I kept waving and so did he, and then he got smaller, and the person next to me said, "How are you doing?" and I said, "I have dirt in my eye," and she said, "All right," and we taxied and took off and then we landed and exited the plane and someone from the airline waited with me for my mom, but she didn't show up.

For what felt like six hours, but could have only been twenty minutes, I sat in a waiting room in a weird little plastic chair and I was sort of hungry, and eventually my mom came, and she was drunk.

Not so drunk that the airline didn't hand me over to her. But drunk enough that I knew. She was silly drunk, not weepy drunk. She was ready-to-drive-me-home drunk.

She swerved and sped and actually drove up onto a median and our house was like forty minutes from the airport, on the edge of the Phoenix desert. Plenty of time for her to get caught zooming in and out of lanes while we laughed and listened to the radio.

She wasn't nice to the cop. She was embarrassed, mad. She walked an imaginary line. She tried to touch the tip of her nose.

I had to stay in the car, but I watched through the window. Just like looking at my dad standing in the terminal. I didn't wave this time, though.

We were shuttled into the cop's car, Mom in the back and me in the front, and we were at the station and I saw her being photographed, standing straight ahead and then at a profile, and I was in another waiting room—a friend of my mom's who I think was named Amy was coming to get me—and I sat there and was still hungry and no one was talking to me until I met the big man with glasses.

He led me into the men's room. It was just the two of us in there. We stood in the middle of the room and he said, "Watch how strong I am."

He did some stretches, bending down, swinging his arms about to loosen up his muscles. He even jogged in place for a beat.

"Do you think I can do it?" he said.

"I guess."

"I can," he said, "I've done it before."

"Okay."

He flexed. Grunted. Leaped at the urinal. He bent down. He put one hand under it. He put the other on the pipes above it. He made that power-lifter grunt. He made it again. And again. But it wouldn't budge.

He sweated and swore, shaking out his arms.

Gripping again. Grunting again. Giving everything.

"I can do this, goddamnit!" he said.

I stood in the middle of the bathroom watching. You have to understand that five hours earlier I'd waved at my dad through the window of the airplane. Five hours ago, I didn't know my mom would pick me up soused, didn't know I'd ever meet this grunting man with his wet-spiderweb glasses. Five hours ago, I was just a boy hoping to hear his father say some simple words: "Stay here with me."

If he'd said that, so many other sentiments would be conveyed, too. He'd be answering all the lamentations crackling in my guts. *Why did you leave me with her? Why am I so impossible to love? Why won't you be my ark?*

Five hours ago, I saw my father through the airplane's window, and then my mom through another window, and now there was no separation between the big man and me. Only a few feet between us.

Swears again, grunts again, lifts again.

"I'm loosening it, I think," he said.

But he wasn't. He would give it a couple more useless tries, but the urinal never budged. Certain things in life were just too incredible to carry.

"Shit," he said.

"Sorry," I said.

He took off his glasses and wiped the lenses on his shirt. "I want to show you something else," he said, leading me into a bathroom stall.

There should have been no safer place on earth. A boy, in a building filled with cops.

He and I went in there.

You should stay out here.

The day after I met the Big Man, it was show-and-tell in my second-grade classroom. I raised my hand, the first to volunteer because I had a good story.

I had no idea that the night before should be kept a secret. Had no idea that these things didn't happen in other houses. No idea that booze and pills and men didn't traipse across everybody's life.

So I stood up in front of the class and told part of the story—Mom picking me up and getting arrested, leaving the Big Man and his wet-spiderweb glasses out of it.

If a child told the same story to his second-grade class today, Child Protective Services would rescue him before the sun went down. But not back then. There was a phone call; there were the mechanisms and motions of hollow Caring. All it did was make Mom mad.

"Use your head." She wasn't screaming at me, was speaking in whispers, speaking between sips of wine.

"I'm sorry."

"That can get me in trouble."

"Okay."

"Be smarter than that."

"I will."

We lived way out on the edge of the desert, way up Shea, and behind our housing development was just desert. I'm sure it's all paved now. Even a place as terrible as Phoenix is gentrifying. Every place is. There are too many of us. We'll ruin every last inch of dry land.

Which reminds me of the snakes.

See, the snakes liked the warm roads. Rattlers would hide most of the day in an Arizona summer, but once dusk rolled in, the snakes would slither to the pavement and stretch themselves out, absorb the warmth. But when me and these two crazy brothers whose names I can't remember first saw a snake stretching its length out on the road, we made a decision: let's hit it with our bikes.

One of the crazy brothers ran right over the snake, which immediately coiled and hissed. But we were biking away, celebrating our victory—we had really shown that helpless animal who was boss. Good job, us!

There were rumors that snakes' fangs could bite through a car's tire. We'd all heard that on the playground but had no idea if it was true. It made our game even more exciting. I was always too chicken to run over the snakes, though. I imagined one sinking a fang in my foot. I imagined dying right there on the road.

But I was about to turn twelve years old, which meant that the law was going to allow me to choose which parent I could live with—and I was going to move to California. I was going to move in with my father. And his new wife. And their new daughter. I was going to join a happy family.

"He's too chickenshit," one of the brothers said about me, making the other cackle. I had to do it. Had to see what it was like. To understand how hard a human heart can beat, how fast, how arrhythmic. To hope I didn't get bit, didn't learn what it felt like as venom diluted into a bloodstream.

I pedaled and pedaled, got closer and closer, could see the snake, make out the texture of its skin, see its quiet rattle, its glittering eyes, could see it sitting there, minding its own business, doing nothing wrong, and I was scared but I was going to do it. I was going to hurt this sunbathing snake.

Right up until I couldn't do it.

Right up until I swerved.

Right up until hearing the brothers calling, "Chickenshit, chickenshit!" but I didn't care.

I was leaving.

I was finally getting out.

It was almost like my bike became magic. Its earthly wheels and chain were miraculously replaced by a kind of engine, requiring me to exert little effort to cover vast stretches of land fast. I didn't even pack a suitcase, didn't say goodbye to anyone. Didn't need an airplane ticket. Didn't need to make any arrangements. I left the rattler and I was free.

So I just biked through Phoenix to I-10 west, and my magical bike topped out at the legal speed limit, making my travel easy in the far right lane of the highway. People waved at me. People honked encouraging honks. I pedaled through the Sonoran Desert, through Palm Springs, toward Los Angeles. My bike was so magical that my butt never got tired, my legs never cramped, never got hungry or thirsty, never sweltered in the sun, no, sitting there and knowing I was going to a hopeful place, a place where I might know kindness, and I hung a right turn toward I-5 north, moving up through California, speeding through Bakersfield on a magical bike, and holding my nose through the barnyard stink of the Central Valley.

I made incredible time.

The whole journey took, maybe, three hours.

And Phoenix was gone and my mom was gone and her drinks and pills were gone and her men were gone, and my bike knew exactly where my father lived, and when I pulled up, he waited outside of his perfectly painted house, waving at me, smiling—he was ecstatic to see me!—and my stepmom stood next to him, holding Jess, my new baby sister, and the bike braked and I let it crash to the ground and I sprinted to this happy family and threw my arms around them, and my stepmom said to Jess, "This is your brother. He's going to live with us now. Isn't that wonderful news?" and I couldn't help but bury my face in their freshly laundered clothes, couldn't help but bury my face in the hope secreting from their pores, and the magical bike picked itself up off the ground and pedaled away to help some other trapped child, and we all waved to it, thanking the bike for its noble dedication, and things were going to be different now, yes, my life was going to be better.

13

Here's the thing: relapse makes us uncomfortable. We don't like it, conceptually. We want clean arcs. We want characters who overcome adversity. We want progress, lessons learned. We want to be tidy at the end, nothing wrinkling our botoxed souls.

We have good reasons to want such things, too. It isn't because we're dumb. Not at all. It's because we care. It's because everyone has an alcoholic or junkie in their family, and we don't want to think about them going back out. They are our mothers and fathers, our children, our siblings. They are grandparents and lovers and spouses and friends we love like blood relations.

We don't want to imagine them being so susceptible, so delicate in their recovery. No, we want them impervious, battle-tested. We want them fixed, cut off from any earlier iteration of their being that blares self-destruction. We evict such possibilities from our minds.

It's fine to have a checkered past. In fact, we dig people with histories splattered in mistakes. It gives them perspective, wisdom. We like it when they regale us with stories from their tawdry mythologies. So long as these stories are told from a removed distance. So long as they fit into a tidy, bleached binary: These people used to be dirty, and now they're clean. Complimentary opposites. Cause and effect.

Or maybe it's not about someone you love.

Maybe it's about you.

Maybe you're like me.

After the bad ultrasound, I don't hear from my neurologist or my cardiologist or my neurovascular surgeon for a full week.

I would freak out, except for one important detail: I'm still on blood thinners. So even if some rogue bubbles are trickling through our new dam, the security of the thinners makes me think that the likelihood of throwing a blood clot is minimal.

Is that true?

I have no idea but thinking so makes me feel better.

So I allow myself to be a husband, a teacher, a dad. Ava only goes to day care for half days right now, so from 1:00 p.m. on, she and I are usually together. We go fairy hunting in the forest. We wrestle in the grass, paint watercolors. We eat serious amounts of ice cream. We go scooting, by which I mean she rides a scooter crazy-fast and I sprint behind her, hoping she doesn't knock out her teeth on my watch. Let her knock out her teeth when Lelo's in charge.

Finally, my doctors make contact. Not a phone call, mind you. God forbid. No, they send a curt email that says, *The bubbles aren't clinically significant.*

I'm pissed getting such weird news without a call, an opportunity to fling questions back at them—I want to know how they can measure clinical significance, how they determine if I'm safe.

I want to know how they'd feel having surgery and learning via email that it might not have worked. I want to know how they feel safe in their own bodies.

I sit at my desk and think, *What a bunch of assholes, saying these bubbles aren't significant!*

Then I address these bubbles directly, as though they're wearing fedoras and smoking cigars in the corner of the room: "But that's doctors for you, Bubbles, always talking down to you."

I wish the doctors had called, so we could have been on a line together, and I'm 99% positive that it would have sounded like this:

"What does 'clinically significant' mean?" I ask. "I need a definition of the phrase."

"Just stay on the blood thinners and you'll be fine."

"But the surgery might not have worked?"

"We don't know yet."

"Can you operate and fix it?"

"We'd only go in if the device somehow became unanchored in your heart."

"Jesus, I didn't know that was a possibility."

"Fine print, amigo."

"Are there symptoms I should watch out for, so I know if it's become unanchored?"

"You'll have a massive coronary."

"Maybe I should've just stuck with the email option."

"People think they want the personal touch, but does this feel good to you?"

"How do you know they're not 'clinically significant'?"

"Harvard—it's a little school in Cambridge."

"Why can't you just say that I'm going to be fine?"

"Because nobody is fine."

"Harvard must be some asshole factory . . ."

"When people call us names, we roll up hundred-dollar bills and lodge them in our ears."

"I'm going to watch Ava grow up."

"Okay."

"And I'm going to live a life I can be proud of."

"Give it the ol' non-Harvard try!"

"Fuck bubbles and fuck blood clots and fuck you."

"Neurologist, hand me a hundy, will ya? He's starting with the names."

"What if my heart doesn't heal and this amount of bubbles gets through forever?"

"We can't hear you with hundys in our ears."

"What if I have another stroke?"

"We can't hear you."

"What if the next stroke strips me of my lucidity and I live drooling in a wheelchair?"

"We can't hear you."

"What if I'm at the park with Ava and I throw a blood clot right in front of her and I fold down to the grass and I mutter those meaningless moaning sounds that came from my mouth when I've had strokes before, and Ava watches the whole thing, and that's her only memory of me, moaning and dying? What if that's the first thing her conscious mind records, moaning and dying? What if for her whole life every time someone asks her about her earliest memory, she'll see her dad fall and moan and die right in front of her?"

I was thrilled to be living with my dad, but by junior high I was drinking and smoking pot and my grades slipped, and I got popped shoplifting and my dad lost it. "I'm so ashamed to have a son like you," he said. "You are disgusting." He took everything out of my room, and I went to school and came straight home, was supposed to sit in the stripped room.

After doling out the punishment, he refused to talk to me, and by the third day of my sentence, I wanted out of my cell, and so I left without permission, walked to a bridge close to our place that ran over a creek. My friends and I would sit under it sometimes, smoking bowls and bullshitting, yet on that day, I sat on the sand, threw rocks in the water.

I'm not really sure how long I stayed under there, though it was long enough to scare my dad. When I walked on the road toward home, he drove toward me. He looked frantic and furious and he braked, and I climbed in and he smacked me in the face.

"I thought you were dead!" he said.

I just held my cheek.

"I thought you hurt yourself," he said. "I thought you were swinging from a tree."

"I'm fine."

"What's the matter with you?"

"I don't know."

"Let's go home."

I didn't belong here. He was right to exclude me from their family initially. No matter the grades I got. No matter the songs I sang in church. No matter the games we played or the prayers we said at bedtime, I wasn't one of them. I belonged in the desert.

In high school, I found LSD and E and Vicodin and codeine and mushrooms and I popped tabs of acid before school, stumbling around the halls, should have flunked out my sophomore year but the vice principal went to my dad's church so there was always clemency, and I found punk rock playing in garage bands with a guitar case full of malt liquor and that ire kept getting louder and louder in me, like it had been plugged into one of our amplifiers, and the band found cocaine and we found crank and then I ventured into narcotic destinations that didn't interest the rest of the band—I smoked PCP and I smoked heroin and I smoked crack, and all these drugs, these wonderful drugs, were a perfect facsimile for freedom.

I can't stop thinking about the "clinically significant" email and all my practical armchair doctoring about blood thinners and my team knowing much more about the present dangers of my heart post-surgery and blah blah blah, and it all makes me surly, which makes me thirsty . . .

Cocktails.

Craving things I never even drank back in the day. Peach margaritas. That's what sloshes around my cocktail-shaker brain.

Then cocaine shows up. I can actually make myself salivate thinking about blow.

Shooting Special K, that wonderful boneless feeling.

Pills that fill up bathtubs and wash me and warm me.

When these cravings come on, it's like I never stopped.

I tell myself—*you've never consumed a peach margarita so you're not really wanting a peach margarita and just shut the fuck up about peach margaritas, all right?*

"I need to hit a meeting tonight," I say to Lelo.

"That's a great idea."

"I just can't stop thinking about these bubbles," I say. "I'm mad about it."

"That's understandable," she says, "just take care of yourself."

"The surgery was supposed to fix all this."

She's supportive, sure, but it's more than that: It's muscle memory for her, too. We've built a life together, and she doesn't want me to ruin it.

Neither do I.

At least not most of me.

There is that filthy faction in my mind that loves ruin—adores the idea of a wrecking ball bringing down our life. It sounds despicable, especially with a kid, but it's the truth. These cravings aren't just about drinks and drugs. These cravings are about dismantling happiness, saying to each and every wonderful day of our sober life that I don't care—I don't fucking care—I'll wreck anything and everything, anyone and everyone. I'll wreck my wife and I'll wreck my daughter and I'll wreck myself.

One of the things about Lelo that I cherish: I can tell these dark thoughts to her. She knows that I work hard to stay sober, but she also acknowledges that drugs have their hooks in me, and it's almost impossible to rip a hook from a fish if it's been swallowed.

Just like the device in my heart, if the hook stays in long enough, the tissue grows around it, anchoring it, welcoming it. Soon, the hook *is* the fish.

◻

"Hi, I'm Josh. I'm a drunkard. And an addict. I'm pretty confused today. See, I had heart surgery about eighteen months back, and I just found out that it might not have worked. They said I'd be fine, and now maybe I'm not fine, and I don't know what to do with that. It makes me mad. It makes me want to hit them all. Those doctors. They were so smug and self-assured and now they tell me it might not have worked and then they say that they won't do anything to fix it. They make a mistake. They make a mistake in my human heart, and they won't try to right their wrong? They make a mistake and now I might not see my daughter grow up? It's been like this forever, man. These people who are supposed to help us. These people who are supposed to do right by us. Rehab was supposed to fix me, but I'm always thinking about booze and drugs. And the heart surgery was supposed to fix me, but they haven't done anything, not really. Right? It's up to us. It's the people here. The ones who show up. The ones who acknowledge that the world isn't fair, but that there's nothing we can do to make it fair. It's flawed and that's the way it works and you can whine about it and debase yourself and boo-hoo your way through an existence, or you can try to make it better. That's what we're doing, right? I have to think that's true. Because I don't want to be sober today. I hate my sobriety today. I want to go get lit and forget all this shit for a few hours. That's the hard part of being sober that no one talks about: the fact that we're always here and there's no quick escape. People having their martinis after work, or some wine, or a bong hit. But we don't ever get to escape clarity. No, we're aware and present for the whole shebang, bad and good. And I hate that about being sober. At least, today I hate that. I want to crawl in a cocktail and forget. I just want one day off from all this reality. I know it doesn't work that way for us. If we could drink for one day and then get back on the wagon, none of us would be sitting here. I hate that about myself. I hate that I'm so weak, so incredibly weak. I wish rehab and my heart surgeon could fix me, but it's becoming more obvious that no one is going to come help. I have to do this. But I can't do it alone. I need help. I need phone calls. I need people to say that it's all worth it—that all this struggle is worth it. I see people drinking too much all the time and I admire them. I want one day like them. That's what I want. 'One day at a time' but not like us—like them. I know I'll never get it. I know that if I go back out, my wife will leave me, and my daughter will hate me. And I'll never put her in a position to feel about me the way that I feel about my own mother. I just don't know what to do with all this anger. I haven't felt it fire through me for years. It's like I'm on cocaine again. Like I did a big old bump of ire and it's stomping through my bloodstream. I don't know what to do. I'm rambling. I'm sorry. I should've thought about what I was going to say tonight and organized my thoughts, but maybe it's better this way, this barreling anger. I won't drink. I'm not gonna do that. I won't get any drugs. But I just wanted to stand up in front of all of you tonight to tell you that I hate my sobriety. It's not a gift. It feels horrible to be clean today. It probably feels more horrible to be an addict today, so I'll stay on the sunny side of the street. But I hate it. Do you? Do you ever hate it? Am I alone here? I know it beats the alternative. I get that. But why are we supposed to work so hard when everyone else half-asses their way through life? Shit. I'm sorry. I'm scattered. I'll stop. I'm just mad and don't know what to do with it. Don't say yoga. I'm gonna goddamn strangle the next person who tells me to do yoga. I'm not Yoga Guy, all right? I'm a guy who has a heart that's supposed to be fixed, and now I'm not. I might have a stroke tonight, tomorrow, next week. It will be my fourth stroke and the docs say it will be the one to kill me."

◇

Driving home and there are some cars swerving, maybe fifty feet ahead of me, and I slow down to figure out what's happening. I see it: There's this big ball bouncing in the street, and it's painted like a globe, like Earth. I can see the world bouncing in the road and then a car runs over the world and it doesn't pop or anything, it just bounces a different way and then another car hits the world and again it doesn't pop, just springs over some, and when I pass it, the world's still bouncing there, right in the middle of traffic.

I watch it in my rearview, but I don't know the outcome.

Tell me.

Please.

What do you think?

What do you think happened to the world?

14

I often thought about people from the old days leaving AA meetings. Wondering where they are. Wondering if they made it out.

There was Sally, who Blue and I used to do cocaine with, hanging out at her house all night and exchanging stories, the bad ones, the treacly binges on childhood traumas.

One night things were getting heated between the three of us, something about how Sally's old man didn't want to knock her up. It was quite a sight, seeing her talk about children with a straw in her hand, a pile of yayo on the living room table. Blue and I were being self-righteous and that in and of itself was laughable, us espousing wisdom on healthy relationship dynamics, and Sally didn't appreciate our coked-up coaching, so she said, "I just want a baby and Jose can't even talk about it with me. And why not? I'd make a good fucking mother."

We tried consoling her, but she was on the verge of tears.

That's when she said, "I want a child so much that I let my cat suckle my breast."

Uh, what?

One more time, please.

Blue had a terrible poker face. I tried to soothe Sally by saying, "Well, um, that's nothing to be ashamed of, I guess."

"It's weird," said Sally. "I know it's weird. But it makes me feel better."

When I look back at these nights, all I see is our desperate ache to belong, to be loved: The compulsion to have genuine affection such a gale-force craving that we tried assembling beauty from all the rank bits. To get far away from our eight balls of cocaine. To be lifted from this sweating squalor and dropped into a child's nursery. To be in a moment of such purity. To be keeping someone alive with the food of you, that sustenance, that joy . . .

To Sally, there was no cat.

She fed a baby and life was full of wonder.

Lelo lies in bed, laptop on her lap, watching an old sitcom on Net-flix. "Did the meeting help?" Lelo asks.

"I'm not drunk."

"There you go."

"Thanks for being so supportive."

"Wanna watch a stupid show?"

Ava is asleep, and we get a couple hours of dumb TV together. I lie down next to Lelo, snuggle in so my head rests in her armpit. It's been a long day, and she's ripe. I love the way she smells. You could nuzzle me in a hundred other armpits, and I'd always know her smell.

I feel relaxed and calm. I can do this. So what if the surgery isn't healing in an ideal way. They haven't said that it didn't work— just that some bubbles are slipping through. Focus on the positive. Most bubbles are blocked. And that's a good thing, a great thing, the best thing.

But I'm just not wired to see the bubbles that are blocked. I'm one of the masochists who only see the bubbles that bypass the device—the ones running up to my mind. The ones seeking to kill me.

More exercise. More meetings. More talking.

Less moping.

This is my second chance. Immediately after the surgery, everything had shimmered. It was a life made of diamonds, the value shining so bright you couldn't look directly at it. I felt privileged by the simple fact of waking up—and I wanted to feel like that forever, the power in realizing you're lucky to be here. It faded, though. It fades, an infinitesimal dulling to the luster, the human eye unable to register it in real time—till you look up a year and a half after the surgery, and my life isn't a diamond.

No, now it's a peach margarita.

I'm halfway down the stairs, heading into the BART station, when I see some crusty punk stealing a lady's purse. He's pulled it off her shoulder, but it hasn't slid all the way off her arm, and they both tug, swinging their bodies back and forth, using momentum to jerk the purse, and she's saying, "Stop! Help!" and he's saying, "Just give it to me!" and I'm to the bottom of the stairs, and I fall in love.

Not with her.

Not with him.

I fall in love with opportunity.

To be violent.

To release rage.

I fall in love with my fist.

Fall in love with the way knuckles crack as I squeeze harder and harder.

It's like every clinically insignificant bubble is in my palm and I'm strangling them, killing them, no bubble will survive the grip of my fist and my heart will heal properly and Ava will have a father and I will be fixed, there's a future for us, there has to be, and tomorrow and tomorrow and tomorrow.

Crusty jerks the purse another time, but the woman does *work*, holding on to her treasure chest. She says, "Get away from me!" and he says, "Hand it over."

What I'm hoping for is for him to win, rip the purse out of her hands, and begin his triumphant strut in the other direction. That way, I get to swoop in on my invisible white horse. That way, I get to hear his nose break, taste his blood. But unfortunately for me and Crusty, she wrenches it out of his grasp and spins away from him.

A bubble bypasses a defective wall mounted in a defective heart that beats in a defective human. A bubble is like a thought—a shape, self-contained and perfect in its curves and angles. The thought has its geometry and inside it lives a compulsion—something that can't be reasoned with or cornered or conquered. A compulsion knocks us over like we're liquor stores being robbed.

I can sell this after the fact. I can talk about the crusty punk accosting an innocent woman. I can tout civic duty. Watching out for my fellow traveler. We are all in this together.

I wonder, *Will I hurt the punk?*

Will he hurt me?

Do I know the difference?

They're maybe twenty feet ahead of me, and nobody else is really around. This is midday in Montgomery BART station, a part of downtown SF that bustles before and after the banker's hours but can seem ghostly in the early afternoon. So it's just the three of us, save the occasional stray—just the woman, Crusty, and me.

She wrenches the purse from his grasp and spins away from him, calling him an asshole and walking away.

"Bitch!" he yells, standing there.

It doesn't matter that he doesn't have the purse. Doesn't matter that she's out of harm's way.

I don't care about those things anymore.

I'm walking fast.

Seven more steps.

That's all it takes to turn a punk into a bubble. Turn him into a blood clot. There's no human standing there. In front of me. Smiling with "bitch" blasted from his lips seconds ago.

He's just a clot.

A six-foot blood clot in combat boots, hard-to-read tattoos that look like signatures written in wet cement, hardened into meaningless, gnarled shapes.

Five steps.

I've done everything they've asked. I eat clean. I work out every day. Drugs and drinks stay far away from my system. I sleep. I laugh.

Three.

I'm to him fast. A fist throwing a hook. Hitting a cheek. A fist and a face and fucking magic happens when they come together.

A clot going down, Crusty not moving.

The woman wheels around and sees me standing over him.

"I'm helping you!" I say to her.

She doesn't answer, darting out of the station.

"You're okay!" I say. "I'm here!"

The cops will arrive soon, and I'm not in the market for an assault charge. I run in the opposite direction of the woman, so as not to spook her anymore.

Sometimes, I can come on a little strong.

I sprint up the stairs and into the sunshine, and it's like I'm a miner who has been trapped underground after a cave-in, enduring days deprived of supplies, stumbling up to the surface, squinting into the sun, stunned at the light and his luck—lapping up the simple fact that he's still with us and the world is a beautiful place.

I run away from the BART station and call Lelo. I am ecstatic. A convert. Being reborn, suddenly standing in a body of warm water with a preacher, and he says his magic preacher-words and works his magic preacher-moves—my past being painted over—and I plug my nose and he tilts my head, my body, back into the water, and it is instantaneous, this cleansing, this scrubbing of my existential grime, and I open my eyes in the water and look up at the blue sky, not one cloud, and I see the smiling preacher, and I'm submerged in peace, drenched in righteousness.

These are the bipolar moments that feel so fulfilling. That racing elation. Even when it's coming from something cruel.

I'm standing on Market Street in San Francisco. Adrenaline canters through my body. My fist throbs from the punch. Each pulse thrumming through my bones is electric and splendid.

I dial Lelo and say, "I had to help a woman."

She's not skeptical per se, but she's heard me talk like this paint-by-numbers Neanderthal before. "What happened?" she asks.

"This guy was going to hurt her."

"Who?"

"A woman in the BART station."

"Are you okay?"

"I punched him to help her."

"Are you in trouble?"

"She needed my help."

"Are you in trouble?"

"He deserved it."

"Are you in trouble?"

"I had to do it."

"Are you in trouble?"

"I'm fine," I say.

15

I have this dream that I drive a hearse. It's the middle of the night, and the roads are empty, and I'm alone in the hearse. Or what I mean is: I'm the only one alive in the hearse, on the abandoned road. It's some sort of highway and the hearse doesn't have any working headlights, but I can see where I'm going because there are streetlights, every few feet on the side of the road. There are too many lights, in fact, so I squint as I speed ahead. And it would be maddening if I had the bandwidth to wonder who in their right mind planted so many streetlights in such tight proximity, running on the outside of the highway like teeth on a zipper. I'd probably be getting super pissed about the brightness—how I don't want so much light, how I don't need it, just let me drive my hearse in peace in the goddamn darkness—but there is no space for such thoughts.

Because of the sound.

The sound of the coffin sliding around in the back of the hearse.

The sound of the coffin sliding around in the back of the hearse and bumping the walls and windows.

The sound of the coffin sliding around in the back of the hearse and bumping the walls and windows and some of them crack. And some of them shatter. Some of them crack and some of them shatter and now there's a knocking noise coming from inside the coffin.

Because of the sound of the coffin sliding around in the back of the hearse and bumping the walls and windows and some of them crack and some of them shatter and now there's a knocking noise coming from inside the coffin and that's what I hear—coffin sliding, windows shattering, someone knocking—and that's what I see—the blazing streetlights blinding me—and I steer the hearse and I was supposed to be the only one alive in here but someone is knocking and the windows are breaking and the lights are blinding and now there's a voice—I can only assume it's coming from the coffin-knocker and the voice is a man's, and I don't recognize it, there's no accent, and by that I mean—the voice sounds like mine, a West Coast kid, someone who's smoked, someone who didn't take very good care of himself, this raspy coffin-knocking corpse, and he says, "Take me home," and I say, "Where do you live?" and the coffin keeps clattering against the walls and the windows keep shattering—they never stop shattering—it's like someone's stomping a chandelier with steel-toed boots—and the coffin-knocker is getting impatient and he says, "Take me home!" and I say, "I don't know where you live," and he says, "Yes, you do," and I speed the hearse straight ahead and there are no exits on this bright highway, which I try to tell the coffin-knocker, who is not having it: "Take. Me. Home," he says, and I say, "There's no way for me to get off this," and since I'm driving aimlessly and that's making him mad and since all the noise is making my head overheat, I slam on the brakes, and they smoke, and we squeal, and we stop.

Our apartment is empty. It's Christmas Day 2015.

I've spent the morning and afternoon loading one of those moving pods mostly by myself, though a pal came by at the end to help with the huge stuff. But for the most part, the pod was packed by me and me alone, a lovely way to spend Christmas.

I'd posted official signs from the city that no one could park in front of our apartment building so the pod could be dropped off. But people don't really read signs, so when I awoke that Christmas morning, I experienced the Yuletide miracle of towing cars. It felt like the equivalent of dressing up like Santa and leaving eviction notices under people's trees. Four cars towed.

A few hours ago, a man stormed up to the pod while I was packing: "You towed my fucking car?! On Christmas?"

My only company at that point was the Cramps, their rockabilly curses ricocheting around the pod. If they couldn't cheer me up, it was hopeless—and now there was this belligerent intruder.

I'd felt sympathetic to these fictitious tow-sufferers right up until he raised his voice. In my imagination, they were all orphans, with one leg and black lungs, eye patches, cleft palates. In reality, though, this guy was middle-aged and wore moccasins.

If I had any sympathy, it vanished once I saw the fucking moccasins. "*You* towed your car," I said.

"What?"

"I posted signs."

"So you towed me."

"I get it, man," I said to him. "This sucks. But the signs have been up all week."

"Asshole."

"Get! Out!" With one step in his direction, Moccasins exited the pod, calling me an asshole one last time as he disappeared.

That was a couple hours ago, and now I'm in the empty apartment by myself, wandering around, wondering if moving is the thing—if this will be the thing that will take my brittle sobriety and crack it like a candy cane.

Lelo and Ava are up at the park with some friends. We're having a picnic, a send-off before we move to Seattle.

We've officially outgrown our one-bedroom apartment in SF, and we are in the wrong tax bracket to even contemplate getting another flat here. The tech boom has priced us out. Ava sleeps in a closet. Don't get me wrong: it's big, and it has a window, so before you light torches and swing pitchforks, the closet is better than it sounds. Still, though, she'd eventually ask questions: "Are you kidding me with this closet bullshit? Can you get your shit together, Dad?"

So we're leaving town for good reasons, selfless reasons. Taking care of Ava is our job, always seeking to do right by her. Even when we don't want to, even when leaving here feels like a threat to my sobriety.

I had been up at the park with them, but I had to come back to meet the man who will pick up the pod, load it onto the back of a truck, and take me away from my home.

I've written six books about this city. It's the only home I've known in my adult life and despite all evidence to the contrary, it's been good to me. I met two wives here, had a daughter, went to graduate school, tended bars, sold vitamins, bussed tables, swept chimneys. Yes, I've told you about other things that happened here that are hard to live through once, let alone relive in these pages. I've told you about debasement and crimes. But I love San Francisco.

And maybe this is the moment I actually become a father. Displacing myself, leaving my home of twenty years, all to get Ava out of the closet and into a proper bedroom—this represents the most selfless thing I've ever done.

I'm crying for San Francisco. I'm crying for Seattle, the place I don't know or care about. I'm crying as I wander from room to room: Here is the kitchen, the place where I fed Ava her first bite of solid food, yams. Here is the bathroom, where we take showers and play this silly game where we spit water on each other's chest and laugh and laugh and laugh. Here is the living room, where she sits on my lap as I play her songs on the guitar, Ava tracing all the tattoos on my arms while I sing to her. Here is the bedroom, where I dump warm clean clothes, straight from the laundromat beneath our home, and Ava climbs into the middle of the bed, burying herself in the clothes, beaming.

And here is her closet, the culprit, the reason we need to leave, but also a place that I adore. Here is where I learned to console her in the middle of the night, snatching her from the crib, whispering comforts, where she played with my earlobe as she fell asleep.

My phone rings. I know who it is. He's here to rob me. "Hello?" I ask.

"Is this Josh?" says a man.

"It is."

"I'm here for your pod."

"Oh."

There's a beat, but I'm trying to catch my breath.

"Hello?" he says.

"I'm downstairs," he says.

"I'm here for you," he says.

Ava is four, I'm forty-one, and Lelo is thirty-nine. I'm thinking about our ages today because when I was four, I had a good life. My biological parents were still married. We were in LA. He had his church, and my mother volunteered, played piano and organ to accompany various choirs. There was nothing wrong in our life yet. We hadn't gone to the desert.

We'd wash the car together, my parents and me, and I loved to crawl in the bucket with the soapy water, and they'd pretend to be mad: "Don't crawl in that bucket! Don't you do it! You need to get out of that bucket right now!"

And the soapy water would slosh all over the driveway, and we'd all laugh.

Or one time my dad was taking the old shingles off our house's roof, and I wanted to help. Ministers don't make much money, and we were living in the parsonage, a home that the church owned and let its clergy bunk in for free. That meant that my pops did a lot of the repairs himself to save the church the expense of hiring professionals. So he was up on the roof and I was making a big stink of wanting to be up there, too.

Good parenting, 1970s style: he tied me to the chimney, with just a few feet of rope, so I couldn't fall off. It's one of my happiest memories of my childhood.

By my fifth birthday, we'd move to the desert. They'd be divorced soon. My mom's drinking and pills would rise up like saguaro cacti, huge and prickly things, casting barbed shadows over our lives.

I think about this all the time now that Ava is four: how a life can be happy, and then it's unbearable. I had no idea about my parents' particular problems when we lived in LA, though I certainly know more about them now.

Being in that bucket with the soapy water and being tied up on that roof, those are the only happy memories I can hunt down. I don't know about your earliest memories, but mine are mostly harrowing. My mind has a certain nostalgia for trauma. It becomes something to savor. Or fetishize.

My mind has built a shrine to devastation. It took me ten minutes to find two benign memories—in a bucket, on a roof—but I could scroll through so much cruelty.

I could see my dad hitting me.

I could see my mom leaving me.

I could see my dad shaming me for wetting my pants when we were out playing miniature golf—and what I couldn't explain to him back then was I just wanted to be with him—I didn't want to miss one second of being together and going to the bathroom would've interrupted our time—and it's just urine, Dad. Do you understand how much I love you? Do you have to say such mean things?

I could see my mom, driving, just the two of us in the car, her up front, me in the back. This is my earliest memory in life, the first beam erected in my cathedral to trauma. I must've been three. We were coming home from a pool party at one of the parishioners' houses, and I was still wearing just my swim trunks. It must've been a warm night because I wasn't cold. I was happy. And my mom and I were laughing in the car, having a blast in the car, sometimes she was so silly with me, and I loved when she was so silly, and we lived at the bottom of a big hill and we drove down the big hill toward our home and we laughed and I was in my car seat, in my swim trunks, and pool parties were my favorite, loved being underwater or floating on a raft or hopping off the diving board, and Mom and me were almost home and an animal darted out into the middle of the street and she swerved to save its life and we careened into someone's front yard and she steered our Pinto head-on into a tree.

Black.

A cloud of smoke.

Quiet.

That's all I remember, that hush. The world holding its breath. Maybe a hiss from a crushed engine or some moaning from a semiconscious Mom. Maybe. But I can't hear a sound now and I couldn't hear a sound then. Maybe I started crying. All I could see was smoke. If you told me we were in a cloud, that we'd somehow crashed into a cloud, I'd believe that. Yes, in the center of some storm cloud. Maybe we did drive into a thunderstorm that night. Maybe we never made it out.

The thing that finally flew through the cloud was a blanket. It wasn't there, and now it was on me. And the blanket had hands, patting me. And the blanket had a voice: "Are you hurt? Hold still. Don't move." And the blanket had fingers unbuckling the car seat, and the blanket had legs to lift me up, and the blanket had feet crunching us away from the wreck, and finally the blanket had a woman's face looking down at me, telling me everything was going to be okay, everything will work out, and the blanket carried me out of the storm cloud and into a house.

I remember sitting on a couch. Remember the lights of the fire engine's sirens springing to life on the living room walls. Remember my dad showing up. Remember the sounds of the tow truck as it pried the Pinto from the tree.

I remember seeing the mangled thing every time we passed it. What must that have been like for my mom? What horror to have to see that tree every day driving home, knowing she almost killed us?

I remember the firefighters checking my little body: I was fine, barely a scratch. Remember them making me laugh by talking about how tough I was, crashing into a tree like that.

I'd have my own DUI with Blue, and I couldn't stop apologizing as the cops loaded me into their cruiser, but I'd go on to have many other nights like this, many other accidents. I smashed a different car into a bunch of parked ones, only discovering when I tried to flee that the impact had snapped the drive shaft—the steering wheel spun uselessly while the tires stayed stuck in one place. That time I tried to get rough with the cops pulling me from the police wagon at the station and ended up face-first in a puddle. I ended up in county jail with a man who had one of those tiny red Swiss Army knives and he had those scissors out, and all night as he screamed at me, "I'm gonna cut you, white boy, I'm gonna cut you up!" I wondered how he had even gotten the knife past inspection while I'd had to take out all my piercings. I smashed up a different car driving drunk through North Beach, rear-ending some poor woman, breaking my nose on the steering wheel, and she refused to stop her car, didn't want to be alone with me and my nappy dreads in the middle of the night while we talked insurance, didn't want to deal with my deranged bleeding face. I ended up in a ditch or in the wrong city or with the wrong people or I ran out of gas, out of time.

We shouldn't have been allowed to have cars, my mom and me. We weren't capable of driving in straight lines.

16

Here I am, in Seattle, unloading the pod by myself on Valentine's Day.

Not totally alone—I did have one visitor. Some spokesperson from the Worst Welcoming Committee had sauntered across the street to tell me to get my license plates changed from California to Washington ASAP. He spoke in a nervous singsong, spitting out his words in little jingles, and I came to think of him as the Gratuitous Crooner.

"So no one keys your car," he crooned.

"It's not in anyone's best interest to key my car."

"Seattle is sensitive to people from California."

"Right, but I'll beat them to death."

"I don't know what to tell you," sang the Gratuitous Crooner, before wobbling away.

Now it's raining as I lean on the pod. Not hard rain, but enough that I squish around while I walk. Several new neighbors have seen me unloading said pod and no one offered to toss a box inside the house. Fair enough: it allows me to work slowly, to avoid going back to my mother-in-law's place, where we've been staying the last six weeks while we scoped out a house to rent.

I need to conjure the energy to knock off my pod-slack. It's time for another run inside, so I heave up a couple boxes, shimmy toward the front door. We have a house. I've never lived in a house as an adult, and finally, at forty, here I am. It's a little bungalow, with front and backyards, a bedroom for Ava.

These particular boxes are full of books, and so I cart them down to the basement, where I'll have an office. So on one hand, it's like, yay, I'll have a dedicated place to scribble, and on the other, more morbid hand, how many hours, days, months can you spend by yourself in a basement before you're watching a YouTube tutorial called "Top-notch Noose Cinching"?

Six months later—a different state, a different city, a different home, a different doctor's orders, a different needle in my arm, different saline bubbles shot into me, a different lab tech, different scrubs on her body, different art on the walls, a different black-and-white monitor showing my deformed heart.

But the same leakage.

The same rate of bubbles slipping through to the chamber of my heart that should have been protected by the surgery, the chamber supposedly liberated from these guerrilla bubbles.

So what do I do? I ask my neurologist in an email.

Keep taking the blood thinners, and we'll keep tracking the progress.

The word feels sarcastic. Progress? Nothing is getting better. The bubbles have burrowed a cogent hole, a route to smuggle blood clots, to end me.

I am exactly the same, and it appears there will never be any meaningful healing.

"Nothing has changed," I say to Lelo. We are in our new living room, moving furniture around, deciding where the couch and TV should go.

I'm filling her in on today's bubble test.

"Okay," she says, "so what does this mean?"

"Means I stay on my blood thinners and hope they're doing the job."

"Okay," she says, "but what does this *mean*?"

It's a good question, a scalpel cutting away all the skin and fat obscuring the essence, the evidence. "I don't know what it means," I say, "and that's why this is fucking with me so much."

"Can you ask the doctors more definitive questions?"

"They can't say for sure that the device will ever be totally anchored. And if the saline bubbles can get through, so can blood clots. So here's hoping the blood thinners are strong enough."

She points toward the window, meaning she wants me to move the couch over a few feet. I slide it under the window and ask, "Like that?"

"Better, right?"

We stand back, admiring the room. "It looks good to me," I say, "but you're the decorator in the family."

"The blood thinners are doing their job, Josh," she says. "Don't worry."

"I've had three strokes. It's hard not to worry."

"Your doctors are on it."

"I'm trying to stay steady."

"I know."

"And I'm not freaking out."

"People who aren't freaking out never say that they're not freaking out."

"I am a calm and rational person," I say.

"Now I know you're lying. I like the table better centered with the windows," she says, pointing.

I nod in agreement and make the adjustment.

I don't ever want to hurt Lelo in the same way I did Blue. I know that. I believe that. I'm trying to live up to those beliefs.

But the only way that seems to work is to force myself into nightmares, the memories. These are things I don't want to think about—they are certainly things I don't want to tell you about—and yet I have to because otherwise I'm going to fuck up again.

I'd closed the restaurant I ran in the Mission and came straight home. Blue was on the couch, cooked on wine. She wanted to get into a scrap—that was obvious, and she glared at me. We lived in a pyromaniac's dream, reams of botched intentions and promises stacked everywhere.

"Did you fuck someone tonight?" she said.

I was on a few grams of cocaine and couldn't get my dick hard for a million dollars. But I'd told her I was taking it easy with the blow, so I argued from a different angle: "I came straight home after closing up. When would I have been with another woman?"

"I don't believe you."

I moved toward the kitchen for a beer, wine, whatever. "It's the truth."

She followed me. As our short marriage got increasingly unhappy, she wore this bathrobe, patterned in light blue clouds on a white background. But she kept smoking cigarettes in the thing and not washing it, and ash stained its clear skies with storms.

"Let me smell your dick," she said, falling to her knees in front of me like some feral believer praying to a rotten prophet. Blue working off my belt. Ripping my fly open. Shoving my pants to my ankles. Blue burying her face against my cock and balls. Checking to see if the condiments of some other woman were smeared all over me.

I stood motionless, watching her. She was broken; I'd broken her. Not permanently—she's fine now, shacked up with a nice dude, a daughter of her own—but I'd temporarily picked her heart clean of meat.

Finally, she stood and walked away, returning to the couch and her wine and the TV as though nothing had happened. I stood there with my pants around my ankles. I stayed like that for months.

So when she kicked me out, all I had to do was lean down and pull my pants up.

I know I'm making a mistake in Seattle. Too much time by myself in the basement. I'm middle-aged, in a monogamous relationship, sober, which are already the ingredients of the Antisocial Cocktail.

In SF, I belonged to an artists' collective, a whole floor of us in the South Beach neighborhood, all in offices, working on our art. Fiction and nonfiction writers, poets, journalists, screenwriters, we were all there, bringing out the best in one another's work simply by proximity, the heat emanating from one person's office throwing a spark into the adjacent space, until we were all on fire. It was the healthiest kind of competition because we weren't competing with one another. We were competing *for* each other. We were rooting, hollering. We were patting backs. We were cheerleaders and confidants and friends.

In Seattle, I'm in the basement. Writing alone. Working out alone. Working out twice a day, actually. Don't get me wrong: my abs look great. But I need some fucking friends.

I'm not complaining about working from home, so much as I'm acknowledging the fact that I should be putting in more effort to get to know new people. I need an escape plan from the basement, which requires effort and energy, which requires will, which requires me to prioritize it, though really, how? By the time I run my business, teach my classes, play with Ava, be a husband, how much time is left? And I try to use those crumbs to actually, wait—what's that word?—oh yeah, WRITE every once in a while.

It's a bit of a catch-22, but I make a reminder to work on it. I even write it on a sticky note and put it on my office's wall. GO OUTSIDE.

It's still there.

I'm still in the basement.

It's snowing ash in Seattle. It's the beginning of September and three wildfires roar in the Pacific Northwest. And because of the time of year, it's hot, in the upper eighties. The sky is hazy with smoke and the sun is unlike any color I've ever seen. A kind of fluorescent orange, tinged with wings of red and gold. It looks man-made. Or alien-made. Or maybe nuclear: a hue you only see when the worst has happened.

I can imagine it was this dubious hue when it shined down on all those dinosaur corpses, slowly watching them decompose, witnessing extinction. It's seen a lot, this sun of ours, this radiant spectator to the earth's blunders.

Ava and I are out of the house early this morning, about 7:30, because of the ash storm. She says we need to "find all our flakes."

"All of them?" I say.

"Not all of the ashes, Daddy. Only the ones that are ours."

"Okay," I say, "it sounds like we are ash detectives."

She nods, leads the way, picking up her pink butterfly net from the front yard. We walk down the stairs to the sidewalk.

"I can catch them!" waving the net around.

"Of course you can," I say.

Ash must be lighter than snow because it billows this way and that, in a way I haven't seen snow do. The ash almost touching the ground and then suddenly climbing ten, fifteen feet.

I point at a larger flake and ask, "Is this one of ours?"

She immediately and emphatically shakes her head in the negative, pointing to the house across the street, where her little friend lives. "That one is Maia's."

"How can you tell?"

"It's Maia's," she says.

"Should we collect it for her?" I ask.

"There," she says, swinging the net. "I got it!"

This is one of the things I love about being a parent: the nonsensical, logic-less games.

"You did get it," I say, "and we need to deliver this one to Maia, right?"

"Right." She scrunches up her face. "But after we get all our ashes, okay?"

She, of course, means this without one dollop of subtext: she means this absolutely literally. That's how she processes all the life around her, from one adventure to another, one tantrum to the next, one negotiation, one fight, but these things are only experienced on a literal plane.

One of the wonderful curses of being a writer is that I see subtext everywhere. See rhymes between the past and the present. See simile. See that fluorescent orange sun up there, like a kind of electric burner set for high heat, cooking each and every one of us. So if I see that with a simple star—the one that nourishes us—what am I supposed to do with an ash snowstorm?

A couple weeks back, because of the latest pissing contest between America and North Korea, Lelo and I had to have a talk about what we'd do if there was a nuclear strike in Seattle—and if one of us was with Ava while the other wasn't, what should be the plan of action—how would we find each other?

"I'd want you to leave me," I said. "I'd want you to get her as far away from the blast radius as possible, assuming that's an option."

"I won't leave you here."

"You absolutely will."

"We're a family."

"Your loyalty needs to be to her, to protecting her."

Lelo thought for a minute: "Then you have to leave me, too."

"Okay," I said, "I will."

We were two people who loved each other and had been together for twelve years. Who couldn't even imagine living without the other one around. And yet, if a nuclear bomb was dropped, we made a promise to abandon each other. It was one of the most romantic moments of my life.

"I'd leave you to die alone," I basically said to her.

"I'll leave you too," she said back. "You might be instantaneously incinerated. Or you might die of radiation exposure within the first week. Or that initial shock wave would have left your body badly burned, and some topical infection will end you. Or you might be slowly poisoned by the air, fallout radiation, cancer—you'll live in the rubble and hunt for food and die a painful tumor death, just like your dad, except you'll be utterly alone, screaming into the concrete ruins."

It was a pre-apocalypse love story.

And we meant it.

We mean it.

If we have to, we will desert each other, forsake the other to a hateful fate. And it would be the right thing to do. Ava will never know that we love her so much that we'd leave the other to die in merciless ways. And for the one of us who hopefully survives with her—for the one who escapes the blast, moves north, say, into Canada—the survivor will find a flower blooming and will lean down and say to Ava, "Smell this," and she will sniff that lilac, and the survivor will find a glass of ice-cold lemonade and say, "Taste this," and she will, smiling at the tang. And the survivor will draw Ava a warm bath and say, "Touch the water, sweetie," and she'll crawl in, floating on her back, her blond hair haloed out around her head. And the survivor will say, "Listen to this," and will whistle one of the songs from the *Moana* soundtrack, and Ava, who has recently learned to whistle as well, will join in. And the survivor will say, "Look at this," and show Ava an old picture when our family had three people, and the survivor will say, "Do you remember? Always remember," and Ava will say, "I will. I promise."

But again, this has nothing to do with today, with this morning, and I don't want to think about fluorescent suns and nuclear bombs. Goddamnit, I'm an ash detective, and so's she, and we need to get them all—we need to retrieve every last flake of our ashes. Didn't you hear her? Don't you understand how important this is?

Don't you get that without the ash, without Ava, there wouldn't even be anything left of me to burn?

Now she has her pink butterfly net tracking a cluster of flying ashes. She walks on her tiptoes, sneaking up, looking at me and laughing. Ava takes a swipe.

"Was that all of them, sweets?" I say.

Ava scrutinizes the sky. Finally, she nods. "Yeah, we got all our ashes, Daddy, and we don't need the rest."

"What do we do with them now?"

She plants the butterfly net on her shoulder, like a soldier with a rifle. "Come on," she says, "I'll show you."

17

Me and Michael were completely naked and stapling each other. There were other naked people around, too. Shany and Veronica and Marc and Blue. They had all passed out in various parts of the house, leaving Michael and me unsupervised to do what we did best—find creative ways to debase ourselves.

In 2004 or thereabouts, and on this night, that meant stapling. I'm not sure exactly how it started. I mean, I know how it started. I saw a stapler sitting on Veronica's desk and picked it up and hit myself in the chest with it, sending a staple deep into my flesh, and then Michael—god bless his malfunctioning soul—somehow took it as a challenge and snatched the stapler from me and sunk one in his chest, too.

So I guess what I mean is that I don't know *why* it started. I'd seen thousands of staplers in my life and yet this one stapler on this one night spoke to me.

It said, "Hey, stupid, let's be stupid."

And rather than answer it, I let my actions do the talking.

But let me back up. Before the staples started flying, it was the weekend of Michael's birthday celebration. He was Shany's boyfriend and one of my favorite drinking buddies. Michael had a despondent and splendid sense of humor. He also had a Death tattoo on his forearm: a skull wearing a sombrero and across the hat's rim it said *muerto*. I'd never been so jealous of a tattoo and knew instantaneously that we'd drink troughs of whiskey together.

We had spent the night before at Jumbo's Clown Room, in Hollywood, Mike's favorite strip club.

Tonight we were at Veronica's house in Tujunga, some weird town in the Valley. We had gone out for sushi and walked home—I think Veronica actually fell into a hedge—and then eventually everyone took their clothes off, which wasn't unusual. When Shany and I lived together, we had Topless Thursdays, where we sat around with our shirts off and listened to music and drank tall boys.

At one point, Michael, Marc, and I were having a naked dance competition and I remember Shany and Blue sitting on the couch and hearing Blue say, "I really want to have a baby," and hearing Shany say, "You want to have a kid with him?" while pointing at me naked dancing and drinking straight from a whiskey bottle, and Blue said, "Yeah, is that crazy?"

The look on Shany's face said, *You mean staple guy?*

The look said, *Pick someone else, anyone else, because that guy will fail your child in all the conspicuous ways.*

In that moment, I realized I was my mother.

Right at the end, when my old man could no longer speak, when he had to wear an eye patch to help with double vision, he'd only eat fast food. Jack in the Box.

We'd hit the drive-thru and I would narrate behind the wheel— "Dad, do you want cheese? Do you want lettuce, tomatoes, pickles? Would you like fries? Extra ketchup? A drink? Yes? Coke, diet, orange soda? Okay, orange soda!"—and I knew the answers to them all, asking only to tease a syllable from him, one that never came. He just stared at me with his single eye, like *I'm dying, asshole. You think I give a shit about pickles?*

I finished ordering and we waited in silence.

For months, he'd been hearing birds. This was due to the metastasis in his brain, or maybe an anomalous by-product of all the meds. "Do you hear that?" he'd ask before asking was impossible. Now that he couldn't talk, I always wondered: Did the birds stop cawing, or did they get louder and louder, until he was finally gone, until the birds flew through the window to carry him away?

Truthfully, we didn't care about his birds, the flock chirping in his skull. We only wanted him to say goodbye. After his death, my stepmom hunted around the house, convinced he'd left her a note, that he must've felt compelled to offer closure. They'd been together twenty years, and there's no way he wouldn't say goodbye, right? She knew—she fucking knew!—that she would stumble across a handwritten letter, an impeccable explanation. A letter of gratitude for all they shared. A note recounting their many adventures. Something to let her know that all the anguish of monogamy had been worth it. He didn't leave her a letter. He didn't leave one for Jess. Or for Katy. He didn't leave one for me.

There is, however, a horrible irony to his illness. He was doing these last desperate steps, the gamma knife surgery, the experimental trials, to stay alive, to live longer so he could know my sisters, especially Katy, the youngest. But the pills, especially Decadron, turned up his temper. He hated noise, hated messes. He hated how children were children and birds were birds. He hated how his god wouldn't issue a pardon. Hated being so feeble and ugly and cold, always cold. So he endured outrageous treatments to get some extra time with Katy, but she was only eight or nine, and he was always snapping at her, scaring her, and Sarah and my sisters started calling him Decadron Man behind his back. I didn't live there, so I only heard the stories. When I came to the East Bay to visit, he was always on his best behavior. But when I wasn't around, Decadron Man scared Katy so much that most of her memories of our father are negative. So his plan to know her more made her know him less.

That's not irony; that's a noose.

And since we never get to see him again, let's remember more than Decadron Man, let's remember not simply the philanderer, the self-preservation expert, let's also remember how he endured having a helmet, a literal helmet, drilled into his skull for the gamma knife surgery. He let them mount it, screw it into position; he had to hear and feel each turn of the screw—and he did it for us. There was real love there. Decadron Man was only a malicious impostor.

Back at Jack in the Box, we got our fast food from the window and drove off. He had some fries in his hand, a limp and greasy bouquet. I was too hungover to eat. See, I had an eye patch, too. Kept it in my glove compartment to help with double vision when I drove drunk. But that doesn't belong here. We aren't talking about me, my secrets. We are talking about a man who has birds singing in his brain. We are talking about a tumor taking language. Trying to know your daughter and in so doing, corrupting her memory.

He took a nibble off the fry bouquet. He'd be dead in days. We'd have our unanswered questions forever.

"Dad, should I go straight home—or should we drive awhile?"

He answered by pointing ahead, through the windshield, the open road, that freedom, and we merged onto the highway, speeding— I could outrun anything he wanted, if only he'd ask.

I won't make his mistakes. I won't make Ava ache to know me, the real me. No, I'll overcorrect, overshare. I'll write these books that confess all sorts of crimes, literal felonies and those of the heart. I'll scream myself hoarse so Ava can know exactly who I am, what I did, where I came from. I want her to sift through the rubble of her old man like a possessed archaeologist, assigning value to certain artifacts and reducing others to junk. This book is a plot of earth allowing her to work her dig, so she can form an understanding of me, of our life. She needs to see how hard it is for me to get out of my own way in order to understand the joy she's brought. That's the way to show her unconditional love.

One by one, Shany and V and Marc and Blue all fell asleep, leaving me and Michael alone to staple ourselves.

"Watch this," I said, jamming one into my forehead.

With each new staple, our placement moved toward more dangerous locales, one-upping each other with every new blast.

A cheek, a nose, a nipple, an ear, these were all fair game, but we stopped ourselves, deciding to call the competition a tie before either of us stapled our eyelids or pricks.

The one thing we hadn't really factored into our stapling game was how the hell we were going to pick these things out of our bodies.

On the Discovery Channel, I'd seen gorillas harvest dirt and ticks out of each other's fur. That's what it must have been like, watching me and Michael pry staples out of each other's bodies. We were the most magnanimous gorillas.

Marc's disco nap was over. He came into the kitchen, nude, holding a golf club.

"The sun's about to come up," said Marc. "Should we hit some grapefruits with this and watch the sunrise?"

A top-notch suggestion, indeed.

Soon all three of us were in the front yard at 5:00 a.m., drinking beers, each taking turns hitting grapefruits with the golf club. The grapefruits were scattered under a tree. They were old and caving in, and not particularly aerodynamic. Some of them exploded when we hit them. Others were too soft, turning immediately to pulp.

But a couple of them flew.

Whenever we hit one that got some air under it, traveling thirty, maybe forty feet, landing in the street or in the neighbor's yard, we'd howl and high-five. I wasn't having as much fun golfing as them because I kept thinking about Blue wanting to have a baby with me. Each time another grapefruit flew, it was like a maybe-child, a giant egg, and I knew I couldn't have a kid. It would be like that Philip Dick novel *The Minority Report*, in which technology allowed the police to predict crimes before they happened. Before our child could even be conceived, I'd have marred our relationship. Even before I met the baby, we'd have no chance, all our futures exploding like these grapefruits.

Marc hit another and it sailed sadly into the distance, thumping down, lying in a macerated mess.

I'd abandon this kid. I'd put my happiness ahead of his or hers. I'd make the decisions that were the easiest, the most convenient for me, the ones that poured down my throat like alcohol. I'd do anything to protect my secrets.

In that instant, I realized I was my father.

No one ever told me the truth. I didn't know the real reason my dad left me in the desert with my mom until after he died. For years, I'd carried these desolate questions around: How come she was so alcoholic that he had to get away from her, and why would he leave me behind? If he loved me, why didn't he take me with him?

The truth, it turns out, was self-preservation: The minister was getting run out of town for screwing a woman in his parish. If there was a custody battle with my mom, his secret would come out. But if he left quietly, no one ever had to know. So he saved himself, moved to Berkeley, and started over.

Giving my mom full custody. Giving him a cover story.

My father loved me—I have to believe that—but he loved himself a little bit more.

I want to write something judgmental. I want to write how as a father myself now I'm appalled, say something about how I'd never treat my daughter that way, and I hope that's true, but you never really know. You don't know if you're capable of acting selflessly until everything ruptures around you.

It wasn't until after his funeral that my biological mom told me the truth about his affair in Arizona, telling me it wasn't the first time either.

I said, "Why are you telling me this now, after he's dead? I can't ask his side."

"I was always hoping he'd tell you himself," she said.

"What am I supposed to do with this?"

"It's your life," she said. "You're supposed to know about it."

But the more I found out, the less I knew. My mom was always the villain. The drunk. The disappearer. And now my dad, the hero who fled from a marriage seasick on booze—could he also be the villain?

The fact that he was dead made this so harrowing. All these questions and I'd never know the answers. I wanted to hear his whole side. Wanted to know every fleck of detail. Wanted to burrow in the crannies of each decision he ever made about me, but I'll never get to do that. I'll have to endure never knowing.

And he had to endure the malignant opposite: he had to live his whole life knowing exactly what he'd done.

If it was going to happen—if he was ever tempted to confess the truth to me—it was probably during that moment before my wedding to Blue that I told you about earlier. When he and I were putting on our rented tuxedos. When his hands shook so violently that he couldn't get his shirt buttoned up. When I dressed him like he had dressed me as a baby, a toddler, before leaving.

The two of us, father and son, both miraculous liars, face-to-face. I know he wanted to say, "It wasn't that I didn't love you. That's not why I left you there."

"Then why?"

"It's not simple."

"But why?"

"I'd do it differently now."

"But why?"

"I just . . . I did . . . I thought I made the right decision at the time."

And I'd say, "But she was sick."

And he'd say, "I'm sorry."

And I'd say, "But didn't you love me?"

And he'd say, "I'm sorry."

And I'd say, "But didn't you want to protect me?"

And he'd say, "I'm sorry."

And I'd say, "But . . ."

Really, there would be nothing else to ask. I've spent so much of my life wondering *why*, and yet that's not really the right question. Most of life is just a boiled paste of *what*, a pulp of stewed facts. This is what happened. Period.

Of course, as we finished getting on our rented tuxedos, he chose not to be honest with me, even as he only had a few weeks left alive. Of course, I chose not to be honest with him about booze and drugs, and I had years still, but I was so scared of him knowing me—what I considered the *real* me, liquored up with a cocaine halo, a syringe of Special K crammed in my triceps.

There we were, two men who cherished blind spots. We loved each other and barely knew each other and there's no reason to drag *why* into this. Let's leave it at the pulpy *what*.

We were all still fully naked, and the sun was coming up—the light making Marc see my and Michael's bodies more clearly and he said, "Shit, your skin looks covered in bee stings."

It was true, the staples had left tiny red dots all over us. Covered in our own epidemic of stupidity, except in this example we were both the bees and the doghouse.

"Let's tee off again," I said.

"Let's," said Michael.

"Fore!" called Marc, crushing one of those grapefruits into the road.

When we noticed a neighbor eyeballing us from a nearby window, we decided to do the whole world a favor and put on some pants. Maybe we passed out for a bit. I don't remember. I do know we never really sobered up all weekend, but there's this point where you sort of drink yourself accidentally straight.

For me and Michael that happened in the airport, waiting for our flight back to SF. We decided we needed to remedy this dry horror immediately. We were in the bar and Blue and Shany waited at the gate. They looked at us like we were madmen when we said we needed a couple more before going airborne, and again I thought about Blue saying she wanted to have a baby with me—about our exploding future.

I knew things in my life were getting bad, but I didn't care yet. I convinced myself that life could be no better than being naked while the sun came up, hitting those fucking grapefruits with a golf club, watching the bulbous things wobble into the great beyond!

"We should go to rehab," I said to Michael in the airport bar, over a whiskey shot.

"What?"

"Don't even think about it, or we'll screw it up. Let's go. Right now."

We stared at each other. I was serious and I could tell that a part of him wanted to be serious right along with me. We had a singeing moment, a burst of will that had to be acted on quickly, or all the liquor in the world would whisper in our ears *one more, one more, one more* . . .

In that closing window, I would go, but if we waited even one minute longer, I'd leak gall all over the floor.

"Who cares?" he said, hoisting his whiskey.

"Okay, who cares?" I said, raising mine, too. I almost threw up, but practice makes perfect, swallowing the bile back along with my shot.

A voice came over the speakers and said our flight was about to board.

"We missed one," he said. "On your neck." Mike leaned over and pried that last staple out of me and once it was clear, he held it up for us both to inspect. "Good thing you didn't set off the metal detector. How would we have explained all this?"

"I don't know."

"What were we thinking?" he asked, staring wide-eyed at the staple.

But there was no way I could answer that question, if it even was a question. *What were we thinking?* was a lifestyle. It was an epitaph. It was a different sort of *muerto* tattoo telling the whole world to stay away. A safe house from memories that clanged louder than the worst hangovers. *What were we thinking?* was our natural habitat, the only place gorillas like us could find peace.

A shitty little plastic pool from Fred Meyer. It's blue, with pictures of the various fish. Ava and I have changed into bathing suits, and I've folded up my six-feet-two frame. She sits next to me, pouring cold water over her head and threatening to drench me, too.

Everything in her life, so far, has been a series of phases, and so I know she won't want to cram into the pool with me for long. No one ever told me about the various things I'd grieve as she outgrew them. Nobody mentioned the first time she held her own bottle, her own spoon—I didn't understand that there would be a sense of loss, even if those meant successes, progressions. I got to do them to keep her alive and now she didn't need my help.

And as much fun as we have in the pool, I know the clock is ticking. So I say to Ava, "Can you please please please dump cold water on my head?"

"Really?" she says.

"Please please please."

She kicks her legs in delight and douses me.

It takes my breath away. I was happy in both places, and maybe that's the resourcefulness of our particular animal. We have more than one natural habitat. That night with Michael and the grapefruits is a happy memory. I was genuinely having fun that night, despite all evidence to the stapling contrary. I'm genuinely enjoying my time smashed into the shitty little plastic pool, too.

I love this quiet existence, and I try every day to honor it, to find contentment in dropping Ava off at day care. I say, "Should we do a fence kiss, sweets?" and she doesn't even need to answer with words. She sprints to her side of the fence and waits for me to exit the gate and I make my way to the other side. And when our lips meet through the slats, and when she smiles at me as our heads move away from each other, and when I say, as I do every single weekday morning at drop-off, "I love you like crazy," and she says, "Bye, Daddy," there's no possible way I can consider screwing up our family. This is where I'm supposed to be and life is lovely.

But I get in the Outback and I am unsupervised and weigh the pros and cons of being clean, staying clean, and maybe the cesspool brain starts making some compelling arguments for implosion and maybe you feel your skin breaking out in a relapse rash, so maybe you and Outback enter into a sophisticated conversation. Maybe you push the button on the steering wheel that lets the car know you need to say something to it. Maybe you blurt, "Hey, Outback, you are known to be a safe, reliable vehicle praised by safe, reliable people, so what the hell am I doing in here?"

"Finally," says the Outback, with an Aussie warble, "I've been waiting."

"For?"

"I can't believe you're fucking dumb enough to mess this up. You've never had a better life," says the Outback.

"I'm trying to stay clean for Ava."

"You're supposed to stay clean for yourself. You have to want this, or you'll go back out."

"How am I supposed to do that when I don't even like myself?"

"People like you have two options: abstinence or death. Just fucking accept that and quit complaining."

"I was hoping you'd be more supportive."

"Then you should've bought a BMW."

He hangs up on me.

Maybe you don't talk to your car, maybe you don't need to. But if you're willing to be honest, I bet you feel it too, that tug, that desire to do something you're not supposed to. It might not be booze or drugs for you, but it's something, or someone. A commodity tempting you to run away, vanish in the oblivion of a parallel life.

Rationally, I know being a stapled gorilla doesn't make any sense—not if it comes at the expense of being an ash detective—but I have a hole in me that can only be filled with liquor.

Right now, I'm still in a little plastic pool. She's still splashing me.

"What's next?" I ask.

"We are in the ocean."

"We are?"

She scrunches up her face, disbelieving—*this is obviously the ocean.* Then she says, "I love you a million and twenty bucks."

I can't convey how wonderful it is to hear her say this. Maybe you have your own kids and they've surprised you in some flourish of dented language. It's incredible to be on the receiving end of the sentiment.

"Where did you learn to say that?" I ask.

"I made it up."

"I love you a million and twenty bucks, too."

I'm not supposed to be giving you advice, but if you'll excuse my indiscretion, I can't recommend this highly enough: find the right person, get nice and close to their ear, and say it—"I love you a million and twenty bucks!"—and for a blast of seconds, everything is quiet—every misery muted, every misgiving gone—while we float on our measly oceans, content.

18

I'm teaching at a writers' conference in Northern California, in a small farming town called Surprise Valley. I decide to drive there from Seattle, see Eastern Oregon, which I've never witnessed and is supposed to be lovely. It's about a ten-hour trek and the terrain certainly lives up to the billing, climbing into the mountains, seeing Crater Lake, Klamath Falls. I drive fast. I listen to just the worst punk rock. Songs so fast. Songs so out of tune. I like sloppy art.

I dig tattoos because of their flaws. Maybe the artist is hungry or didn't sleep the night before, fighting with her man and storming to the shop, livid and starved. Maybe there's a lash tickling an eye or she has to sneeze, maybe she hears her phone buzz and a parent is dying, and she thinks: *Is this the message that means I'm an orphan?*

We never know, of course, we only wear their mistakes. A shaky line. A blowout. Colors bleed. Shading that doesn't heal the way the artist expects. It's human error, which is the best kind.

Pretty soon, people will be able to get tattoos from robots, immaculate, perfect in every way. But not me. I won't wear the work of machines. No, I'll keep scrawling my skin in human messes.

Bad tattoos, bad punk rock.

And so I speed along the highway and the slapdash music

blares. I do this because I can—no one bellowing for the *Frozen* soundtrack. No one wanting to listen to a book on tape regarding the venerable Winnie the Pooh.

I drive and swig Gatorade and eat peanuts. I'd even pulled over and hopped in a body of water—I thought it was Crater Lake but I'm not totally sure—which was freezing, by the way, which I could only stay in for a couple minutes before emerging ecstatic and cold, but I didn't care—I still don't, though I'm driving wearing wet drawers. My pants actually ride shotgun, and it's just me wearing combat boots and wet drawers, no shirt, screaming down Route 39.

I love being a dad. Yet these little trips really help me recalibrate. Writers' conferences, especially, are unilaterally fun. It's nerd camp. It's my people, all gathered in one place. I feel very blessed that I get to do these things.

Just the same way I feel blessed to drive right now, sans pants. Is my ass itchy from wearing wet drawers? Yes. Are my feet unimpressed with being wedged in boots without socks? Certainly. Should I put something in my belly besides peanuts? More than likely, yeah. There's time for all those things, though. There's time to take better care of myself. I have four days as a free man.

Two hours later, I roll into the house where I'm staying. I'm sharing a big spot with two other teachers, a poet and a nonfiction writer. We stay out of each other's way, though our interactions are warm and welcoming.

There is no Wi-Fi at our Surprise Valley house. I mean, there is a network listed for the property but no one knows the code. That wouldn't be such a big deal but I discover that I'm out of data. I'd used Google Maps as I navigated down from Seattle and I sucked up the whole plan. So I'm off-line. And this whole town feels off-line. Surprise Valley is basically two blocks, two restaurants, one store. It's quiet and sparse and beautiful, looks like the staging of a Sam Shepard play.

I hear a rumor that the local feed store has Wi-Fi you can poach if you sit outside of it and find the right positioning to your phone or computer. I'll try that later.

First, I need to do the opening-night faculty reading, meet my students and fellow teachers. Then my workshop starts tomorrow. I'll have six or seven people to talk shop with, and we will bandy narrative about, a bunch of happy bookworms.

By the end of the first night, I'm not compulsively checking my off-line phone. I leave it on the bedside table and head out for a midnight walk, meandering the deserted streets of Surprise Valley. The air is still about eighty degrees, and I listen to the alive empty sounds of the desert. Truthfully, I love this climate. It's in my blood, spent too many of my formative years in Arizona not to feel at home here.

Wherever here is.

No signals.

No way to contact anyone.

We are on our own.

My workshop is filled with smart, excited writers. I yammer for an hour because I'm inspired, teeming energy. This is when I feel like the best part of my dad, channeling his career as a minister—that excited piety. I've always thought it's spiritual what writers do, soulful, holy, requiring a peculiar belief.

The next day, we have the afternoon off. Without a phone,

without internet access, without any accountability, my mind has a lot of time to think. I'm not good with free time. I keep my schedule chock-full because if I start thinking, I get myself into trouble.

It's just an itch at first, some rough, irritated part of my brain. I notice its inflammation and it whines, screeching some menacing lyrics: *Why not enjoy a beverage?*

Fuck off. I have steps, defenses against this. I am trained to see this punch coming and counter, move my head, pivot my feet. I can bob out of the fist's way.

I take off my shirt and pants and stand in my drawers and knock out a hundred push-ups. I do some ab work, pistol squats. I throw at least a thousand punches and I'm left spent and perspiring and my brain feels not satisfied, but placated. That itch neutralized.

For about five minutes.

Then it's all: *Just a beer, Josh. Just one. You're not a dad this weekend. Cut yourself some slack.*

I can call someone. Call my sober pals. I can call my wife. I can call my mom. She's got almost thirty years clean at this point, and it would mean so much to her if I could find enough humility to ask for her help.

So why don't I? Why can't I?

So why am I putting on my clothes? Grabbing a wallet?

Why am I walking out of this house?

◇

I touch the beer in the Surprise Valley general store. It's cold, almost electric. Yes, I have the beer and I tuck it under my shirt, not in a shoplifting way, but in an I-don't-want-anyone-from-the-conference-to-peep-me way. So I walk fast. To the register. There is no one else in the store. I plop the beer down. I pay. I ask for a bag.

Tuck that under my shirt. I am sweating. Approaching the rental car. Get in. Sit down. Hold the bagged beer.

But where do I drink it?

I can't in the car, don't need some Surprise Valley cop giving me another DUI. Can't bring it back to the house with the other teachers, at least one of whom knows I'm clean. It's almost a hundred degrees outside so I don't want to hike somewhere and sit in the desert.

So that leaves . . . what does that leave? It means I'm in the car driving around, the beer sitting next to me. I salivate. My heart pounds. It's almost sexual the way I want it.

I turn the car right, holding the beer up so it doesn't tumble, doesn't turn into a sudsy grenade. I see a small park, across from a church. The same church that I gave a lecture at yesterday.

I don't see anyone I know, don't see anyone, period. It's too hot. I hold the beer under my shirt again just in case anyone's watching me walk. Shit. I can't sit outside. I'll be discovered.

Then I see it. My best option.

My Versailles. My Graceland. My grave.

In the middle of the park, a public restroom.

Me and the beer zoom to it, a squat cinder-block building cooking in the middle of the park.

I throw the bathroom door open and am mauled by the forgotten swamp of the toilet, stewing in the June heat, some of it missing its target, splashed on the floor. The metal sink is tagged with graffiti and grime. A small window is covered with metal mesh and offers no fresh air.

It must be a hundred thirty degrees in here, but I don't care.

I have the beer.

We are together, the beer and me.

We are ready.

On one of my last days in rehab, they had this role-playing exercise. Had a makeshift casket and corpse, the body representing our addictions. Each of us, one by one, was to get up and commemorate, eulogize, insult, tease, tell off, tough love, beg our vices to torture someone else, to leave us alone so we could clutch a teaspoon of happiness.

I'm supposed to chastise some Halloween costume and find peace? Please. But I had no choice if I wanted to complete the program. I took my turn, approaching this treacle and trying to take it seriously.

The scarecrow lay there, and I spoke at a whisper: "Get up."

It seemed so trite and simple. I'd planned on mailing this in but suddenly the casket and corpse weren't window dressing. Suddenly, they turned into the real things. Turned into tools, an external representation of the hauntings and blazes.

"Get up, you fucker," I said, "you're not dead. Get up and kill me."

It surprised me, speaking passionately to this staged scene, and soon I was raging at it: "I know what you're trying to do! Trying to trick me and kill me when I let my guard down! Well, I won't, I won't, I won't!"

A hand holding beer. Solitude. Heat. Humidity. Like a greenhouse. But there's no life in here. This is the opposite. A deathbed. A slaughterhouse. An electric chair. A relapse. A redundancy. A dad. A beer in a hand and I am alone and off-line and there's no reason to do this. No reason to be holding the beer. But here I am. Here is me. Here is a full, forgotten toilet, the sun macerating the contents, turning its stew to a perfume that wanders into my nose and sticks to my clothes and my hair and the beer is in my hand and Ava is in my deformed heart and I hate being sober—hate it because I want to be the sort of person who can moderate, who can have a beer, a glass of wine, whatever—I don't want to work so hard, I want to unwind like all of you, I want happy hour, a pint after work, pinot with dinner, a spliff, a recreational pill—I don't want the lockjaw of abstinence. And hey, maybe I'm fixed now. Maybe I can moderate. Maybe I can drink one lone beer in a hundred-thirty-degree filthy bathroom, and everything will be okay.

To drink is to abandon and to abandon is to drink. I'm trying to make you fully understand how something so significant can happen for no obvious reason. Maybe the answer is Occam's razor, the simplest explanation being the best: it was simply my time to make a wrong turn in this maze of gaffes we call *life*.

Can you understand how thirsty I was in that bathroom? How much my body ached for a taste? I am talking about the glorious sweat of temptation. That sheen of risk. A sip. I'd be ruining my life, but wouldn't that mistake taste magnificent?

Yes!

No!

Please tell me: Why don't I know how to be whole?

There's a thumb and an index finger.

These mischievous digits pop the can open—that hiss, that foreplay, the nudity of it. The beer is open, and it is in my hand and my hand is connected to my arm and the way a body works is simple: a brain sends a message to a limb, letting it know the score, the plan, the dirt.

Because arms bend and beer pours into mouths.

Beer pours into my mouth. All I have to do is swallow and I'm free.

There's nothing in the world I want to do more than drink this beer.

There's nothing in the world I want to do more than *not* drink this beer.

Because Ava. Because ash detectives aren't stapled gorillas. They can't coexist. You have to decide. You have to honor one compulsion or the other—to take care of her, or to make her suffer.

Maybe, to you, that doesn't sound like a difficult decision, but for me and those from my thirsty tribe, it's almost impossible.

So the only thing to do is spit the sip out, pour the beer in the toilet.

The only thing to do is throw the empty can against the wall.

The only thing to do is buckle to the bathroom's dirty floor.

I sneak back in the house I share with the other teachers and hop in the shower and scrub and scrub and scrub, but it doesn't matter, the soap makes no difference, I can't escape it, it's everywhere, that bathroom, that stink, it is me. It won't go away because I can't.

Like a lovely liar, I lock all this away. I teach the final morning. I kiss new friends. I sign books. I thank the people who put the festival together.

I drive away from Surprise Valley, leaving that maybe-sip of beer and the bathroom behind. I can't be any further away from that man who sped down here—who jumped in that frigid body of water—who cranked the punk rock—who ate peanuts and drank Gatorade and felt so happy.

The person leaving here is his opposite. Has all the information. He's snatched the beer, ended up in that bathroom.

The person leaving here has plenty of time to ponder—has a whole ten hours in the car to contemplate: Can a maybe-sip of beer become a nuclear weapon? Will one maybe-swallow take our family of three and make them a family of two?

PART IV

YOU LOOK BEAUTIFUL IN THIS UNFLATTERING LIGHT

19

Another dream: I'm sitting in a wheelchair made entirely of bees.

They fly so close to one another that they form something solid, a shape to take my weight. They don't sting me, just buzz.

Hold me up with their sounds.

◻

Outside in Seattle, it's partly sunny, fifty degrees.

Or so I've been told.

I'm in the basement again and both the washing machine and the dryer roar right now, next to me and my desk, my office-cum-coffin. I'm solving this problem of the machines screaming, not by walking up into the partly sunny fifty-degree day. Hell no. I solve this problem by listening to the saddest music I've ever heard in my life as loud as it can play in headphones.

The band is Mount Eerie. The record is called *A Crow Looked at Me*. It's written by Phil Elverum. He wrote it for his young wife, who had recently passed. Actually, he recorded the whole record on his wife's instruments, tracking all the songs in the *actual room* where she died.

It is one of the most intimate pieces of art I've ever interacted with—it creates this odd relationship, this triangle, an audio voyeurism that allows me to enter this sacred space, see Phil singing these songs, see his wife's ghost smiling and listening, while I am off to the side, blinded by the blips of hope that gleam through trauma, of the sounds of a man using art to articulate something that can't possibly be understood, singing desperate wrenching melodies to ease his suffering.

It will not offend me in the slightest if you stop reading so you can listen to the record. I promise it's time well spent.

I wish there was a way for us all to hear it at the same time. Some grand coordination: we all hit play at this precise second and take the grim ride together. We all sit in that room with her, the one she died in, the one where he recorded all these songs, all of us packed in there, sweating and moved and comforting one another. Wipe your nose on my shirt. Sure, you can have a hug. Yes, let's rest heads on shoulders. Yes, let's kiss each other on both cheeks and maybe sing along.

Do you know that I've been waiting my whole life to hear you sing?

All I need to do is take the buds from my ears. Put on shoes. Walk into that partly sunny fifty-degree day. So why can't I? What's holding me hostage?

I look at my sign: GO OUTSIDE.

There should be another sign, too: TELL LELO ABOUT THAT BEER. But since that one doesn't exist, I'm under no obligation to follow its edict.

"*Last time it rained here,*" Phil is singing to his dead wife, "*you were alive still.*"

It's five months after Surprise Valley, and I'm back in San Francisco, teaching for the weekend. I'm staying a block off Union Square, across the street from the American Conservatory Theater, my favorite playhouse in town. There are things I could be doing, granted—I'm teaching two online courses for Stanford this quarter, and I have a handful of editorial clients. But I don't want to do those things. It's a sunny day, about sixty degrees, and I want to walk, listen to music, hoof around SF.

Chinatown. North Beach. I snag an espresso and sit in Washington Square. Then I'm ready to go to church, which in my life means only one place of worship: City Lights bookstore.

These people are my pals, and after doing a lap around the store, smelling that intoxicant of a roomful of books, I make my way to the office and say hi.

Since it's Saturday, the publishing arm of their enterprise is closed, but the events coordinator is there. Peter. He's the best. We've done a bunch of events together over the years, and it's a warm conversation, sitting in the mezzanine, overlooking all those bound stories, all the customers circling the artifacts, hunting for the right one. It's the ideal setting for me to catch up with a friend, in nerd church, seeing all these readers milling in the rows of pews, praying.

Peter says, "How's Seattle?"

I don't know how to answer.

It's a place?

I live in a house there?

It rains and there's no state tax?

Space Needle? Nirvana? Hendrix? Heroin? Salmon?

I certainly can't say: I spend too much time alone I'm not taking care of myself emotionally I'm isolated and continuing to isolate I'm not doing anything to fix it and I'm in the basement again and it's hard having a four-year-old a full-time job on top of a full-time gig on top of ah you get the point and that's not mentioning being married and I love my wife and I'm not trying to be disparaging only acknowledging that everything takes effort and tending and shit I'm in that basement again I am alone again and I'm working out twice a day to tamp the temper and how do you meet new people in a new city when you're middle-aged and sober and I'm not the sort of cat to join a fucking kickball league or some shit and I know I should go to AA meetings especially because I haven't told anyone anything about Surprise Valley and who knows and who cares we shall see and I'm in that basement and I'm in that basement and it's raining and Ava has a cold and I need to tell Lelo how much I'm struggling and I'm in the basement but I don't want to admit to being so feeble which is male and dumb which is redundant I know and there's that maw of the basement swallowing me up again and I'm so tired and I forget Peter what was the exact fucking question?

"Seattle's fine," I say to him.

I tell him that I sold a new book—the one you're holding in your hands—and he's happy for me. It's all over his face. Men's mouths might evade tenderness but it's often in the eyes.

We make plans to have a party for this book when it finally comes out and we hug and offer pleasantries and he goes back to work, and I go outside.

I make it two steps.

I stop walking and start crying.

The sun is out, and the tourists are out, and I can't remember this ever happening to me before, stone-cold sober crying on the street. For no real reason. Or No Reason of Physical Pain. If I'd been bitten by a pit bull or stuck with a screwdriver, then by all means bawl on the street if need be. But this, just walking out of a store, even if it's one of the best places you've ever known?

I don't really know how to explain it. A spontaneous emotion rushing up. I've seen women cry when they orgasm, and maybe this might be something similar: a biological reaction from a body being overloaded, too much stimuli, too much licking the pleasure centers.

Then I see it. Vesuvio. Right next door.

I had walked up this same street, striding past this bar without even knowing it was there. It isn't lost on me that this is the place I had been the morning of *Check Out Time*.

Not lost on me that opening the door is a bad idea.

So who's moving these legs?

Whose mouth says to the bartender, "A pint of Guinness?"

She does a double take. "It's on me," says the bartender. "I love your books."

There are two thousand bars in town and none of their bartenders even know I write books, but here she is, this one woman, destroying me with kindness.

I haven't picked it up yet. There's still time.

But the stout settles, blond ripples floating in the murk, and I'm trapped. I've finally put myself in a situation that I won't weasel out of, won't have a last-second burst of clarity or desperate carefulness. I can't. Not watching that pint settle. Not seeing the waves of color dance in the glass, a lullaby. Not knowing that it's for me. She's buying it for me. She loves my books, that angel.

"Thanks," I say and tip her five dollars, snatch the pint, and walk upstairs and sit at a table. There are no talking dogs or duffel bags or Nazi doctors.

That first sip!

There is none of the self-hate slipping into me like Surprise Valley. This is just a Guinness and it tastes like kissing an old lover. How long has it been? And why, why did we ever stop? The suds come up to my head and wipe the tears, make shushing sounds, stroke my skin to calm me down.

Another sip another sip another sip.

It's gone and I'm fine.

I'm fine because I carry the glass back to the bar, set it down, thank the bartender for her hospitality, and then do the unthinkable thing: I leave.

One simple beer and out the door.

I walk and notice that there are other bars around. Presumably, they were there when I walked to North Beach, but it's like I'm seeing them for the first time, not just seeing them, no, I hear them, these Sirens, singing to me. I crawl past all these hoarse screechy bars without going in.

I am in control.

Since I'm so close to ACT—and since I'm not drinking anything else today—I decide to see a show called *Hamlet*, which is the new William Shakespeare joint. Have you heard of him?

For this particular production, the theater had updated and created a mesmerizing set design, its new look and aesthetic based on photographs from the Fukushima site, postnuclear, colors drowning in browns and deathly earth tones. But there are also jolts of kinetic color that give the set the feeling of a Nine Inch Nails music video. It's a juxtaposition that lures me in right away. It is masculine and feminine, life and death, young and old—it's a living exhibit to each phase of our short experience here.

The actor playing Hamlet is one of the most charismatic performers I've ever seen in person and embodies that peculiar consciousness with such heft and pop that I'm eating from his palm the whole time. I'm actually relating to Hamlet in a way that you amateur psychologists out there might say *no shit*. But it's those ghosts, right? Those ghosts that are there forever. Some to be avenged. Some to be tolerated. Some to torture or ease our burdens. Some to drive us insane. Some to scream, to seduce. Some to hiss. Some to be so frustrated with our shortcomings. Some to let us cry in their laps.

Because we breathe means we suffer. We suffer because we love. We love because it's the only way to feel. To abate loneliness, which is like a plastic bag pulled over our hearts, asphyxiating the organ.

I'm aware that there is a bar in the other room of ACT, but I don't order anything during the intermission. Instead, I simply stay in the great theater, looking at this lovely Fukushima; instead, I stew in my own wasteland, knowing that this might've been the day of my own nuclear disaster.

I think of my failed bubble tests—how my heart's not fixed, how I might never be. None of us will. We might picket heaven's gate, may march on our leaders and froth for an inoculation against all the self-destruction, but no one is coming to repair us.

We are unrepairable.

Whatever wipes us away in the end, the details don't matter. It can be an army of humiliations and we won't know the particulars of our shameless fates until it's too late. It might be Alzheimer's, turning whole lives into alcoholic blackouts, erasing every conscious recollection. Or cancer going on a cell bender, bingeing on our bodies. Maybe some cirrhosis of the soul, making it impossible to take care of ourselves, even though that's what we claim to want: a way to finally dote on our bodies and flawed hearts. Every drunk and junkie wakes in the morning pleading with their own sloppy senses, *stop, let this be the day we stop, let this be the day we try to take care of our shit.* And they mean it! They are ablaze with earnestness, and for two minutes they are resolute in these newfound convictions.

But then their brains, these brains caked with crusty memories, like microwaves that never get cleaned, on the ceiling and bottom and walls, these caked brains cook up alternatives. They imbibe on other styles of sustenance besides newfound convictions and suddenly what had been steadfast wilts.

Tomorrow, we say. *I'll start trying tomorrow.*

Which never comes, this fictitious tomorrow, because a life is simply a sky of todays.

Or it's leukemia. An accident.

Or we drown. We choke. We settle into a nap after a meal and never wake up.

Or we never get that surgery for a congenital defect.

Or we do, and it doesn't work.

And we are unrepairable. We will never be anything other than what we are—a snarl of cells and desires and shames. That doesn't mean we can't be happy. All it means is that we should stop striving to be fixed and simply settle into that gruesome realization: life is always messy, and no one will ever fix us.

20

A cab drives me home. When I get there, Ava is at day care, Lelo at work. Ava calls our spot "the house with the green door." As the taxi drops me off and I stand looking at the place, it's been redecorated.

Halloween.

My girls have been busy. There are fake spiderwebs in the front hedge, as well as a big skeleton hiding the door. There is also a "person" sitting on the porch with a skull head. This person consists of my wife's Chuck Taylors, a pair of her jeans, and an old brown sweater stuffed with newspaper to mimic body mass. And of course, that skull, creepy smile on its face with eyes lit up purple, the person sitting there to welcome you. Either my wife or a hysterical newspaper delivery person has placed *The New York Times*, in its blue rain bag, on the person's lap.

The last detail I notice is another swarm of fake spiderwebs, this bunch above the porch, almost making a kind of roof right in front of the door. I stand under it and look up, spotting black and pink spiders in fixed positions on the web, seeming to say, *Welcome home, phony. Welcome back to the life you're turning into a tomb.*

Or maybe I'm projecting.

It's overcast but not yet raining, though the report is a big storm will hit this week. I am happy to be home, almost religious in my newfound devotion to sobriety. The beer had given me a test and I'd passed. I had been in SF all weekend, unsupervised in a hotel room, and I didn't have one more sip. I shadowboxed. I did push-ups. I jogged. I jerked off. I wrote.

I didn't have one more drop to drink. Is it clear that's an accomplishment? It might not seem like one, but trust me, that beer gliding through my bloodstream felt like a gentle cleansing rain. But I stopped at one. I fought the cravings. I did right by my family.

Now I am home.

I call a sober pal and tell him about the beer.

"I don't think any less of you," he says.

Wait, was that an option?

"Uh, thanks," I say.

We talk for about half an hour. I'm honest and he's smart, caring.

The conversation makes me feel less alone. "I need to tell my wife," I say.

"Yup."

"I was hoping you'd tell me not to worry about that."

"Nope," he says.

I tell Ava about my bee-wheelchair dream while we do pull-ups in the basement. "What do you think it means?" I ask her. "Why would I dream about a wheelchair made of bees?"

I realize she's not my therapist, nor skilled in Lacanian dream analysis, but I'm stupidly hoping for some words of wisdom. Here's all she says: "The bees are probably pooping."

"I'm Josh, addict, alcoholic, though it's only booze that's got me all up in my head right now. It's booze that's calling. I was down in SF this weekend and I had a beer. Hadn't had a drink in seven years and ordered a pint. Simple as that. What's got me so twisted about it is I can't tell if I care. It's only a beer. I didn't go on a run, never thought I'd be able to order only one drink and stop, but that's what happened. Drank the pint and went to my hotel room. So what does that mean? What am I supposed to do with that? And I don't know the answers to these questions. I can only put my finger on one thing—I don't value my sobriety the way I used to. Relapse? So what. So you go on a run, then go back to treatment, start coming to tons of meetings and work the steps again. My sobriety felt so precious, so important, and now it's . . . it's something else. Some prop. It just feels so temporary, whereas it used to feel like something I had to protect at all costs. Something that needed to be pristine. And I know that our addictions change the way they talk to us, always looking for a new way to bring us down, to compromise and corrupt us. That's not lost on me. I just don't know how to care right now. I don't have the energy or the will. It's so much work and other people get to have pints after work and turn the volume down on their woes, and I want that. I'm tired of being so available. Tired of working so hard for so little. I'm complaining and making excuses and I'm sorry. This is all so confusing. I don't want to go back to the caveman life, but maybe I don't have to. I mean, I stopped after that one beer. That's how a normal person behaves. Am I normal now? Did I magically cross over? I'm not even gonna look any of you in the eyes right now because I know how stupid that sounds. I know people like us don't suddenly learn how to moderate. We're the 'all or nothing' chain gang. I get that. I just don't want to. I'm tired. I'm lonely. Any of you who have kids—you know that trick, how you can be surrounded by your wife and kid and still feel so alone. It's so kid-centric all the time. I can't remember when someone really asked me how I'm doing. And I probably wouldn't have been honest, anyway. All of this is my fault and I get that. Seven years clean and you drink a beer and now I'm supposed to confess to my wife, supposed to ask for forgiveness. Forgiveness for a beer? How inane. I should've had twelve beers and twelve shots and should've thrown up on the floor and crawled to the toilet, that confessional, to see my reflection in the water, where I'm most comfortable. So is a beer a relapse? Did I relapse? What a dumb thing to do. Should've gotten my money's worth. What's scary to me is how divorced I feel from the severity here. What it might mean. I have a daughter. And I want to protect her from who I used to be. She shouldn't know that man. But the only way to protect her is for me to start to care again, to value that sobriety. How do you go back? How do I find that frame of reference when a clear head felt like a gift? Or this is what I do. I screw up. I might take some time off but inevitably I end up buying that beer—and I delude myself into thinking I'm 'better'—then I pretend everything is fine before I really fuck up. It's like I can see all that on the horizon and I don't know how to course correct. I don't know how not to let that happen. Do you? Maybe we can grab coffee after. I'd love to hear people's thoughts and experiences. I keep thinking about this girl who used to be friends with my youngest sister and she was a cutter. And her parents didn't know how to help her not cut herself. Nothing was working. Therapy. Drugs. Family counseling. It didn't matter. Got so out of hand that her parents took her bedroom door off the hinges and every morning they'd make their daughter stand before them in a bathing suit, so they could examine her body for new wounds. One of them had a book, a legend telling of all the preexisting cuts so they could determine if there was any new mark on her skin. Imagine that. One parent holding this bible of desecration, while the other inspected their daughter's body. Who had it worse, I wonder? The one with the book, all that evidence of how unhappy and fragile their daughter was? Or the one combing over the skin, desperately hoping not to find another cut? Or even the daughter, simply standing there almost naked, fingers traipsing all over her, in the name of helping. Maybe that's me. Maybe I can't have a door. Maybe I need daily inspections, constant supervision. Because I'll tell you something: I don't want to become a drunkard again but that beer tasted good. And I stopped. I controlled it. Or that's the knife tricking me. The blade. It gives me the illusion of control with that first cut until it turns itself loose, unleashes that despicable wrath that brings a life to its knees. That's probably it— addictions play the long con. Convincing you slowly to go back to an awful way of living. I've tried to kill myself before and I don't want to be that. I tried twice, really. But I'm here and I have so much to be thankful for. My life is good. How sad is that? I can't see it. I can't understand how to value it. I am incapable of feeling content. Liquor has its hooks in me good. I'll cut myself. I know that. What I don't know how to do is care enough to *not* do it. For years, it's been about my daughter and that worked. It kept me on the straight and narrow for seven years, which is a long time to stay clean, and I'm appreciative of that. And it was only one beer. That's it. I can't tell my wife, not yet. I don't know how. I'm not scared of the consequences so much as I'm afraid of comforting her. Of comforting her when I need the comfort. When I feel so on the verge of fucking up. If I tell her, the conversation immediately becomes something else and it doesn't feel like the time for that. Or I'm rationalizing, stalling. I should just go home and tell her, huh? Blurt it out. Clean. Easy. I won't, though. I'm not ready to stand there in my bathing suit being scrutinized. I know her parents were only trying to help her, but I can only think about that kid's humiliation and unhappiness. It makes me want to keep the beer a secret. It makes me want to never tell a civilian. You all don't count. You can't say a word and who believes us, anyway? Thanks. I can't remember being this confused during my clean time. This feels different. I don't know. But I should come here more. I need to meet people in Seattle. I'm pretty new and have no friends. I spend a shitload of time in my basement, which is probably sadder than it sounds. So yeah, coffee. I'd like to get some coffee after this. Can I take anyone out for some coffee, please?"

What I didn't say to them because it wouldn't have made any sense: "Nazi doctors don't die. They migrate, hide in your heart like it's Argentina after the war."

A guy agrees to get coffee with me after the meeting. We sit at a vegan café. I'm eating yams and kale. He's drinking a smoothie. "AA is hard for smart people," he says. "You think too much."

"I guess."

"Lucky for me," he says, "I'm dumb."

"Don't say that."

"I mean it as a compliment."

"It's a good thing, being dumb?"

"It has its perks," he says, and we both laugh.

His smoothie is gone, his straw makes that scraping, sucking sound drawing the last drops.

"You," he says, "need a fucking sponsor."

"You're probably right."

"It's a wonder how you made it as long as you did without much help."

"Is that supposed to make me feel better?"

"No," he says, "it's not."

In addition to the Halloween decorations, Ava bought one more thing at the store. A pink flashlight. A flashlight that is now her favorite toy.

So at six in the morning, the day after I get home, Ava wakes me up with her new flashlight, the beam bouncing off the ceiling as she jostles it around. "Daddy, do you want to flashlight dance outside?"

"Flashlight dance?"

"It's so fun."

"Now?"

"The flashlight is brighter before the sun comes up," she says, smiling at me.

"Okay."

"The sun is a girl, Daddy."

There's no way of getting out of this, not after I've been away, so I brew a shot of espresso, put on a jacket. We stand in the darkness, dancing with the flashlight.

"Watch this," she says, twirling with it. "Now let's jump!"

"Aren't you cold?"

"Giraffes can dance on the moon."

"Really?"

"Their hooves dance all over it."

I should go inside and tell Lelo the truth right now. That I'd had a slip, but that was on Saturday and now it is Tuesday. What's stopping me? What's preventing me from leveling with her? All I can come up with is the calendar: that it will mean more if I confess with a stretch of time *without* alcohol. If I have, say, two weeks clean, not merely a couple days. Then, only then, there's ample evidence to support my claim that it was a one-off mistake.

Or that's what I'm trying to convince myself of . . .

Really, there's nothing else to do except dance in the dark morning, watch the arc of Ava's flashlight cut through the blackness like the lights from a rescue plane.

It feels violent, the secret. A fang. A fist. A missile lifting, listing, landing—a fallout future. It feels like a home invasion, the secret, and maybe that's what it is, as it returned home with me. It came in my suitcase and brain. It rode a taste bud back. It snuck a lift with my liver. The secret was happy to squat in our house. To take up illegal residence. To book time here like an Airbnb and refuse to vacate the premises.

After our flashlight dance, we retire inside for a bath, an omelet, a *Cat in the Hat* cartoon.

"Here it comes," I say. The weather report had been right, and the rain taps our window. Ava and I sit on the couch watching cartoons. "We should go puddle jumping after school today. How does that sound?"

Lelo had an early meeting so it's just the two of us. Ava sits on my lap, playing with one of my earlobes, eyes on the TV.

"Sweets, should we puddle jump?" I ask.

I'm not even in the room, hell no, not with the Cat holding court. I decide to use this narcotic trance as a time to get her dressed, braid her hair. I even have time to give her a temporary tattoo on her forearm ("We love tattoos, don't we, Daddy?" she has said to me a hundred times. "My arms look like yours!").

The show ends and she remembers how to talk. "Blue shark?"

That means she wants some candy. The local grocer is one of those overpriced co-op travesties, so on our way to school—not every morning per se, because that makes me sound like a crappy parent, but, conservative estimate, 92.7% of our mornings—we go by the co-op so she can shoplift some candy. Okay, maybe having sticky fingers isn't what I'm supposed to be teaching her, but the way I see it, Ava is a little Robin Hood every time she sneaks a gummy shark, gnawing on it while we're in the store and then carrying its half-chewed body out to the car. The co-op charges me $8 for a dozen eggs so if we enjoy the occasional (see: daily) free shark, that's frontier justice.

Right?

Regardless, we are avid shoplifters of gummy sharks, my little Marxist doing her part to redistribute wealth.

We are dressed and ready to snag another blue shark, but as I throw open the front door, our path is impeded. Our porch is clogged with dripping, wilting spiderwebs.

These aren't all-weather webs, apparently. Lelo must've gotten the cut-rate ones. I hold Ava and bend at the waist so we can weave underneath.

"What happened to the webs?" she asks.

"They're heavy."

"Why?"

"Rain," I say as we walk down the stairs, approach the Outback, but I'm thinking of my secret. I buckle Ava into her car seat, and she asks her favorite question one more time. "Why?"

"Because the rain makes the webs heavy," I say, "so they're sagging down."

One last instance, for the cheap seats: "Why?" asks Ava.

"Don't worry. I'll fix it later."

Ava and I are playing a game with the new flashlight: Find the Spooky Noise.

It's sort of like hide-and-seek, except we are trying to find a nonexistent noise. We pretend it is in the basement. We pretend it's in the pantry. We peek under the bed, but we never find the spooky noise.

That's the part of the game that Ava finds hysterical, the fact that we can never find it.

I don't think this game is as funny as she does because it reminds me of the secret. And *reminds* is too civilized a word for what it does. No, this feels like a horror movie to me, as we move through the house, hunting for this hiding monster. Because it's the secret she's looking for, even if Ava doesn't know that.

And what if we see it? What if we throw open a closet and it's there? Just standing there, animated and inhabited? And what would it look like? Would it be tall, a dwarf, a dog? Would it don a sombrero, a kilt?

Would it wear my mother's face? My father's?

No, it would simply look like me, as I am that slapdash cocktail of their legacies. I am his cruel capacity for self-preservation, the kiln that cooks the secret. I am her pain pills and booze, the maids that tend to the secret, keep it warm and safe. So the secret would spring out of the closet, and there it would be—nude and emaciated, the way I looked right before the heart surgery, sick and scared—looking back at us. The secret would see me and Ava standing there, and it would warn her: "Your father's life was just like yours, fine at four years old. Until his parents drove his childhood into a tree. Now he's doing the same thing to you."

"Shut up," I'd tell the secret.

"But that's exactly what you are doing. And she should know!"

"You don't live here."

"I do."

"I'm kicking you out."

"You can't."

I try to put my hands on the secret, to manhandle it out the front door, but it turns into vapor. My hands are empty. I can't evict it.

"Fine," I say to the secret, "I'm politely asking you to leave."

But he laughs. And Ava cries.

The three of us standing together.

Lelo and I are hosting a bunch of four-year-olds tomorrow for an early Halloween party. The house is decorated with orange streamers and pumpkins. I'm standing in the kitchen, watching Lelo stuff a skull piñata with plastic spiders, fake fangs, and candy.

We are good parents and sometimes that comes at the expense of being solid spouses. Most of our conversations are logistical, tactical. We give all our energy and attention to Ava, and there's often not much intimacy left. Not much time to come clean, especially if you don't want to.

Say the secret, says a voice in my head. But I actually say to Lelo, "What time are the girls showing up for the party?"

"Eleven in the morning."

Say the secret.

"And what games are we playing?" I ask.

"We will paint little skulls, dance, and of course, smash this," says Lelo, tapping the piñata.

Say the secret.

"Are we feeding them lunch?"

"Pizza."

Say the secret.

"Will everyone wear costumes?"

"I'd imagine so," she says. "There. All done." She holds the piñata up and lets it sway back and forth. "We'll need something to hit this with."

Say the secret.

"This is going to be fun," I say.

"Do you still have that old baseball bat?" says Lelo.

"We can use a broom handle."

"Okay. That's your job."

"I'm glad I can help."

"Are you sure?" she says, giving me some shit and I deserve it. She's done the heavy lifting, planning this party. She's even sewn Ava's flying squirrel costume.

Say the fucking secret!

"I am known for my broom-handle selection skills."

"Thank god," she says.

"A lot of guys aren't up to this task."

"Lucky me."

I am a piñata and no matter how hard you knock me, I'll never spill.

Now the webs stretch all the way to the porch. I can't sneak underneath, can't just duck and weave out of their enclosure, emerge on the other side free of their captivity. No, it's a perfect prison, webs all the way to the wood. I can barely see through them, barely make out the world.

Ava is in my arms and I try to use my free hand to pull the webs apart, to break free, but I can't. Not with only one limb. Not without having both hands free to work me out of this mess.

"We are stuck," I say to Ava, setting her down. "What should we do?"

But she doesn't answer, instead smiling and trying to shove herself through, which doesn't work, which just makes her mad, being tangled in these webs, and so I pull her back, then reach down and grab the webs from the bottom and hoist them up, holding them above both our heads.

"Ready?" I ask.

She nods and we both jet underneath and stand on the front stairs, laughing as they crash down again, hiding the house, the webs wobbling, heavy with the weight of rain, my cascading guilt.

"I'll fix it later," I say again, then drive her to day care.

21

Getting divorced from Blue was one of the hardest things I've ever endured. That flop. Those pieces of paper. Those acerbic words outlining all the days I botched and burned. Even if we weren't happy in the marriage, and we were definitely not happy at the end, it was the divorce papers that mangled me—the unflinching and objective document that was a record of us imploding. I didn't want a paper trail. In fact, I yearned for a crime. Craved the ability to erase and deface these documents. I remember when it was my turn to put the pen to the page, to notarize my failure, I saw a bottle of Wite-Out on the desk and wanted so badly to smear my palms in it and, like a child finger-painting, soak and vandalize those papers. Expunge the universe of any written record of my disasters.

◻

It's possible that I'm not a strong enough person to ever tell Lelo the truth, though I try to convince myself to be a strong person. It reminds me of a couple weeks back, Ava and me at the playground. We had been playing chase, until we spied two boys sitting on the slide, seven or eight years old, and they took turns flexing their biceps while the other squeezed it.

We watched for a minute and I said to Ava, "You're stronger than those boys, aren't you, sweets?"

She didn't answer for a minute, still watching their game, and then she said, "Feel my strong muscle, Daddy."

I assumed she wanted me to follow the strategy of what we'd been observing, and so I wrapped my hand around her upper arm and said, "Wowee!"

"No," she said. "My heart. I was talking about my heart."

"You want me to feel how strong your heart is?" I asked, placing my hand in the center of her chest. Did I ever have a strong heart? Or has mine always been wriggling with drinks and pathologies?

"Sweets," I said, "you are so so so strong."

"I know that, Daddy."

My hand was still in the center of her chest, and she nodded at me, and what I wanted to ask her was this: *How can you possibly know that about yourself?*

Happiness turns our hearts into hot air balloons, and they can leave our bodies, our floating hearts tethered back to earth by veins: we don't die, mind you, no, we simply watch. It's an intimidating enterprise at first, seeing these organs shimmy out of us and rise up to take flight. But once we realize this won't kill us, we can all gawk at the beating sky. They are all up there. Mine. Yours. The sky is suddenly a harbor of hearts, and we are going to be okay, even if we'll never be as strong as we'd like.

◦

I haven't told you as much about Lelo as I have about Blue. It's easier for me to talk about a relationship that's fixed in the past, something finished. I can analyze that affinity in a way that's more difficult with a marriage that's a moving target. And there are Lelo's feelings, of course: My loyalty is to her, the real her, not the one in the book. That makes it hard to grapple with the fettering circumstances of my relapse.

But I still need to tell you more about her, and here's where I'd like to start: Lelo was a big baby when we dated. You should've heard her whine when she didn't get eight hours of sleep. You should've heard her whimper when she got a little cold, lip quivering as she asked me, "Why is this happening to me?" as though she had pancreatic cancer. She was a terrible patient, and I loved taking care of her.

Then she became a mother, and everything changed. In the best way.

I, of course, loved her before we had Ava, but since, my love for Lelo has multiplied. First, as I watched Ava slide out of her—it was the most violent and the most beautiful thing I'd ever seen, will ever see. I stood up next to my wife's head, whispering into her ear, my shaking hand fluttering on her cheeks and forehead, saying, "There. We're almost there. Keep pushing," and one of the nurses held a mirror up so I could witness Ava being born. I got to be in two places at once, and I'm very thankful for that.

I remember not even caring that much about Ava in her first few minutes here. I hadn't met her yet, and yes, I biologically cared about her, but my loyalty that morning was to Lelo. I wanted one thing and one thing only—for her to be okay.

From there, though, my love kept growing. It was unruly. It's nasty the way I love Lelo. It wasn't manicured or tended or trained. We didn't have time. We were new parents, bewildered and tired. But Lelo was unstoppable. Once her maternity leave expired, she sucked coffee up through an unlit cigarette and stormed out of the house, pumped her breasts while sitting in rush-hour traffic. I'd never been in love with a warrior before, and now I love her the way you love your lungs for drawing breath.

The other thing you need to know about Lelo is that her biological father was a violent drunkard. Luckily, he was only in her life for a few years. Her mom married an incredibly nice and generous man who raised Lelo most of her life. Tim, a different Tim than I've mentioned before. He's as solid as they come, and I'm very thankful for the stability he provided during my wife's childhood, which could have easily veered in the direction of mine.

She had been estranged from her father for years, the whole time I've known her, basically. He'd emailed Lelo a bit around our marriage and the birth of Ava, wanting pictures of his grandchild. He'd seen news of these things through social media and wanted to be included, in some small way. But he never entered our life. Lelo didn't want it, and that's her story to tell. And then he died. His ashes are in our basement. We keep meaning to scatter them somewhere, to get them out of our house, but Lelo hasn't figured out where or how she wants to let them go. And even if she has, it's not a priority. There's such little free time in our life and it's hard to want to give a Saturday or Sunday away for such a task, scattering the cremains of an estranged parent. The brutal truth of parenthood is how if we aren't careful, we end up ashes in our children's basement. Lelo's father is on a shelf between board games and blankets. Sitting on top of his box is a coil of Christmas lights, wound tight and looking like a green crown. He was her father. And now he's here. If he'd been better, his ashes would be displayed prominently perhaps, or we'd have already released them, made a celebration of the ritual, a way to help Ava understand that the people we love might physically die.

That's if he'd done his job correctly, of course. If parents focused on their jobs. Raised kids right. Stopped drinking. Stopped fucking around. If they put away their fists and dicks and lies. If not, this is their fate. A shelf. In the basement. The final fuck-you from someone they used to love.

It's never lost on me that Lelo's dad and I share vices. Never lost on me how sad it would be to end up ashes in Ava's basement. To be such a regret, a nuisance. To be valued so little that you're shelved and forgotten.

Anonymous. Obscured. Valueless.

All of this makes me want to see him. To commiserate.

All of this makes me want to hold him, obviously.

I walk to his box. Pop off the top. Peep the plastic bag. His home. Undo the knot. Carefully. So as not to create a mushroom cloud of my forgotten father-in-law. The man I've never met. Until right now.

Face-to-face.

Face-to-ash.

I thrust a hand in the bag, balance a pile of him in my palm. Hold him up. Close to my face. For inspection. For a sniff.

I've robbed his basement grave, brought a dune of him out of his plastic-bag crypt, exhumed him: for a chat.

For a plea.

For a warning or any wise words.

Ashes can't talk. I know that. I'm not totally unhinged. Though holding a pile of Lelo's dad's ashes doesn't speak to being well-adjusted. Though no one's ever called me well-adjusted in the first place.

So:

I stand with ash-mountain in my spread hand and he looks like instant oatmeal. Before you pour the water in. Once the dust slides from the pack. Lumps. Moguls on the mountain. Pieces of bone, maybe. A tooth.

This isn't actually her whole father. No, this is half of him. The other half is in Florida with his older sister. Lelo hadn't wanted to deal with the mortuary or the bureaucracy of his death. Not that she couldn't have handled it—just didn't feel compelled to work hard on his behalf—so I dialed in these details. Asked them to divvy him up, as though they were drug dealers, weighing out bags of powder.

Math even works with ashes.

Math is never sentimental.

The ashes aren't imparting any wisdom. The dust doesn't divulge any tricks to stay on the straight and narrow. There will be no knowledge transfer in the basement, it seems, except for the simple fact of their presence here in the board-game graveyard.

"Last chance," I say to the ashes. "Carpe diem, you dune!"

I never held my dad's ashes like this. I did hold the box of him, did peek inside at his own bag of instant oatmeal, but I never held him without the prophylactic of the plastic bag, never saw his nude dusty body.

"Last last chance," I say to the ashes, hoping for something stupidly meaningful and getting what I deserve: nothing but a dirty hand.

He can't drop any wisdom because dust doesn't know anything. They say water has memory, and I'd hoped maybe cremains did, too. Hoped the soot of his cursed soul might help me keep mine from turning radioactive.

My fingers twitch, my palm tilts, her dad's ashes slide back in his bag, his sarcophagus.

Knot it again.

Close the box.

Banished to the basement, forgotten ashes under a crown of Christmas lights.

Rest in peace, you terrible father.

Then a quick sprint to the bathroom. To wash the evidence off my hand, wash him away. To be clean again. But it gets weird. Part of me wants to wear him. To wear a dead dad ash mask. To carry him on my skin. To look like him. To play him. I swipe my ashy hand over my cheeks and chin. I haven't shaved in a couple days and the ash gets trapped in the stubble. Some of him might seep into pores, then he'll be a part of me. I've read accounts that this was one of the ways Jimi Hendrix took acid, tabs of LSD wedged between a bandana and his forehead, so as he performed onstage, the drug trickled into his body through pores.

That's how I'm taking her father.

That's how I welcome the drug of her dad into me.

This way, I'll never forget, always remember and remember and remember: never lose sight of how a decision today can poison tomorrow—to hold on to the fact that Ava doesn't hate me, and to be mindful of how easily that can happen if I slip, if I fall.

If I was still tending bar, all this would lead me to invent a drink, a tincture of sorts, some of a dead father's ashes floating on a double shot of whiskey, looking like pond scum. Call this tragic potion "the epigenetic."

One swig and you're an ash father, forgotten.

The mirror is quite rudely showing me my reflection. *Our* reflection.

The dead dad ash mask.

Another dream: I'm in a rowboat, in the middle of the ocean. The water is calm, Caribbean blue. The sky is bright and clear. I can't stop gritting my teeth. Can't stop grinding them. Can't stop biting down so hard that they are cracking, they are shattering, and I hold my hands up to my mouth and spit these little seashells of teeth out and no matter how hard I try to stop myself from biting down, I can't and can't and can't, keep spitting more seashells, my hands full of teeth and blood.

22

There are other boxes in our basement. They're not all filled with ashes. No. One of them has the busted gun.

This happened when I was eighteen, living in an SF punk house. The place didn't start out as a punk house, but I guess they never do. My friend's grandmother had recently died, leaving her home in the Sunset District vacant. My friend's mother said that he and I could live there for $250 apiece so long as we were enrolled in college. That was the deal. But punks multiply like mushrooms in manure. First, it was just Ryan and me. Then, poof, there was Germ. Then Derek. And Icky Mike. And Clark. Nicole the Biter. Then there was Downtown and Leslie and Sonya. And Rory. And a small runaway whose name I can't remember, but her lip piercing was infected, and she could drink malt liquor with the best of them.

One night, I poked around in the basement and found a gun in one of the boxes left over from the grandparents' stuff. The trigger was so rusted I couldn't pull it.

I'd found one other gun in my life. It belonged to a man my mom and I lived with for a couple years when I was in elementary school. Felipe. He had a .357 Magnum and kept it under his waterbed. Seriously. That might describe our early-1980s existence perfectly: dude kept his .357 under his waterbed.

I can't remember if I found it, snooping around one day, or if he showed it to me. All I know is that the gun was under the waterbed, which meant I was often under the waterbed, hanging out with the .357. It was never loaded. He kept it oiled and clean. I loved spinning its cylinder. Loved cocking the hammer. Loved drinking box wine and then holding it to my head.

I knew it wasn't loaded. I wasn't risking anything. I just loved that what-if—that click noise. That release. That chance. That hammer coming down that meant it wasn't bringing any bullets. That meant I'd keep living. I'd be under the waterbed with my wine and a .357 and I'd be laughing and laughing and laughing until they came back and I crawled out.

In the punk house, I held this rusty gun to my head and yanked the trigger with all my might, but no matter the force, it wouldn't budge. I still dug holding its silver body, its black handle. I brought the busted gun to my room upstairs and showed it to May, my girlfriend at the time.

"Where'd you get that gun?" said May.

"Let's go to the movies," I said.

All three of us went—me, May, and the gun—a late screening of *Pulp Fiction*, which had just come out—we left the theater, arm in arm, nursing the last of a pint of tequila, and the gun wasn't good at sharing liquor, selfish little gun, but he was just learning to drink, and I said to May, "We could rob something too, just like the movie," and she said, "We could rob something too, just like the movie!" and I said, "Why not a liquor store?" and she said, "Why not a liquor store!"

Then the gun shouted, "I love you guys!"

It was coming on a little strong, sure, but you spend years boxed up in a basement and you might fall in love on the quick, too.

That was how we decided to commit a felony. A gun, some tequila, a film. Maybe other petty criminals scrutinized their decisions; maybe they had better reasons than us. Hell, we didn't even have reasons. Or none that mattered. We were mad kids, and the animosity over our childhoods lit us up with fantastic and furious watts, and we were humungous in our anger and we could do anything we wanted to this world, because this world never did anything for us—this world that saw us as easy marks—it spun and the sun rose and the moon rose and birds chirped and the levels of lakes changed and a polar bear ate a harbor seal and a gorilla got shot and a rhino got shot and a mosquito sucked blood and a baby was born, the mother bringing that baby to her nipple, the mother feeling the pleasure of feeding her child for the first time, and someone won the lottery and a lawyer cashed a six-figure bonus and a homeless woman found a still-warm bagel in the trash, but who gave a shit about any of that when the world was wrecking you—when you couldn't get ahead—couldn't fucking deal with this day and the next and the next—and so what if we raided a liquor store—why shouldn't we, why should we care about a world that only showed us its wick and wrath and fire?

May and I spent the next couple weeks scoping out various candidates. Even though we cooked this plan up drunk, both of us were committed. We needed a liquor store with semi-direct access to a freeway, I posited, so we could get lost in the chug of traffic. But what did I know? I was basing that opinion on absolutely nothing.

Finally, we found one that fit, which left us with only one last detail to dial in, something that had to not fit. Our clothes. The ones we'd wear during the robbery.

Here was my plan: I wanted both of us to dress in baggy black clothes. I wanted us to look like two dudes. That way, as we fled the robbery, we could change out of our thieving outfits and look like what we were, young lovers. May was a beauty, a five-foot-three Mexican with hazel eyes. I had these stupid white-boy dreadlocks at the time. Other aspects of our "alibi": a sandy blanket, an acoustic guitar in the back of my truck. So if we got pulled over, I could tell the cops that we just had a night picnic at the beach.

I parked my truck in front of the liquor store. It was about midnight. We pulled stockings over our heads. I ran into the store. May waited by the front. I had the busted gun. I never even raised it. I just held it by my side. Realized what a horrible idea this was as soon as I entered the store. I've heard stories of jumpers, people planning on committing suicide leaping from the Golden Gate Bridge, but right as their feet left the bridge's railing, they immediately recognized their mistake. They wanted to live! That was what happened to me as I stood in the store.

As I'd crossed the threshold, the front door made that beeping noise. The sound some doors make when you enter that means: "Hey, a stranger is here."

I was alone. It didn't seem like anyone was working. I stood next to the chips.

But the beeping did summon a worker. Maybe the store's owner.

A woman. Asian. In her fifties or sixties. She had been in the back. Now she walked out and up the aisle.

Now she saw me and my stockinged face and the busted gun.

She was not speaking. I was not speaking.

She was still. I was still.

We just looked at each other.

A second went by. Or a year.

The busted gun in my hand was a boulder.

She stayed halfway down that aisle. Still not saying a word. Or doing anything. Then she turned around and bolted to the back of the store. Slamming that little door that led to all the rest of their supplies. Since she just ran away, I took that as my cue, too. I could never raise that gun and point it at her. I could never empty her register. Suddenly, I saw consequences, real consequences. I saw prison. I saw a whole life snake out in front of me that I didn't want. Worse, I just made another human being fear for her life. This was her store, most likely. She owned it. She'd be back tomorrow and tomorrow, and on each of those awful days she'd wonder: *Will he be back too?*

That's the question I'm always asking myself—the question that compels me to scribble this memoir: Will that part of me ever come back? Can I guarantee I'll never be that animal again?

"We need to get the fuck out," I said to May, and then we were to the truck, and we were driving. I was taking corners and speeding. We stripped, taking off all the black clothes while the truck squealed. Trying to make the highway.

We were in our normal attire now, with the busted gun and baggy black clothes wedged under my truck's bench. We sat on the edge of all that evidence. On top of our felony-future.

That was when the cop car's lights went wild in the rearview.

That was when we were pulled over.

My mom and I got pulled over once just a few blocks from our house. She was giddy, and there was music playing and any consequences couldn't reach her, not yet, not with wine and pills turning her indestructible.

She was laughing about it, which made me start too, and we kept it up all the way until the cop reached Mom's window.

Then I stopped laughing.

She kept going, couldn't quit that incriminating laughter, even after he asked, "Have you been drinking?"

Even after he made her exit the vehicle.

No matter how close we were to home, we weren't going to make it there that night.

I couldn't outgas the cops, not in my '86 Ford Ranger. I pulled over to the shoulder and two police officers walked up, one on either side of the vehicle, their cruiser lights still flashing and a spotlight on me in the driver's seat.

May squirmed and asked, "Are we going to jail, Josh?"

"We'll be fine," I said. "I'm too pretty for prison." I didn't believe anything that I was saying, was trying to keep her calm. But I had those shimmering malfunctions—the heat and sweat of an adrenaline spike.

One cop nearing my window.

The other behind the truck, hand on holster.

"I'm scared," said May.

Me rolling the window down.

The cop was right there.

"This truck matches the description of one used in an armed robbery," he said. "Where are you coming from?"

"Ocean Beach."

"Why?"

"We had a night picnic."

The cop took his flashlight and aimed it at May. I had her dress nice and sexy underneath her clothes from the robbery.

"I played her some songs on my guitar," I said.

The cop inspected the back of the Ranger, gazing at the blanket, the guitar. "Hold on," he said, walking back to his cruiser.

Me and May in the truck, the busted gun and baggy black clothes wedged under the bench, the cop walking away from us for a minute, a whole congregation of seconds, devout, chaste, that was the thing about seconds: they couldn't be corrupted, couldn't be contaminated by misshapen human hearts, hell no, the seconds beyond fallibility, stomping out their march—one, two, three, four—uniform and pure, soldiers believing entirely in the monotheism of *time*—five, six, seven—and these seconds start singing, as congregations are wont to do, belting it out, in unison—eight, nine, ten—totally on pitch and perfect, the harmonies creating a song so structurally sound it becomes its own church, these seconds, these believers, all harmonizing and happy and me and May squirming and sweating, knowing that the cop will soon be back with his not-busted gun drawn, demanding that we exit the vehicle, that we exit our status quos, pitching us in prison.

The waiting, the unknowing.

Imagining days and nights in the pen, years to impale myself on these faults. Twenty-six, twenty-seven. The seconds swelling their lungs to sing the song's final chorus, its crescendo, my demise, the end of a life, the beginning of another. I'd meet Kae, though I wouldn't be his teacher. We'd share a cell. We'd share stories, decapitated dreams. He'd still have that unbelievable confidence in himself, but convict-me wouldn't know how to help—wouldn't know how to do anything except remember this one night, trying to rob a liquor store for no reason. Stupidly standing by the chips with the busted gun and the stockinged face. Scaring that woman—I'm so sorry for scaring that woman. Forty. Fifty. The suicide of certain decisions. Seventy. May was gonna do time, too. Eighty. The facts of our new lives like their own little jails.

Ninety.

One hundred.

Hemorrhaging.

Here he came walking toward us again.

Here he came to tear us apart.

At the window.

"Okay," he said.

"Can we go?" I asked.

But he was already running off. The cop car peeled out, lights on, maybe hunting down another late-'80s pickup.

All he'd had to do was search inside and our lives would have been over.

When May and I got back to the punk house, there was a party roaring, the rooms filled with smoke and trampling music. We didn't tell anyone what we'd done. Just grabbed forties and joined the soiree.

I hugged everyone. I loved them all. I can't possibly make you understand how lucky I felt that night, and so I celebrated by bear-hugging every stinky punk I could get my arms around.

So what if I'm sorry, so what if I'm sober, so what if I'm a good parent, so what if I'm a good husband, so what if I pay my taxes, so what if I drive a Subaru Outback, so what if I volunteer my time at halfway houses, so what if I take the neighborhood kids for ice cream, so what if I listen to NPR, so what if I try to help people, so what if I give and give, so what if I write this, so what if I try to find a rhythm in the beat of a deformed-fruit heart, that mad kid doing something so reprehensible and getting away with it, and getting away with it, and getting away with it?

I want to have a heart that's gentle, peaceful—a heart like those drawings of a placid Jesus in the manger—or maybe that's wrong. Maybe the baby wasn't calm; maybe he was crying, scared, cold in his barnyard sanctuary. Maybe this just-born lord shuddered with disgust, seeing how we treat one another here. How we are endlessly creative with the ways in which we self-destruct.

◻

Spoiler alert: May and me didn't work out. We burned too white-hot to stand the trials of time. We were strangers and then we were fast friends and then we were best friends and soon we were locked in liquor-worlds like bugs frozen in amber, and it was a good life, a goddamn great life to be bugs, happy bugs with alcohol all around us.

May broke up with me in the only way a relationship like that could end: she stole a bunch of my stuff and disappeared back to Guadalajara, leaving me with a $700 phone bill. She was a near-perfect woman.

23

My father and I were the happiest with each other when we read the newspaper. This was our morning ritual my senior year in high school. He'd open my bedroom door early, before my sisters were up, so my room would fill with the smell of brewing coffee. I'd sniff the caffeine and emerge, joining him on the back patio, and we'd sit swigging and passing various sections of the newspaper back and forth.

There was never much talking. That wasn't our thing, and we'd spend hours like this. Sure, if something caught our attention, we'd make jokes or observations based on what we read. For the most part, there was nothing except the sound of crinkling newspaper pages.

"It's going to rain next week," he said, "so I'll pray for rain on Sunday."

He was joking—or it seemed like he was—but there he was in his pulpit praying for rain a few days later. Some of these parishioners read the paper, right? They had access to the weekly weather forecast? So why, the following Sunday, after it had rained, did they thank my father? Why did their eyes shine with gratitude?

They wanted what everyone in a place of worship seeks: to be in the right place, with the right god, with the right minister messengering their prayers straight to the holy ear.

A simple chain of humdrum events could morph into a miracle: he read the weather report, and he prayed for rain, and then when the storm started, every believer got to stand in the downpour, dance in these hallowed drops, and there was something concrete to their faith now, something they could feel land on their bodies and drip along their skin, something giving them goose bumps because of the wonder falling from the sky.

For a moment, as they danced in this shower, there was order in the universe and god was listening. Yes! Their god was hearing the whole clog of believers, prayers ringing out like whale songs in the ocean, schools of noise alive in the water.

Their minister, their meteorologist.

I'm still not religious, not after living with a minister who had abandoned me—and yet his congregants lauded him as pure, as good, a person to emulate. That dissonance was unbearable for me. How could I consider someone holy who I'd heard scream at me, demean me, while wearing his preacher robe and stoles?

I didn't know nuance back then. I couldn't contextualize his human inconsistencies until I was an adult, too. Until I had friction from various parts of me making sparks in my body.

And life has a way of challenging us about the things we think we know. Life likes to strip our certainties, humble them with evidence to the contrary. I was agnostic on a good day, an atheist on the rest, and life wanted to test my convictions of nonbelief.

And so started the strokes . . .

I had my first one behind the bar. I was in my twenties, ripped on cocaine, and I lost the feeling in my right arm, and I said to a coworker, "I might be overdosing," and he said, "You're just too gakked. Have a whiskey," and so I had one to slow my heart down and I felt better, but the numbness wasn't going away in my arm and I took a cab to the emergency room.

It was a Saturday night and numb arms didn't get top billing in the Mission District, so I waited my turn, and my arm eventually got the feeling back and when I had my time with the doctor, she exhibited very little human sympathy. I told her what had happened, and I leveled with her about the drugs.

The look on her face said: *Wunderbar, another junkie, lucky me.*

She ordered zero tests and told me to stop doing so much cocaine.

She was right, of course—the coke wasn't helping anything. But just because I was a junkie didn't mean there wasn't something else wrong. She was supposed to be a doctor, which meant she needed to be curious and compassionate, two traits that never showed their mugs in my exam room. She could've ordered a CT scan of my brain, and the stroke's lesion would have been right there, scar looking like some thumbprint. Instead, she dismissed me.

For years after, it didn't occur to me that this was a stroke. It was Lelo who said, "Hey dumbass, do you think maybe that 'mysterious' first stroke was the time you lost the feeling in your right arm behind the bar?! You know, the same thing that's happened with all your other strokes?!"

Okay, she said it *much* nicer than that.

My second stroke was the most serious of the three. I've told you about this one already. Staying in Los Feliz for the LA Times Festival of Books. I'd been sober for a few years at that point, so the doctors couldn't blame cocaine and turn off their Hippocratic oath like muting a TV. They did order tests. Lots of them. And that was the first time I had a diagnosed stroke (and they saw the scar of the previous one).

Lelo was with me, and we drove back from LA to SF—they let

me out of the hospital Sunday night, and I was supposed to teach an MFA class that Tuesday evening. I had one day to figure out how to talk again.

Because that was a real concern: I couldn't talk.

On that whole car trip between LA and SF, all six hours of it, I couldn't speak coherently. In my head, I'd compose these illustrious sentences, but when I opened my mouth, I made these moaning sounds.

My third stroke felt like a pregnancy, once you'd already given birth before. I knew immediately. Felt numbness and within thirty seconds I told Lelo to call the paramedics. And here's where faith comes into it. Here's where I'm one of my father's desperate parishioners.

Back then, my wife was the one with the "real job," the one who got insurance for the family. And it just so happened that her company was changing insurance providers on January 1, 2015. So if I'd had my stroke six hours and one minute earlier, before midnight, making it New Year's Eve, I'd have ended up back at Kaiser, under the previous health-care plan. Because I had my third stroke at six in the morning on New Year's Day, I was under the jurisdiction of this new insurance policy. So when the ambulance driver asked where I wanted to go, I said, "Where would you go for a brain injury?" and he said, "You go to UCSF. They're the best."

Because I was a kind of medical anomaly, and because UCSF was a teaching hospital, I had a gaggle of frothing neurologists on the case. They wanted to discover a disease! They wanted to name some new syndrome after themselves!

It took them a couple weeks, but they ordered an expensive test called a transesophageal echocardiogram. What was that, exactly? They were going to numb up my throat—I had to actually gargle lidocaine—and I was to swallow a kind of camera to take pictures of the back of my heart. They snaked it all the way down my esophagus to the stomach, and slowly pulled it up to show the germane angles. If they had only relied on the frontal view of the heart, as Kaiser did, they would have made the same misdiagnosis.

Maybe to you, this story doesn't seem spiritual, the fact that my third stroke happened only six hours after our insurance changed providers. I'm not going to say I was spared. Not even I'm that self-involved. But I can see my father on our patio, shuffling the pages of the newspaper, viewing the weather report. I can see him deciding what to pray for, what miracle to bestow his flock. And even if that's what I'm doing, choosing to believe this coincidence is more than chance, well, that's my right. I can sit in any congregation I see fit.

I can worship whatever brings the rain.

It's a brisk day in Seattle, drizzling, but I have a triple espresso and I'm walking around our neighborhood, talking to my mom. I tell her the City Lights story, the beer. It's scary to say it out loud, especially because it's been difficult for me to be mature about my mom's sobriety. I'm happy she's sober. Of course. I'm glad she found the way to do right by herself. Every year on her sober birthday I hope to be a better son, send her a card, call with congratulations. But it's hard for me to want to honor it, after everything that happened. I know that's petty. Now I need to admit that I'm floundering, need to admit that I'll never make it to thirty years clean, like her. Might not make it back to thirty days. So I leveled with her.

"That bartender knowing who you were probably kept you from getting drunk," she says.

"I walked by a bunch of other bars on my way to my hotel."

"You left that first bar, Josh. That broke the trance. That was the hard part. I'm glad you were able to stop at one. I don't think I could do that."

"I didn't think I could either."

"Why did you do it in the first place?"

"I'm just . . . I'm tired, Mom. Being a parent is so hard and running my own business and teaching classes and trying to write and trying to be married and blah blah. I'm whining."

"You can't always work so hard."

"I have no idea how you raised me on your own."

"Well, I didn't do a good job."

"You did a better job than I would do," I say.

It surprises me, saying this to her. I certainly hadn't planned on bringing the past up, but that's what it does, leaks out, like a cocktail's condensation melting into a napkin. And I mean it. Yes, my mom failed me in many ways. My childhood had too many drinks and too many men, and yet now that I have a child of my own, I can't even imagine the job of single parents. I was so judgmental of her and the way she brought me up, and yes, she deserves her share of shit for that chaos—but goddamn: having a kid is rough, and I have a spouse to help. My mom worked two jobs. I respect her now in ways I couldn't imagine before.

"I need to tell Lelo," I say.

"You do," Mom says, "but only when you're ready to comfort her. Right now, you're comforting yourself and that's okay—that's allowed. But soon she needs to know."

○

Of course she needs to know. That's obvious. What's not as evident is how I pry this secret from my heart. As though the organ is an old-school safe. As though I kneel in front of it with a stethoscope, hearing the clicks of the proper combination as I spin its dial.

I crack it, open it, see its tawdry contents.

The thing that's really fucking me up is presumably a simple detail, though to me it feels anything but simple: I was sober. I was clearheaded when I decided to order that beer. I mean, obviously you have to be sober to order your first drink, but what I mean is this—what am I supposed to do with that information? For anybody sober, we blame a lot of our mistakes on booze and drugs. We say, "Of course, I wouldn't have acted that way with a clear head," but it always starts with a conscious decision. I *chose* to walk into Vesuvio and order that pint. I *chose* to charge into that liquor store.

The doctors can't seem to figure out what's wrong with me, they can't fix me, and so far, I can't seem to stay out of my own way, I can't fix me, and after so many years clean, shouldn't it be more difficult to screw up your life?

Let me rephrase: it should be more difficult to screw up your life, but it's effortless. Drunkards have some sort of alcoholic muscle memory. It's a breeze for us to ruin things. The horror stories of staying sober are all the relapse anecdotes that have no calamitous triggers. The stories of brutal ubiquity. The ones where a woman has nineteen years clean and it's a Wednesday and she goes to a party at a coworker's house, and someone she doesn't know there offers her a glass of wine and she, for no real reason at all, accepts this invitation to demean her life and she slurps a glass, and another, and another, and she embarrasses herself and she wakes up fully clothed with the self-hate blazing through her hangover and she is so righteously humiliated that she can't go to a meeting, she can't admit that nineteen years clean disappeared for *nothing*, and that shame keeps her drinking and she blinks her eyes and a year has gone by.

Another dream: I am a cat, the kind who likes to kill birds or mice or snakes and leave their dead bodies at the front door. An offering to their owner. A gift. It's a fine vacation, being a cat. Being four-legged. Having whiskers and a tail. I can get used to having fur.

But the dream isn't about me test-driving another species. No, the dream is about me being a hunter. It's about catching a mouse, killing it, carting its corpse to the doorstep of the house with the green door. Using my little cat paw to knock. The bloody thing splayed on the welcome mat. Me looking up through cat eyes and waiting for my owner to open up.

I hear her feet pad across the hardwood floor. Hear the tumble of locks open. Hear the creak of rickety hinges swing. There she is, my Lelo.

"Not again," she says, disgusted with my offering.

There's so much to say to her, to explain, to articulate these bloody compulsions, to kill, to parade these carcasses about, leave them on a doorstep like my sacrifice to an angry god.

"Why do you keep doing this?" she asks her horrible animal.

And since I'm a cat, I can't explain. I try. Believe me. I open my cat jaws, jonesing to bring some clarity to the subject, to try to explicate my behavior to her, to me, to the whole species. But fact is, I'm a fucking cat and all that runs out of my maw is "Meow meow meow," and she says, "I don't understand you," and I clear my kitty throat and retort, "Meow meow meow," and she says, "I don't want this. I don't want this anymore. Stop doing this," and I stand my cat ground, "Meow meow meow," and she says, "If you can't quit, you won't be a part of this family. I'll have to give you away," which is my biggest fear so I conjure a compelling cat speech and say, "Meow meow meow," and she asks, "Why can't you stop acting like this? Why can't you just behave normally?"

That's what I'll be giving Lelo: the present she doesn't want. My confession. Its body on the welcome mat. Entrails exposed. Eyes wide. Rigor mortis.

Mostly, it is spayed female cats that do this. The majority of these treats are from barren would-be mothers: They are maternal hunters and have an evolutionary pull to pass on their skills to their young, and without any offspring, they attempt to share their killings with their surrogate family, their owners. "I love you so much," these cats say with the left corpses, "that I want you to know how to murder your food and I want you to eat this dead thing to build your strength. I want you to eat it so you can learn how to make your way in the world. You'll never survive unless you understand how to hunt."

Most owners, though, treat these presents like they're shit on the rug. "What? Jesus! Why?" That's the easy, obvious response of the cat's owner, repulsed by these gifts, never occupying these treasures from the cat's point of view. Yes, the easy thing is to get frustrated—stop blocking the entryway of my home with slain creatures—and these at-the-end-of-their-ropes owners swear under their breath and sweep these cadavers up into a dustbin and scoff *dumb cat, dumb cat.*

But is it dumb?

I mean, are they?

I mean, are we?

Cats kill little creatures because it's their nature; I kill little beers because it's mine.

And it's time to give Lelo the gift she doesn't want.

Today has been busy. Soccer in the morning. A birthday party in the early afternoon. Lelo and I have been together all day and not spoken a complete sentence to each other.

The secret, which has been growing in time-lapse brutality, from baby secret to prepubescent to young adult, is now full-grown.

It's been six days since I got home from SF, and that's enough keeping her in the dark. Is this an ideal time to tell Lelo? Of course not. But there is no ideal time in our life. Not with our full-contact parenting style, giving everything we have to Ava, leaving us to subsist on emotional scraps and crumbs.

As our car pulled up after the birthday party, Ava saw her pal Maia across the street, helping her father unload groceries from the back of their van. "I want to play with Maia!" Ava said and ran across the street.

Lelo wanted to do some gardening while Ava was otherwise occupied—pull some weeds, sweep the front stairs.

"Let me change my shoes and I'll help," I said.

"Great."

"I'll start in the backyard," I said.

"I'll help once I'm through up here," she said.

Now I am back here alone, under our cherry tree that only produces inedible cherries. I'm wearing these big green gardening gloves, which give me grasshopper hands. Since Lelo has our only rake, I'm using a kind of metal dustpan to scrape the brick and build mounds of leaves, making a noise like a robot's asthma attack.

I look up and the tree is completely bare. This will be the last time I have to take care of this useless thing, at least for a couple months. I drag the compost bin from the alley behind our house and wheel it under the tree. All the piles of leaves, like piles of mistakes, the dead memories we can't fix or alter or clean.

And I am here, holding my confession and a metal dustpan.

Lelo comes into the backyard carrying a rake and a broom and begins sweeping off the porch. I am using the green gardening gloves to pick up a pile of leaves.

"I need to tell you something," I say.

I fill her in on the specifics—City Lights, crying on the street, the love-your-books bartender, the beer. I keep bending and picking up piles while I talk.

I'd been worried that once I was done, she'd look at me like I'm no better than the ashes in the basement, and she'd have been right. I've been looking at myself the same way. Yet I don't see any anger and animosity on her face. I only see sadness, which is worse. Welling eyes. Processing the information. Holding the broom.

"If you want me to, I'll go back to rehab," I say. "I'll go to meetings more consistently. I'll start seeing a therapist. Whatever you want."

"I knew it."

"What?"

"You didn't call all weekend, only text."

"I had a Guinness and stopped there. I shouldn't have had anything, obviously. But I stopped after one."

"You're unhappy here," she says.

"In Seattle?"

"You haven't been yourself."

"I can find reasons every day to relapse if that's what I want to do," I say. "That's not the problem. The problem is I'm having some kind of seven-year itch with being sober. I don't value it like I used to."

"Why don't you value it?" she asks.

"It used to be a diamond."

"What is it now?"

I scoop another load of leaves into the compost bin. "Not a diamond."

"Do you consider this a relapse?" she asks. "A beer?"

"By the letter of the law," I say, "even one drink is a relapse."

"Can you control it now?"

This is the question—the one I've been asking myself—the one that part of me wants to believe. I remember reading an article in *Vogue* written by Mimi O'Donnell, Philip Seymour Hoffman's widow, who talked about this con, this lie, the idea that maybe an alcoholic can learn to moderate. So he started with a drink or two, then five or six, then it was pills, then it was heroin, then he was dead.

Alcoholics and addicts aren't the exception to the rule. We are the rule. If it can trick Hoffman into euthanizing himself, it can do the same to me.

One of the most memorable and terrifying pieces of advice I got in rehab has stayed with me, thundering around my head ten times a day, keeping me on the straight and narrow until it didn't. And it's simple—*what are you willing to lose?*

If you're willing to lose your marriage, start drinking again.

If you're willing to lose your child, by all means hoist a cocktail.

Maybe you can control it now.

Maybe you can act like a normie.

Maybe.

If you drink, you have to be comfortable with never seeing them again, have to be comfortable aching for the life you tossed away like a wine cork.

Or you say to yourself, it's not worth it. Those risks are too severe, stakes too high. I don't want an alcoholic life and so I'll err on the side of sobriety, because even though it's not always a fun way to live, it beats the hollow alternative.

"I don't know how to answer that question," I say to Lelo.

"Try."

"I have a feeling it's just me trying to trick myself. Make that one beer seem like a success story. And I do it again, can still stop at one. But—I don't know—three weeks later or three months and I'm bingeing again."

It's that concept of the long con. Addictions are learning viruses. Mine has consistently changed its ways of manipulating me. Tried many routes to incite a relapse. Many psychologies and rationalizations to let alcohol slide down my throat again, and its persistence was finally rewarded. It's not lost on me that I might be the long con, too. I might be the confidence man rolling into an unsuspecting town, knocking on someone's door, and Lelo answers holding her daughter, and I smile and pitch her a phony product, lie to her only thinking about myself, selling her something she obviously doesn't need.

"Okay," she says, "so what should we do?"

"I don't know."

"What do you want to do?"

"I don't know."

"Mommy!" says Ava, arriving at the ideal time, storming through the side gate. She's cranky and hungry and wants one of us to help her put on a temporary tattoo.

"In a minute," Lelo says, trying to smile.

"It's cold out here," says Ava.

"Play inside, sweets," I say to her. "We'll be in soon. Once we're done cleaning up."

"Tattoo!"

"We're almost done," says Lelo.

Ava is up the back steps and barrels inside, but we both know the clock is ticking. Seems like our only child can entertain herself in thirty-second bursts.

"You don't know what, exactly," Lelo says.

"I don't know . . ." I say again and trail off, letting my green hands scoop up another bundle of leaves. "I know I don't want to go back out."

"I'm glad to hear that."

"I don't know what happened."

"But that's *how* it happens," says Lelo. "It's not the big thing. Never is. It's something you never see coming."

"I guess."

"You know that."

"Yeah."

"Maybe we should find a way to get you back to the Bay Area," she says.

"This isn't Seattle's fault. It's mine."

"But you don't like it here."

"I need to do a better job of participating. Get out of our basement."

"Or we can move."

"I need to change my way of thinking."

Then we hear this coming from inside the house: "Help! Help! Help!"

Our four-year old thespian has recently learned that if she screams that word—*HELP*—one of us will come running. Just last week, I'd been in the shower at seven in the morning and Ava said, "Help!" and I jumped out of the tub and ran into the living room, dripping wet. She sat at the table and said, "Watch me eat this pancake."

Now I know this is probably another false alarm, but I take off the green gloves and walk inside. Ava is in the kitchen, smiling at me. "Can you help me with this tattoo?" She shakes the little square back and forth.

"Sure." I set her on the counter and get a washcloth, run it under warm water, and use it to hold the tattoo to her forearm. "We need to count to twenty and then it will be there."

In unison, we count aloud all the way, slowing down as we near it, smiling at each other.

"Do you think it worked?" I ask.

She nods at me. "Look, please."

I peel the washcloth off and the tattoo is perfect. Just like that, her interest in it is over and she says, "Let's play Legos," hops off the counter, and runs to her room.

"I'll be there in two minutes," I say, "once I'm done helping Mommy."

I'm back outside, putting the green gloves back on, and say to Lelo, "Do you want to know the emergency?"

"The tattoo?"

"A mother's intuition."

"I'm scared," she says.

"I'm scared too," I say.

"I don't know what we're supposed to do."

"Neither do I."

"So where do we start?" she asks, my wonderful fixer. She's been like this the whole time I've known her, seeing problems as having solutions. The only answer for me is abstinence, to always remember that I am the rule and that drinking and drugging will kill me.

Analytically, of course, I know that, and it's easy to cast practical assertions, though they're useless, like the inedible fruit from the cherry tree. It's not about my brain; it's about my deformed heart that won't heal. It's how a drink is a kiss and a drug is a bathtub. It's how a pint of Guinness swirls and settles and takes a stethoscope and listens to your chest like it's a concert hall, all the music ricocheting off your rib cage. It's so easy to see weak pieces of shit, to see the worst of us, so easy for alcoholics to be burdens and letdowns and wretches. Right? Rake us up. Form piles of disappointments. These little dunes of drunks to lose in the compost, lamenting all the squandered potential.

"I want to see a shrink," I say. "I'm pretty fucked up right now."

"Okay, let's place some calls."

"Someone who does dual diagnoses. Those bipolar conversations that started in rehab. I need help. What's been happening in my head isn't normal."

"What's been happening in your head?"

I haven't told her about the incident with her father's ashes, and that feels like too much information to heap on her, especially on the heels of the beer. So I say, "I need to be proactive with this."

"Okay, I'll look some therapists up who do dual diagnoses."

"There was a dual diagnoses group while I was in rehab. I need someone to help me with my head."

We don't kiss. We don't—or not until later that night—even hug. She has her broom and I have my dustpan and gloves. Most of the piles are gone, and we work on the rest of them for the next five minutes, which is right on time for our next scheduled interruption.

"I'm hungry!" says Ava from the doorway.

"Almost," Lelo says, holding the broom still, but now she's done using it on most of the yard. She's toward the back fence, next to Ava's playhouse.

Ava throws on her rain boots and runs up to her mom, trying to see what she's doing.

"Just sweeping the leaves from behind your princess house," says Lelo.

"It's dirty in there," Ava says, looking in her lair like it's the bathroom in Surprise Valley.

"Should we clean it?" Lelo asks.

"Of course, Mama."

They are a team, a bond existing between them that I'm not a part of, something beautiful that happens when you carry a fetus, feed it with your own sustenance. I had been instantaneously jealous the first time I watched Lelo feed Ava. I had expected breastfeeding to be meek and quiet, gentle and placid. That's not how Ava ate. No, she sounded like a raccoon looting garbage cans. An unstoppable and unquenchable animal. That's what it's like to be an alcoholic.

I'm done moving the compost bin back to the gate, waiting to wheel it into the alley. First, I need to help Lelo with Ava's little house. Lelo goes in to sweep out the leaves. The windows don't actually have glass and thus leaves have poured in and collected for months.

She's in there with her broom. Ava isn't far away, she's picking rocks off the ground and placing them through the playhouse's windows, setting them on the counter, between the fake burner and the sink. She's into the next game, narrating to herself as these rocks stack up.

"Here," I say to Lelo, setting that metal dustpan by the front door.

She sweeps all the leaves toward me and once they're in the dustpan, I place a green hand over them, so they don't get caught in the wind and ruin the work we've already done, the places we've already cleaned up.

Ava's playhouse has no basement, no place to keep a deadbeat dad's ashes.

Her house is only ground level, one floor, just big enough for us to fit inside, so we can all live in the sunlight.

24

After I confess to Lelo, I read an article about these broken musical instruments, casualties of the public school system in and around Philadelphia. The kids' ambivalence about treating their instruments with care and respect mixed with the school district's neglect and lack of funding left these horns and drums and pianos in disarray. Some had been beaten and bent so extravagantly they don't even work anymore.

That's when someone got an idea: What if we use all these broken instruments? What if we play them? What if we have professional musicians get some semblance of notes and tones out of them before they're fixed, as a way to fundraise for their care, as a way to rehabilitate them?

A composer was brought in and he penned "Symphony for a Broken Orchestra." To hear the musicians tell it, some of them couldn't even get their wounded instruments—a phrase the composer insisted the players employ when referring to their battered charges—to play in their traditional ways, having to get creative to usher any sounds out of them at all.

But they made them work, one way or another. They made music.

All of these injured things that had been cast aside, abused, demeaned, forgotten—finally, someone saw them for what they were, broken, yes, but they could be brought back to life, changed.

25

We are playing Where Are You?

These things evolve organically, games tangling into new entities. Hide-and-seek suddenly becomes tag becomes wrestling becomes chasing each other around the house becomes a hybrid of all these, screaming, laughing, and one of us—more than likely Ava—says, "Where are you, Daddy?" and I'm hiding in a different room, or under our kitchen table, sometimes behind a door, and I parrot her, "Where are you, Ava?" and emerge from my hiding place, and we stand before each other, and I say to her, "I'm looking for my daughter, Ava. Have you seen her?"

It doesn't register with her at first and I smile, nudge her shoulder. "I'm looking for my daughter, Ava," I say. "Can you help me find her?"

"I haven't seen her," she says.

I push past her into another room into another into another, all the while asking, "Where are you, Ava, where are you?"

The game clicks for her and she's doing it too, wandering from room to room. We walk right past each other screaming these names, hunting for these missing people. Every once in a while we stop the other and ask, desperate and earnest and scared: "Have you seen my daughter?"

"No, have you seen my daddy?"

"Have you seen my daughter?"

"Have you seen my daddy?"

These games, where do they grow from? What are their seeds? They seem to simply sprout out of nothing. It reminds me of my father's backyard. As he was dying, a cornstalk miraculously appeared in his rose garden. We would sit on the back patio and watch it grow. One foot, three feet, five high.

"Life," my father liked to say about the corn, "always finds a way."

Maybe that's true, but I'd add a dismal amendment: Life always finds a way until it doesn't. Death always finds a way, too.

◎

Three weeks ago, I had another bubble test, lie on the table, watching that spray light up my black-and-white heart on the ultrasound monitor with fireworks, turning me into a sky. Those bubbles looking so miraculous when in fact they still reveal my defect, some bubbles slipping past the wall. "Not a lot," they tell me. "Nothing to worry about. You're fine."

Stay on the same regimen of blood thinners.

Watch your diet.

Exercise.

Come back in six months and we'll do it again!

And I leave and stew and stew stew and stew stew stew.

So we push ahead in time to three weeks later, meaning we're back to the present, meaning it's *now*—right now—meaning you're with me—we're together—and I'm folding laundry and watching an old Cassavetes flick in the living room. It's about two in the afternoon, and nature calls as I'm mismatching my argyle socks on purpose, haven't worn matching socks in probably twenty years, #HipsterPower, and I toss the latest horrible, clashing pair of patterns in the pile, jump up to hit the head, and as I walk, shit, a pop in my head, the feeling vanishing from my right arm, numb, utter dead weight, won't respond to any of my mind's commands, and it's impossible—this can't be happening again—I've been fixed! So I maybe pretend like it's not a stroke, though I know it is, I actually take a shower, why, I don't know why, I stand there and breathe deeply thinking that might solve the problem and my right arm doesn't work and I'm talking slowly, but I am talking, I'm making sense, I think, when I talk out loud, I say, "Calm down, calm down," hoping maybe this is some screaming panic attack and my arm's gonna be fine and this isn't a stroke, it can't possibly be a fucking stroke.

Get out of shower. Don't dry off.

I can hear the Cassavetes flick in the other room. I follow the noise. Now I'm wet and naked and just standing in the living room. Next to that pile of mismatched argyle socks as I stagger around the house still saying, "Calm down, calm down," dripping all over the place.

"I'm okay," I say. "This'll pass," I say.

I shouldn't be having number four because I'm fixed—someone tells you they've repaired your heart, someone tells you that there is nothing to worry about right after the surgery, and not even three years later here I am, wet and naked, a clot cooking my brain.

I'm the only one home, and I'm not getting the feeling back in my arm. It's been about ten minutes since it happened, and I know I need to call it in, know I have to admit it's happening again, there's no way to pretend, to escape, stop being so cavalier.

First, I call Lelo at work, then 911. I'm in an ambulance a few minutes later, and we speed to the University of Washington—yet another teaching hospital so I'll need to remember not to let some first-year student torture me with her first spinal tap again, and it's strange, one minute having two working arms, now only one working arm, and I didn't put the argyle socks away, left those Cassavetes characters talking in my living room.

I've tried to waste this life so many times, and now it's the only thing I want.

CT scan.

Chest x-ray.

Off to the MRI suite, my head in their talking tube, trying to abide their instructions to keep perfectly still, as they bombard my skull with their bonks and knocks and whirrs for forty-five minutes, but I start to cry, convinced I'll miss most of Ava's life. I don't move my face in the tube; the tears just stream. The facts screeching at me: four strokes, four strokes, four strokes . . .

Between blood tests and Dopplers, between visitors and naps, two days pass in the hospital. I still can't feel my right arm. It's gone. I am a one-armed man named Josh. That's just the way it is now.

It's late. After midnight. I'm in my hospital room and can't sleep and I'm out of water and call the nurse and she's coming to help, and I walk into the bathroom to take a leak before she gets there, and I look in the mirror. I've never hated a face more, never been so disappointed and humiliated and ashamed to be myself—the man who can't stop killing himself. The brain that wants to turn into crap and scrambled eggs.

I take my good arm and make a good fist and take a good swing at my face. Boom. Right in the nose. Now one more. Bash. Blood. A lot of it. Gushing on my hospital gown.

That's when the nurse walks in.

She stands.

We both do.

Nose still bleeding.

"I'm okay," I say.

I've been thinking about this scene from her perspective—what she must've seen as the blood forms a puddle on the front of my gown. I want to explain it to her, want her to understand why, with my one good arm, I had no choice but to smash my face. I'm down a limb.

Look, I know we aren't promised anything, know some of us never even make it from the womb, dead before our parents kiss our faces, but I also know something else, someone else: a girl named Ava. So long as I have one good arm left, I'll fight to stay here, to be with her.

Nothing from the nurse at first, looking at me and the damage done, wondering if she should call Psych, tie me up, shoot me loopy with drugs to keep me from further injury, but I want to explain, no I don't want to die, it's the opposite: I want to keep living and I hate that this body doesn't seem to share that wish. This body wants to take me out—so it should be hit—should be punished—until it wants to live as much as me.

"I got a nosebleed," I say, but she sees the blood on my knuckles.

Maybe she's overtired, maybe she's silently punching herself in the face for her life's own letdowns, or maybe she just doesn't care. All I know is she turns and walks out, and I stare at my mug in the mirror. Me, the monster. Me, the man.

How we find ways to be both prophets and predators.

How our parents will remain mysteries.

How we'll remain mysteries to ourselves.

How there are no real answers coming to us.

How a heart is fixed until it's not.

How we are the unrepairables.

These lives of ours, they don't make a lick of sense. If you told me a shooting star was just some disgruntled angel using a lighter to burn god, I'd believe that. Makes about as much sense as anything else in this withdrawing world.

EPILOGUE:
THE LUCKIEST UNLUCKY MAN

The feeling starts coming back, slowly, in my right arm on my third night in the hospital. By day five, it's normal, and I'm finally allowed to go outside for a little while by myself. I limp down four flights of stairs, stand in the sunlight.

I wiggle the fingers on my right hand. I love watching them work. I've never been happier to see these fingers move.

I use two to pluck a blackberry off a bush and pop it in my mouth, and it's the best thing I've ever tasted—this berry's straight from a fucking Whitman poem—this berry was pulled from a bush by a hand that rose from the dead.

Day six, the doctors perform their last tests, so many tests, and here are the results from *all* of them: they don't know, have no idea what caused this latest stroke.

"We stand by the heart surgery; it worked," they say.

"The clots might not be routing through the heart at all," they say.

"We don't know where the clots are forming, what's causing them," they say.

"Unfortunately, in 40% of ischemic strokes, we never know the root cause," they say.

"You'll most likely not live out your forties," they say.

"The big one," they say. "The big one is coming."

They say, they say, they say.

Theysaytheysaytheysay.

I don't say.

I barely hear.

I leave the hospital knowing absolutely nothing, but at least I leave the hospital at all, meaning I'm still alive, with no real legacies from this latest stroke.

I continue to be the luckiest unlucky person.

Even if I only have a few years left alive.

I've coined a phrase, in this new era after Stroke Four, and here it is: cheery nihilism. Not nihilism that's all woe is me, poor me, nothing matters, it's all futile, so I'm going to say fuck it and drink and drug and die, and did I mention poor me?

But a new kind of nihilism, one that's like—life can be meaningless, sure, unless you only put time into what you love, letting the rest of the niggling, narcissistic worries slough away.

Every day, I make art.

Every day, I try to be a proper husband.

Every day, a dad.

I take it easy for a few weeks, and then get cracking on my new plan. Community. I know a few writers in Seattle that I reach out to. Not great friends by any stretch, but people whose company I enjoy. I won't tell them the whole truth, can't call and say Surprise Valley, say City Lights. Can't tell them about my father-in-law's ashes on my head, in my mouth. Won't mention I almost died a bit back. For the fourth time.

I'll just ask if they want to get coffee.

When I had run out of the BART station after socking that crusty punk, I said it had been like a miner emerging from a cave-in, squinting up into the bright sun for the first time in ages. I was wrong about that. I wasn't coming out of anything that day.

This is where I'm hoping to come aboveground.

Here.

Now.

With you.

Lelo and I are on an afternoon date. We're headed to the museum to check out Yayoi Kusama's Infinity Mirrors. We've heard lots of positive things about the show and are excited to check it out for ourselves.

We ride the bus downtown, grab a quick espresso to properly caffeinate.

It's nice to be spending time together during the day. Before parenthood, we did this all the time, nerding out at museums, afternoon screws, hoofing around SF talking about art and the future and books, but now we get very little time together.

The Infinity Mirrors are these exhibits playing with vision and angles and vantage point. There are no blind spots in these rooms. You can see every part of yourself. There are five mirrored life-size dioramas you walk into, and they're all decorated with different color schemes and corresponding setting details.

Besides the Infinity Mirror Rooms themselves, the other part of the exhibit is all white. A house, of sorts. Furnished, laid out like a living room, a table, a couch, some shelves.

As the exhibit launched, this whole room had been a blank canvas, utterly white, and every single person who entered was given a colored sticker, circular and small. And every person who was given one was instructed to place it somewhere in the previously all-white room.

Since the exhibit has been rolling for a few months when we go in, the room has tons of little circular stickers stashed all over it. Primary colors pocking the floor, walls, ceiling.

Lelo puts hers on a table.

I put mine on a bookshelf.

"Do you see me?" my dot says to the others. "I'm this red one. And which are you? Yellow? Blue? Green? I'm glad we got to be in this room together. What an honor to be alive, right?"

I'm not exactly sure why, but these dots feel so hopeful, so unifying. They're just silly stickers, after all, though that's not what I'm seeing. I see people showing up. People marking their time here. Sure, we can be ugly with our stampeding appetites, trouncing everyone around us—and yet we are also incredible, deranged towns of hope.

There are lines, many lines to stand in to get in the actual mirrored rooms. You are only allowed to stay inside these rooms for twenty seconds apiece, and to ensure no one gets greedy and overstays their welcome, museum workers are stationed right outside the small mirrored rooms, armed with stopwatches, knocking on the door and kicking you out as your allotted twenty seconds comes to an end.

To weave toward your twenty seconds, you stand, slide, fidget. You wait in a snake running around these concealed mirrored rooms. From the outside, they don't look like much, could be snack bars, utility closets, bomb shelters. That only adds to their intrigue, only invites that craving to experience them, to walk in yourself, make the most of your minuscule stash of time, that pop and fizzle and split before it's too late.

We are told that there's a workaround, if you don't want to wait in these mammoth lines: we don't have to be together. It would be faster, says a museum worker, more efficient to go alone, skip most of the long line. If we go alone, of course, it doesn't mean that we will enter the infinity exhibits by ourselves. Just means that we can sneak to the front, pair off with another stranger. Lelo and I are of the opinion that it doesn't much matter if we go in these rooms together. We can stand to be away from each other for twenty seconds. We'll survive.

We do it for a room, and it's fine. It is—what is it? A pretty cool thing. But it is nowhere near the amazing art we'd heard it was. No life is changed when I go in that first mirrored room.

I'm with an Asian college student, who takes selfies and spins in circles. Besides all the mirrors, the place is decorated with what can only be described as extraterrestrial candy canes sprouting from the floor.

She turns and I stand behind her, seeing all these versions of me in the mirrors, all these angles, a sort of geometric schizophrenia.

◦

"What did you think?" I ask Lelo.

"It was . . . all right."

My wife is nicer than me.

I say, "But isn't it just what you thought it would be? Mirrors doing what mirrors do? The mirrors are just reflecting. So what?"

She laughs, not with me, but also not exactly at me. "Come on," she says, "maybe it will be different if we go in together."

We're finally to the front of this line, and the museum worker runs her pitch, her spiel. She points to the stopwatch in her hand. "You only get twenty seconds," she says.

"Okay," we say.

She must've been burned by past customers and feels the need to reiterate: "I'll knock and you leave immediately."

Lelo and I look at each other. "We understand."

"I'll let you know when your time is up," she says, not looking at us anymore but at her stopwatch, waiting for the people who are in the mirrored room right now to run out of time.

"That's twenty," she says aloud, knocking on the door, throwing them out. "It is your turn," she says to us.

It feels different with Lelo. How can it not? We know the stats about marriage, know that half of them fail, grasp that if one out of two flame out, those aren't great odds. It's an improbable task: to stay connected over a whole lifetime. We evolve, or we don't. Our interests change. We want a new career. We want a child. We want several children. We want to adopt dogs. We want to adopt new principles. We want to pop oxy and turn the squabbles of status quos down, dim them to cricket chirps. We want orgies. We want quiet. We want to be raucous. We want to reject the ruts we've settled into—that familiarity is like septic shock, infections shutting our systems down, one compromise at a time until it is too late. And all of these problems are so personal, and there are so many of them during a lifetime, and how are we supposed to share them with another person and stay in sync? How is that even possible?

But we shirk logic and vow eternity. We peer into a cracked crystal ball and, in unison, say, "We will stand the test of time. I will love every iteration of you, despite the fact the future is a funhouse mirror, and it will contort us, warp us, degrade us, hate us, challenge our morals and biases and allegiances."

Husband and wife, our twenty seconds here, and I can see her, all these versions of Lelo in these reflections, and she can see all these despicable remixes of me, and I hope she knows that I'm trying, that I'm sorry to be so weak—sorry even for the strokes—sorry my booze Sirens still sing—that with a single whiff the Surprise Valley bathroom bounces through me, rattling bones and organs.

I'd hoped to be nearing a decade clean as this book wraps up, hoped you'd get to see me as a person showing up and honoring his family and responsibilities, even if his mind is its own Fukushima.

Then something strange happens in our mirrored room. All those reflections of me stop listening. They stop following my body. All those reflections become alive and they show my whole life. There I am with the motorcycle man. And there I am in my car seat while my mom hit that tree. There I am having a stroke, and another, and another, and another. And there I am cutting Ava's umbilical cord. There I am on the operating table. And there I am wishing the surgery worked. There I am with the busted gun. Getting married to Lelo. Getting married to Blue. And there I am signing our divorce papers. There I am sitting in the soapy bucket while we wash the car, smiling at my parents. And there I am punching myself in the face in the hospital, relishing the drip of each drop of blood running down my face. There I am in rehab. Holding my father's ashes, smearing Lelo's father's ashes on my face, holding my first drink, writing my first novel, wanting to stop doing drugs. There I am wanting to die. There I am laughing. There I am doing my first public reading. Watching Lelo strip naked for the first time, and there I am getting tattooed. There I am watching a Warriors game with my sisters. There I am forgiving my mom. There I am in the kiddie pool with Ava.

There's even one of me from the future, having Stroke Five, the big one buckling me, this time for good—but I can't see my face in this future; it's obscured, so I have no idea if it's next hour next day next week next month next year.

These twenty seconds—they never stop elapsing.

Here's the crazy thing about being in a room filled with infinity: there can always be more of us to see in these reflections.

We are so many disparate, wrecked pieces, we are a symphony of broken instruments, but once we acknowledge that these different versions are all there, inside us, that's when we get to stand in this mirrored room and bask in the dignity of our complexity. That's when we know that we will always be surrounded by these dancing pasts, these never-ending refractions.

There is a future.

Until there isn't.

Now in our mirrored room, there's a knock on the door.

Slowly opening. "Your twenty seconds is up," the museum worker says.

Twenty seconds? That doesn't make any sense. I've been in here my whole life.

She points at her stopwatch. "Your time is up," she says to us.

"Okay," I say, moving out of the mirrored room with Lelo.

We walk together, holding hands, with all these people stowed inside our bodies.

A NOTE ABOUT THE AUTHOR

Joshua Mohr is the author of the memoir *Sirens* and of several novels, including *Damascus,* which *The New York Times* called "Beat-poet cool." His novel *All This Life* won the Northern California Book Award. He is the founder of Decant Editorial.